TOLKIEN:
MAN AND MYTH

TOLKIEN: MAN AND MYTH

JOSEPH PEARCE

IGNATIUS PRESS SAN FRANCISCO

First Published in Great Britain in 1998 by
HarperCollins Publishers Ltd.
1 London Bridge Street, London, SE1 9GF
Joseph Pearce asserts the moral right to be identified
as the author of this work
A catalogue record for this book is available from
the British Library

Cover photograph:
John Ronald Reuel Tolkien, December 02, 1955
Photo by Haywood Magee/Getty Images. © Getty Images.

Cover design by John Herreid

Reprinted in 2019 by Ignatius Press, San Francisco
ISBN 978-0-89870-825-7
Library of Congress Control Number 98-073639
Printed in the United States of America ∞

For
Owen Barfield
1898–1997
In Memoriam

Contents

Acknowledgements   IX

Preface   XI

1   A Misunderstood Man:

Tolkien and the Modern World   1

2   Cradle Convert to the Grave:

The Child behind the Myth   11

3   Father Francis to Father Christmas:

The Father behind the Myth   26

4   True Myth:

Tolkien and the Conversion of C.S. Lewis   45

5   A Ring of Fellowship:

Tolkien, Lewis and the Inklings   61

6   The Creation of Middle Earth:

The Myth behind the Man   83

7   Orthodoxy in Middle Earth:

The Truth behind the Myth   100

8   The Well and the Shallows:

Tolkien and the Critics   126

9   Tolkien as Hobbit:

The Englishman behind the Myth   153

10   Approaching Mount Doom:

Tolkien's Final Years   182

Epilogue:

Above all Shadows Rides the Sun   209

Notes   213

Bibliography   230

Index   233

Index of Characters and Places

in Tolkien's Middle Earth   241

Acknowledgements

I scarcely know where to begin in the endeavour to acknowledge all the help I have received in the researching and writing of this volume. Perhaps, therefore, it is best to proceed in random fashion, mentioning the individuals concerned without any particular order of priority.

The principal published sources have been acknowledged in the Notes and are listed in the selective Bibliography at the end of the book. I am indebted to HarperCollins for permission to publish extracts from *The Letters of J.R.R. Tolkien*, a short extract from *The Monsters and the Critics and Other Essays*, the second verse of one of the poems from *The Lord of the Rings*, and several lines from the poem 'Mythopoeia'. Various unpublished material was provided by Stratford Caldecott, the Director of the Centre for Faith and Culture at Westminster College, Oxford. I am also indebted to Mr Caldecott for allowing me to quote from his own essay, 'Tolkien, Lewis and Christian Myth', and for the hospitality he has shown me on my visits to Westminster College. While at Westminster College I also received valued assistance from Aidan Mackey, administrator of the G.K. Chesterton Library, formerly situated at the college before its recent relocation to Plater College. Staying in Oxford, I have enjoyed the help and friendship of Walter Hooper, the world's leading authority on C.S. Lewis, and have been helped by other members of the

Oxford C.S. Lewis Society, not least of whom was Richard Jeffery who was kind enough to share his considerable knowledge of both Lewis and Tolkien with me. George Sayer, Lewis's friend and biographer, has been of invaluable assistance, especially in recounting his memories of discussions with Tolkien in the 1960s. Dr Patrick Curry, author of *Defending Middle Earth*, has offered both advice and encouragement, as has Charles Noad, the Bibliographer of the Tolkien Society. Of the clergy who have helped, Father Charles Dilke of the London Oratory and Father Ricardo Irigaray of Buenos Aires, author of *The Theological Style of J.R.R. Tolkien*, deserve special mention, as does Father Robert Murray SJ. I am grateful to Paul Ellis, Elwyn Fairburn, Helene Felter, Michael Ward and Alan Young for help in various ways; to A.F.W. Simmonds who has helped in ways too numerous to mention; and to Sarah Hollingsworth, as ever, for her critical appraisal of the original manuscript. Neither must I omit to mention the crucial part played by James Catford whose enduring faith in my work has helped to bring my efforts to fruition.

Finally, I must acknowledge a debt to Owen Barfield, a key member of the Inklings and a friend of both Lewis and Tolkien, who agreed to meet me even though he was in deteriorating health. Sadly, he died shortly before this volume was completed. I dedicate what follows to his memory and as a tribute to his literary achievement.

PREFACE

When Tolkien's *The Lord of the Rings* was voted the 'greatest book of the century' in a nationwide poll at the beginning of 1997 the critical response was not one of approbation but of opprobrium. Tolkien, it seemed, was as controversial and as misunderstood as ever, prompting the same popular acclaim and critical hostility that had greeted the book's initial publication more than forty years earlier.

It was in the wake of the controversy caused by Tolkien's triumph in the Waterstone's poll that the idea for this volume was conceived. *Tolkien: Man and Myth* is an effort to get to grips with the man, the myth and the whole phenomenon that has delighted millions of readers and perplexed and apoplexed generations of critics. It is an attempt to unravel the mystery surrounding this most misunderstood of men. In order to do so, a biographical approach has been adopted that endeavours to adhere to the 'scale of significance' which Tolkien himself ascribed to the facts of his life in a letter written shortly after *The Lord of the Rings* was published. In this letter Tolkien expressed his distrust of much modern biography:

I object to the contemporary trend in criticism, with its excessive interest in the details of the lives of authors and artists. They only distract attention from an author's work

... and end, as one now often sees, in becoming the main interest. But only one's guardian Angel, or indeed God Himself, could unravel the real relationship between personal facts and an author's works. Not the author himself (though he knows more than any investigator), and certainly not so-called 'psychologists'.

But, of course, there is a scale of significance in 'facts' of this sort.[1]

Tolkien then divides the 'facts' of his own life into three distinct categories, namely the 'insignificant', the 'more significant' and the 'really significant':

There are insignificant facts (those particularly dear to analysts and writers about writers): such as drunkenness, wife-beating, and suchlike disorders. I do not happen to be guilty of these particular sins. But if I were, I should not suppose that artistic work proceeded from the weaknesses that produced them, but from other and still uncorrupted regions of my being. Modern 'researchers' inform me that Beethoven cheated his publishers, and abominably ill-treated his nephew; but I do not believe that has anything to do with his music.[2]

Apart from these 'insignificant facts', Tolkien believed that there were 'more significant facts, which *have* some relation to an author's works'. In this category he placed his academic vocation as a philologist at Oxford University. This had affected his 'taste in languages' which was 'obviously a large ingredient in *The Lord of the Rings*'. Yet even this was subservient to more important factors:

And there are a few basic facts, which however drily expressed, are really significant. For instance I was born in 1892 and lived for my early years in 'the Shire' in a pre-mechanical age. Or more important, I am a Christian (which can be deduced from my stories), and in fact a Roman Catholic.[3]

Accepting Tolkien's premise that the author 'knows more than any investigator' about the important events in his life, his own 'scale of significance' has been employed as the starting point in the effort to unmask the man and unravel the myth. Consequently, those facts which Tolkien considered most significant to his life and work have formed the basis of this book. His academic career and his 'taste in languages' have not been discussed at length, partly because the author is not qualified to do so and partly because this aspect of his life and creativity has been covered extensively in learned studies by T.A. Shippey and Verlyn Flieger. Instead, the crucial importance of Tolkien's Christianity and the enduring importance of his early years in the pre-mechanical 'Shire' are given priority.

One result of Tolkien's Christianity was his development of the philosophy of myth that underpins his sub-creation. In fact, to employ a lisping pun, Tolkien is a *mis*understood man because he is a *myth*understood man. He understood the meaning of myth in a way which has not been grasped by his critics and this misapprehension is at the very root of their failure to appreciate his work. For most modern critics a myth is merely another word for a lie or a falsehood, something which is intrinsically *not* true. For Tolkien, myth had virtually the opposite meaning. It was the only way that certain transcendent truths could be expressed in intelligible form.

One has to understand this in order to understand Tolkien. It is hoped that this volume will go some way to removing the falsehoods and revealing the myth.

CHAPTER I

A MISUNDERSTOOD MAN:
TOLKIEN AND THE MODERN WORLD

'Oh hell! Has it? Oh my God. Dear oh dear. Dear oh dear oh dear.' I'd woken Bob Inglis from deep sleep with the news that *Lord of the Rings* had been voted, by the readers of Waterstone's and Channel 4 viewers, the best book of the century. Inglis's reaction was echoed up and down the country wherever one or two literati gathered together.

These words opened an article by Susan Jeffreys in the *Sunday Times* on 26 January 1997. Like so many other members of the literati she was dismayed by the emergence of Tolkien's *The Lord of the Rings* as the 'greatest book of the century' in a poll of more than 25,000 people throughout Britain. 'Personally,' she continued, 'I won't keep the thing in the house, but I have borrowed a boxed set for the purpose of this piece. It sits on the table like a horrible artifact, giving off a stale bedsitterish aroma. With its awful runes and maps and tedious indexes, the sight of it filled me with depression ... A depressing thought that the votes for the world's best 20th-century book should have come from those burrowing an escape into a nonexistent world.'

Jeffreys' views were shared by others. The writer Howard Jacobson reacted with splenetic scorn: 'Tolkien – that's for children, isn't it? Or the adult slow... It just shows the folly of these polls, the folly of teaching people to read. Close all the libraries. Use the money for something else. It's another black day for British culture.'¹ The actor Nigel Planer was equally dismissive, complaining that those who voted for *The Lord of the Rings* were 'the same lot who phoned in to make John Major Man of the Year and to keep the royal family'.² Griff Rhys Jones on the BBC's *Bookworm* programme appeared to believe that Tolkien's epic went no deeper than the 'comforts and rituals of childhood'.³ The *Times Literary Supplement* described the results of the poll as 'horrifying'⁴ while a writer in the *Guardian* complained that *The Lord of the Rings* 'must be by any reckoning one of the worst books ever written'.⁵

Rarely has a book caused such controversy and rarely has the vitriol of the critics highlighted to such an extent the cultural schism between the literary illuminati and the views of the reading public. More than five thousand, i.e. one-fifth, of those polled in the 105 branches of Waterstone's up and down the country gave *The Lord of the Rings* first-place votes. This made it a runaway winner, 1,200 votes ahead of its nearest rival, George Orwell's *Nineteen Eighty-four*. Graham Kerr, marketing manager of Waterstone's, reported that *The Lord of the Rings* came consistently top at almost every branch in Britain and in every region, with the exception of Wales where James Joyce's *Ulysses* topped the poll. Martin Lee, marketing director of Waterstone's, described the poll as 'one of the widest-ranging surveys of reading tastes ever to be compiled' and added that he hoped it would 'stir a passionate debate about the merits of the century's writing'. ⁶

Debate was certainly passionate, if not always conducted with either charity or restraint. Mark Lawson on the BBC's *Today* programme was the first to suggest that the Tolkien Society had conspired to orchestrate mass voting for *The Lord of the Rings*, an allegation which other critics were quick to repeat. Professor John Carey told Susan Jeffreys that 'I rather agree with Mark Lawson on the radio last week that a Tolkien pressure group had been at work.'[7] Auberon Waugh, editor of *The Literary Review*, also expressed disbelief at Tolkien's triumph, describing it as 'a little bit suspicious' and suggesting that 'the author's fans might have orchestrated a campaign'.[8] Humphrey Carpenter, Tolkien's biographer, joined the ranks of the scoffers, suspecting that the Internet culture had helped mobilize Tolkien's 'anorak-clad troops'. Carpenter was more surprised than most by the success of *The Lord of the Rings* because he 'had the impression that the Tolkien culture had dwindled to a hard core of fans'.[9]

The allegations of foul play were finally silenced when similar surveys vindicated Tolkien's position as the nation's most popular writer. On 25 January, the *Daily Telegraph* responded to the Waterstone's poll by inviting its own readers to vote for the best book of the century. The results were published on 22 February. They revealed *The Lord of the Rings* as the greatest book of the century in the view of *Telegraph* readers and Tolkien as the greatest author, ahead of George Orwell and Evelyn Waugh in second and third place respectively. Two months later, a poll published by the Folio Society ranked Tolkien's epic as Britain's favourite book of any century. The Folio Society had asked its fifty thousand members to name their ten favourite books from any age. More than ten thousand members voted and *The Lord of the Rings* polled 3,270 votes. Jane Austen's *Pride and Prejudice* was second with 3,212 votes and *David Copperfield* by Charles Dickens was third with 3,070 votes. Sue Bradbury, editorial director of the Folio Society, admitted to 'great surprise' at the result. She added, however, that only members of the society had voted, which ruled out the possibility of pressure group voting. 'With two surveys so close together putting it top, I think it has to be taken seriously now,' she said.[10] Commenting on the results of the Folio Society's poll, Ross Shimmon, chief executive of the Library Association, said, 'It's astonishing that *The Lord of the Rings* has this impact. The idea of a parallel world ... I wonder whether it's something to do with trying to make sense of the world around us.'[11]

In spite of the surprise and disbelief of critics, those trying to make sense of the polls needed to look no further than Tolkien's enduring popularity in terms of sales. Tolkien's books had sold more than fifty million copies worldwide, and HarperCollins, his publisher, reported that they 'still sell very vigorously all around the world'.[12] Neither was there any sign of Tolkien's popularity abating. In September 1997 *The Hobbit* topped the bestseller list of audio books for children, even though its retail price of £16.99 was double that of most other titles on the list. Meanwhile, Horace Bent, writing in *The Bookseller*, reported that Tolkien topped the Public Lending Right's list of the ten classic authors borrowed most from libraries.[13]

Bought, borrowed or voted for, it seemed that Tolkien was undisputed Lord of Writers, a fact which caused Chris Woodhead, the Chief Inspector of Schools, to complain of 'low cultural expectations': 'If *The Lord of the Rings* is our favourite book, what is it saying about our attitude towards quality in the arts? English teachers ought to be trying to develop discrimination. *The Lord of the Rings* is an immensely readable book, but it is not the greatest work of English literature this century.'[14] Woodhead, a former English teacher, was echoing the concerns of many educationalists who were as baffled by Tolkien's success as the literary critics.

Victoria Millar, writing in the *Times Educational Supplement*, suggested that the results of the Waterstone's poll 'certainly showed the formative influence of school set texts on a nation's reading habits. George Orwell's *Nineteen Eighty-four* and *Animal Farm* both came in the top five, *The Catcher in the Rye* by J.D. Salinger came sixth.'[15] This observation was repeated by Ann Barnes, General Secretary of the National Association for the Teaching of English, who suggested that the Waterstone's survey illustrated 'that the nation is hidebound by GCSE syllabuses'. 'At least a quarter of the books named regularly appear on GCSE and A-level syllabuses,' she said. 'Some have been on literature syllabuses for at least thirty years.'[16] Yet if this is true, Tolkien's runaway success was all the more remarkable because, as Ann Barnes admitted, *The Lord of the Rings* was 'rarely taught'.[17]

Barnes, like so many of her colleagues, was clearly bemused: 'Are we really so hooked on fantasy as the list suggests? What is it that we – or Waterstone's customers – are so hell bent on escaping from that we look back for solace to *The Wind in the Willows* and *Winnie the Pooh*, or to elaborate sagas about imaginary creatures (Tolkien's *Lord of the Rings* came top) to find expressions of our lives in the twentieth century?'[18] This was both a perceptive and a pertinent question but Barnes was not particularly interested in answering it. Instead she was concerned that the results displayed 'a predominantly masculine tone': 'It is not just that out of the first fifty titles only six are written by women; it is that in the list as a whole, the emphasis is on the sort of fantasy or horror fiction which particularly appeals to adolescent boys.'

In fact, it seemed that adolescent boys had become the particular *bête noire* of feminist writers eager to pour scorn and derision on the Waterstone's poll. For a writer in the

Guardian it was sufficient to point out merely that 'Tolkein's [*sic*] *The Lord of the Rings* [was] a favourite with adolescent boys.'[19] Having made this most damning of all criticisms, no further comment was required. Interestingly, however, the comedy writer Andrew Nickolds remembered travelling on the Northern Line in London in the 1970s: 'You'd walk up the escalator that had all these girls standing on the right-hand side in big long pea coats from Lawrence Corner, all with a copy of *Lord of the Rings* bent open at a page.'[20]

Probably the most bitter attack on Tolkien's triumph came from Germaine Greer. Writing in *W Magazine*, Waterstone's own literary journal, Greer complained that the enduring success of *The Lord of the Rings* was a nightmare come true:

> As a fifty-seven-year-old lifelong teacher of English, I might be expected to regard this particular list of books of the century with dismay. I do. Ever since I arrived at Cambridge as a student in 1964 and encountered a tribe of full-grown women wearing puffed sleeves, clutching teddies and babbling excitedly about the doings of hobbits, it has been my nightmare that Tolkien would turn out to be the most influential writer of the twentieth century. The bad dream has materialised. At the head of the list, in pride of place as the book of the century, stands *The Lord of the Rings*. Novels don't come more fictional than that. Most novels are set in a recognisable place at a recognisable time; Tolkien invents the era, the place, and a race of fictitious beings to inhabit it. The books that come in Tolkien's train are more or less what you would expect; flight from reality is their dominating characteristic.[21]

The nature of this and other attacks on Tolkien's achievement induced Paul Goodman to offer the case for the defence in a review of *The Lord of the Rings* in the *Daily Telegraph*. Far from fleeing from reality, Goodman argued, Tolkien was concerned with the ultimate reality of human life. All humanity has one thing in common, 'the readers and writer of this article, and Ms Greer too: all of us are going to die.'

> Here, surely, lies the most persuasive reason for the enduring success of *The Lord of the Rings*. That circular journey from the Shire to Mordor and back to the Shire again is all about growing older – or, rather, about growing up.[22]

According to Goodman the various aspects of the book's plot 'all point to conclusions as true as they are commonplace: that growing up is painful, but cannot be avoided; that it involves hard choices, which we are free to take; that choices have consequences, and that even good ones will not bring back the past.'

'If the book leaves many parts of the human experience unaddressed,' Goodman continued, 'it none the less explores the parts that are of the greatest importance. Ms Greer was not quite right in implying that Tolkien has nothing to say about war or politics, though what he does have to say may not please her.'

Goodman concluded his article by suggesting that 'the key' to *The Lord of the Rings* was its 'religious sensibility': 'a sense that there is a final bliss to be enjoyed, though neither in Middle Earth nor on this earth. And though it has undoubted weaknesses, do they really outweigh its strengths – its scale of vision, its fecundity of invention, the rhythmic power of much of the writing? No: Tolkien's epic is not the greatest book of the century: but be wary of the judgment of anyone who hates it.'

Goodman was not the only writer to spring to Tolkien's defence. Patrick Curry, author of *Defending Middle Earth: Tolkien, Myth and Modernity*, argued that *The Lord of the Rings* was anything but a 'flight from reality':

> Tolkien did not simply lecture us, like Ruskin and Chesterton, about the dangers of the modern world; instead he wove his anti-modernism into a rich and intricate narrative that presents an alternative. In this version, as in ours, community (the hobbits and the Shire), the natural world (middle-earth itself), and spiritual values (symbolised by the Sea) are all under threat from the pathological union of state-power, capital and technological science that is Mordor. The difference is that in *The Lord of the Rings* the threat is averted – whereas in ours, the outcome still hangs in the balance. Perhaps it does so perpetually.
>
> Tolkien addressed the fears of late-20th-century readers ... and gave them hope. Far from being escapist or reactionary, *The Lord of the Rings* addresses the greatest struggle of this century and beyond. And Greer, unlike the common reader, has completely missed it: certainly in the book, and perhaps in the world.
>
> Who, then, is living in a world of fantasy? Tolkien's critics, not his readers, are out of touch with reality. Never has the intellectual establishment so richly deserved defiance.[23]

On the day after Patrick Curry's article had appeared in the *New Statesman*, Professor Jeffrey Richards of Lancaster University was writing indignantly to the *Daily Telegraph*:

> It was deeply disheartening to hear that Chris Woodhead, HM Chief Inspector of Schools, had joined the sneering

chorus of intellectual snobs who have denounced the choice by Waterstone's readers of *The Lord of the Rings* as the greatest book of the 20th century ... He said that 'it militates against the work of the English teachers across the country'. What arrant nonsense!

The Lord of the Rings is a work of unique power, scope and imagination. Tolkien's language is rich and allusive, his vocabulary extensive and varied. His descriptive writing is wonderful. His evocation of such invaluable virtues as loyalty, service, comradeship and idealism is inspiring. Above all, he creates a universe of myth, magic, and archetype that resonates in the deepest recesses of the memory and the imagination.

Angus Wilson once said that most modern novels are about adultery in Muswell Hill. It was an exaggeration, but a pardonable one, for it drew attention to the tyranny of realism, narrowness, self-absorption and 'relevance' that holds too many modern writers and critics in thrall. Tolkien is an antidote to all that. The more children, indeed the more people of all ages, who read *The Lord of the Rings*, the better it will be not only for the literary level of this country but for its spiritual health.[24]

A similar, though more specifically Christian, defence of Tolkien was made a week earlier by the writer Anne Atkins on the BBC's *Thought for the Day*:

The Lord of the Rings, we're told, is *not* the best book of the twentieth century – though I'd love to know what is. But it's not bad, is it? It isn't a blockbuster by a leggy supermodel. Tolkien was a first-rate scholar, drawing on our vital Norse and Anglo-Saxon heritage, their ideology and poetic language. From this, he created an entire imaginary world, consistent within itself, with its own history, mythology, geography and even languages. He then combined this with a thumping good plot, and characters who are thoroughly credible despite being three feet high with hairy toes.

And his Christianity shines through every page. He understands evil, for instance, and the way it seduces us, as it seduced Gollum, with its promise of goodness. How eventually, if we give in to it, it corrodes our freedom and will and individuality ... Tolkien was a truly Christian novelist, who wrote a great Christian myth.

...Tolkien's Christian faith informed all his writing, and his heroes were based on a greater hero still. One who wasn't flawed, and didn't give way to evil. One who didn't have A-levels either, but who is the perfect role model.[25]

Perhaps the most enthusiastic response to Tolkien's triumph was that of Desmond Albrow, writing in the *Catholic Herald*: 'There is something truly inspirational in a man such as Tolkien, a true Catholic who stood four square for civilised decency, receiving such an accolade in a century that so often applauds the mean-spirited and the scintillatingly meretricious.'[26]

As this mean-spirited and scintillatingly meretricious century draws to a close it seems that Tolkien still has the power to inspire and incite, as well as the ability to divide and conquer. For those he inspired, his work is loved; for those he incited it is loathed. He has divided the critics and has conquered the hearts of large sections of the reading public. The myth he created remains both powerful and enigmatic – and all too often misunderstood. In order to understand the myth it is more necessary than ever to try to understand the man behind it.

CHAPTER 2

CRADLE CONVERT TO THE GRAVE:
THE CHILD BEHIND THE MYTH

'One of my strongest opinions,' Tolkien once wrote, 'is that investigation of an author's biography is an entirely vain and false approach to his works.'[1] His view, which was rooted in a distrust of Freudian speculation and subjectivism, was similar to that expressed by his friend C.S. Lewis:

> Another type of critic who speculates about the genesis of your book is the amateur psychologist. He has a Freudian theory of literature and claims to know all about your inhibitions. He knows what unacknowledged wishes you were gratifying ... By definition you are unconscious of the things he professes to discover. Therefore the more loudly you disclaim them, the more right he must be: though, oddly enough, if you admitted them, that would prove him right too ... this procedure is almost entirely confined to hostile reviewers. And now that I come to think of it, I have seldom seen it practised on a dead author except by a scholar who intended, in some measure, to debunk him. That in itself is perhaps significant. And it would not be unreasonable to point out that the evidence on which such amateur psychologists base their diagnosis would not be thought sufficient by a professional. They have not had their author on the sofa, nor heard his dreams, and had the whole case-history.[2]

A further note of caution was sounded by Tolkien in his fore-word to *The Lord of the Rings*: 'An author cannot of course remain wholly unaffected by his experience, but the ways in which a story-germ uses the soil of experience are extremely complex, and attempts to define the process are at best guesses from evidence that is inadequate and ambiguous.'[3]

None the less, the parameters of possibility within which an author must work *are* determined by his experience. *The Lord of the Rings* could not have been written by William Golding any more than *The Lord of the Flies* could have been written by Tolkien. It is therefore not only legitimate but necessary to examine an author's life if we are to attain a greater understanding of his work. At the same time, being conscious of Tolkien's and Lewis's condemnation of Freudian criticism, the conscientious biographer or critic must seek to avoid the pitfalls of subjectivism and amateur psychology. If one is to understand the man behind the myth one must first avoid turning the man into a myth.

Who then was J.R.R. Tolkien and what were the key events in his life which effected and affected his development into someone uniquely capable of writing *The Lord of the Rings*?

He was born in Bloemfontein, South Africa on 3 January 1892 and was christened John Ronald Reuel in the local Anglican Cathedral four weeks later. Shortly after his third birthday his mother returned to England, taking Tolkien and his younger brother Hilary with her. Tolkien retained nothing of the first few years of his life in South Africa except a few words of Afrikaans and a dim recollection of a barren, dusty landscape. His father, unable to vacate his post as manager of the Bloemfontein branch of the Bank of Africa, was forced to remain behind, intending to follow his wife and children to England as soon as the opportunity arose. Tolkien remembered his father painting 'A.R. Tolkien' on the lid of a family trunk shortly before their departure. It would be the last time he would see him and would be the only clear memory of him that he would retain. Several months after his family's return to England, Arthur Tolkien contracted rheumatic fever and was forced to postpone his journey home. In January 1896 he was still in poor health and Mabel Tolkien planned to return to South Africa to care for him. Arrangements were made and an excited Tolkien, just turned four years old, dictated a letter to his father which was written out by his nurse:

> My Dear Daddy,
> I am so glad I am coming back to see you it is such a long time since we came away from you I hope the ship will bring us all back to you Mamie and Baby and me. I know you will be so glad to have a letter from your little Ronald it is such a long time since I wrote to you I am got such a big man now because I have got a man's coat and a man's bodice Mamie says you will not know Baby or me we have got such big men we have got such a lot of Christmas presents to show you Auntie Gracie has been to see us I walk every day and only ride in my mailcart a little bit. Hilary sends lots of love and kisses and so does your loving
> Ronald.[4]

The letter, which was dated 14 February 1896, was never sent. A telegram arrived to say that his father had suffered a severe haemorrhage and that his mother must expect the worst. The next day Arthur Tolkien was dead. He was buried in the Anglican graveyard at Bloemfontein, five thousand miles from his family who were now living in Birmingham.

Her husband's death left Mabel Tolkien facing some hard decisions. She and her two young sons could not stay forever in her parents' overcrowded suburban villa, yet she scarcely had sufficient resources to establish an independent household. Her husband had only amassed a modest sum of capital which would bring an income of no more than thirty shillings a week, not enough to maintain herself and the two boys on even a subsistence standard of living. She began scouring advertisements for local rented accommodation and in the summer of 1896 she found somewhere suitable and cheap enough for herself and the children to live independently. Their new home was a semi-detached brick cottage in the hamlet of Sarehole, a mile or so beyond the southern edge of Birmingham. Traffic in the village was limited to the occasional farm cart or tradesman's wagon so it was easy to forget the proximity of the industrial city. With memories of South Africa receding into his subconscious and the urban buzz of Birmingham fresh in his mind, Tolkien experienced the contrast of English rural life at a time when his embryonic imagination was most receptive. It was in this tiny hamlet, in days of childhood innocence, that the seeds of the Shire were planted.

It was also in Sarehole that Tolkien's love for trees was born, as well as his loathing for those who destroyed them for no good reason. One incident in particular became ingrained in his memory: 'There was a willow hanging over the mill-pool and I learned to climb it. It belonged to a butcher on the Stratford Road, I think. One day they cut it down. They didn't do anything with it: the log just lay there. I never forgot that.'[5]

Unable to afford tuition fees, Mabel Tolkien took on the education of her sons herself. She was a capable teacher, with a knowledge of Latin, French and German, and she could also paint, sketch and play the piano. From the beginning she realized that her older son had an aptitude for languages. His favourite subject was Latin, with the sounds and shapes of the words delighting him as much as their meaning.

In the hours of the day when she was not teaching her children, Mabel Tolkien ensured they had plenty of books to read. The young Tolkien was unimpressed by *Treasure Island*, *The Pied Piper* and Hans Andersen, but he enjoyed *Alice in Wonderland* and was especially enthralled by the 'Curdie' books of George Macdonald in which evil goblins and good fairies fought for supremacy in a world where implicit Christian morality prevailed. Twenty years earlier, Macdonald's books had also enthralled the young G.K. Chesterton who claimed that *The Princess and the Goblin* had made 'a difference to my whole existence, which helped me to see things in a certain way from the start'. The same could be said of the effect that Macdonald had on the young J.R.R. Tolkien.

Tolkien's imagination was also fired by the Fairy Books of Andrew Lang. In particular, the tale of Sigurd, slayer of the dragon Fafnir, was to make a lasting impression. 'I desired dragons with a profound desire,' he recalled many years afterwards,[6] and at the age of seven he began to compose his own story about a dragon. 'I remember nothing about it except a philological fact,' he recalled. 'My mother said nothing about the dragon, but pointed out that one could not say "a green great dragon", but had to say "a great green dragon". I wondered why, and still do. The fact that I remember this is possibly significant, as I do not think I ever tried to write a story again for many years, and was taken up with language.'[7]

At around the time that Tolkien's love affair with language was beginning, his mother was beginning a love affair which would soon estrange her from her family. Since her husband's death, Christianity had played an increasingly important part in her life. Each Sunday she took her sons on a long walk to a 'high' Anglican church. Then one Sunday they were taken by strange roads to a different place of worship. This was St Anne's, a Roman Catholic church amidst the slums of Birmingham. Mabel Tolkien had been considering conversion for some time and during the spring of 1900 she and her sister, May Incledon, received instruction at St Anne's. In June of the same year they were duly received into the Catholic Church.

Immediately they incurred the wrath of their family. Their father, who had been brought up at a Methodist school and subsequently had become a Unitarian, was outraged. Meanwhile, May's husband, Walter Incledon, considering himself a pillar of his local Anglican church, forbade his wife to enter a Catholic church ever again. Reluctantly May felt compelled to obey, leaving her sister to face the consequences of her conversion alone.

Having brought his wife into line, Walter Incledon sought to put pressure on his sister-in-law. He had provided a little financial help for Mabel Tolkien since her husband's death, but this now ceased with no prospect of any further assistance for as long as she remained a Catholic. When it became clear that she was not about to relinquish her new-found faith, she faced increased hostility from Incledon and other members of her family. She also met with considerable opposition from her late husband's family, many of whom were Baptists and strongly opposed to Catholicism. The emotional strain that this caused, combined with the additional financial hardship, affected her health adversely. Yet nothing could shake her loyalty to the faith she now professed and against all opposition she began to instruct her sons in the Catholic religion.

So it was that J.R.R. Tolkien, at the age of eight, became a child convert. Thereafter, he always remained a resolute Catholic, a fact which influenced profoundly the direction of his life. The realization that Catholicism may not have been the faith of his father but was the faith of his father's fathers ignited and nurtured his love for Mediaevalism. This, in turn, led to his disdain for the humanist 'progress' which followed in the wake of the Reformation.

The conversion of mother and children to the Catholic faith was not the only crucial event in the life of the Tolkien family in 1900. In September of that year Tolkien entered King Edward's, his father's old school, having passed the entrance examination. His fees, which amounted to twelve pounds a year, were paid by a Tolkien uncle who remained charitably disposed towards the family in spite of the controversial conversion. The school was in the centre of Birmingham, four miles from Sarehole, and his mother could not afford the train fare. Regretfully, the family knew their days in the country would have to come to an end. Late in 1900 the boys were uprooted from the cottage where they had been so happy for four years and moved to a rented house in Moseley, nearer the centre of the city. 'Four years,' Tolkien would recall in old age of his days in Sarehole, 'but the longest-seeming and most formative part of my life.'[8]

In contrast, Tolkien described the time spent at the small house in Moseley as 'dreadful'. Although only a few miles from the Warwickshire countryside where he and his brother had played freely, the windows of their new home looked out onto a busy street. Trams, traffic and the drab faces of passers-by filled the foreground, and in the distance the smoking factory chimneys of Sparkbrook and Small Heath dominated the skyline. Yet no sooner had they settled in Moseley than they were uprooted again. The house was due for demolition. They moved to a villa less than a mile away in a terrace row behind King's Heath station. The house backed onto a railway line, so that daily life was disrupted by the roar of trains and the shunting of trucks in the nearby coal-yard. Mabel Tolkien had chosen this particular house because the new Roman Catholic church of St Dunstan was in the same road. It was a far cry from Sarehole and Tolkien remained desperately unhappy at his enforced urban existence. This wrenching of the young boy from the rural life he loved to the urban existence he loathed would have lasting consequences. It formed the basis of the creative tension which would animate the contrasting visions of life and landscape in Middle Earth. The importance of this radical change of fortunes in Tolkien's formative years was emphasized by Brian Rosebury in his book, *Tolkien: A Critical Assessment*:

Much has been made, rightly, of the significance of the idyllic Sarehole years for Tolkien's imaginative development ... But it is at least of symbolic interest (and easily overlooked by readers determined to detach Tolkien from his times) that his intellectually formative years were spent in the busy, noisy, polluted capitalist-nonconformist atmosphere of Joseph Chamberlain's Birmingham; it is as if an American writer of the same generation had been schooled and domiciled in, say, Chicago. If Tolkien was hostile to industrialism, and to the lifestyles and landscapes it generated, it was at any rate a hostility based on a degree of acquaintance than some may suppose ... Tolkien's social origins were (impoverished) middle-class; and the circumstances of his upbringing and education were poorer and more dispiritingly 'urban' than those of almost any, except

D.H. Lawrence, of the major English-language writers of the first half of the century.[9]

Tolkien's time at King's Heath was also short lived. The family moved to Edgbaston early in 1902, to a house that was little better than a slum. The one consolation was the proximity of their new home to the Birmingham Oratory, a large church established more than fifty years earlier by John Henry Newman. In particular, Mabel Tolkien discovered in Father Francis Xavier Morgan, her new parish priest, a valued friend as well as a sympathetic priest. Father Morgan was destined to play a key role in Tolkien's life.

At Christmas 1903 Mabel Tolkien informed her mother-in-law that 'Ronald is making his First Communion this Christmas – so it is a very great feast indeed to us this year.' Aware of the continued opposition of the family to their 'popery', she added almost apologetically, 'I don't say this to vex you – only you say you like to know everything about them.'[10] Ominously, the letter also referred to her ailing health: 'I keep having whole weeks of utter sleeplessness, which added to the internal cold and sickness have made it almost impossible to go on.'

Early in the New Year her condition deteriorated. In April she was taken to hospital where she was diagnosed as diabetic. She made a partial recovery and Father Francis made provision for her convalescence at Rednal, a Worcestershire hamlet a few miles beyond the Birmingham boundary. For a few brief but idyllic summer months the boys enjoyed a return to a rural lifestyle. It was a false dawn. Unnoticed by her sons, Mabel Tolkien's condition began to deteriorate again. At the beginning of November she collapsed in a way that seemed both sudden and terrifying. She sank into a coma and six days later, on 14 November, she died. Father Francis and her sister May Incledon were at her bedside. She had lived for thirty-four trouble-filled years.

Mabel Tolkien was buried in the Catholic churchyard at Bromsgrove. In her will she had appointed Father Francis Morgan to be guardian of her two sons. It proved a wise choice. In the years ahead he displayed unfailing affection and generosity to them. Although their mother had left only eight hundred pounds of invested capital with which to support the boys, Father Francis, who had a private income from his family's sherry business, discreetly augmented this from his own pocket. He also arranged for them to live with their Aunt Beatrice, not far from the Oratory, but she showed them little affection and the orphaned brothers soon began to consider the Oratory their real home. Each morning they hurried round to serve Mass for Father Francis at his favourite side-altar in the Oratory church. Afterwards they would eat breakfast in the refectory before setting off to school.

Tolkien remained forever grateful for all that Father Francis did for him and his brother. 'I first learned charity and forgiveness from him,' he recalled many years later, 'and in the light of it pierced even the "liberal" darkness out of which I came.'[11] Tolkien described himself as 'virtually a junior inmate of the Oratory house' in the years following his mother's death. It was a 'good Catholic home' which contained 'many learned fathers (largely "converts")' and where 'observance of religion was strict'.[12] The effect of these years of strict religious observance at the Oratory should not be understated. According to the writer and poet Charles A. Coulombe, it was in these years that Tolkien's 'religious sense was formed': 'Had he lived away from the Oratory, a living example of Catholic culture, one wonders what the effect on his work would have been.'[13]

The charity and forgiveness that Tolkien learned from Father Francis in the years after his mother's death offset the pain and sorrow which her death engendered. The pain remained throughout his life, and sixty years later he compared his mother's sacrifices for her faith with the complacency of some of his own children towards the faith they had inherited from her:

> When I think of my mother's death ... worn out with persecution, poverty, and, largely consequent, disease, in the effort to hand on to us small boys the Faith, and remember the tiny bedroom she shared with us in rented rooms in a postman's cottage at Rednal, where she died alone, too ill for viaticum, I find it very hard and bitter, when my children stray away.[14]

Tolkien always considered his mother a martyr for the faith. Nine years after her death he had written: 'My own dear mother was a martyr indeed, and it was not to everybody that God grants so easy a way to his great gifts as he did to Hilary and myself, giving us a mother who killed herself with labour and trouble to ensure us keeping the faith.'[15]

Not surprisingly perhaps, Tolkien's biographer, Humphrey Carpenter, subjected this statement to the sort of Freudian analysis that Tolkien and Lewis so despised. According to Carpenter the statement was an indication of the way in which Tolkien associated his mother with his membership of the Catholic Church:

> Indeed it might be said that after she died his religion took the place in his affections that she had previously occupied. The consolation that it provided was emotional as well as spiritual ... And certainly the loss of his mother had a profound effect on his personality. It made him into a pessimist.

Or rather, it made him into two people. He was by nature
a cheerful almost irrepressible person with a great zest for
life. He loved good talk and physical activity. He had a deep
sense of humour and a great capacity for making friends. But
from now onwards there was to be a second side, more
private but predominant in his diaries and letters. This side
of him was capable of bouts of profound despair. More
precisely, and more closely related to his mother's death,
when he was in this mood he had a deep sense of impending
loss. Nothing was safe. Nothing would last. No battle would
be won for ever.[16]

Unfortunately this analysis, or rather this psycho-analysis,
suffers from all the flaws that C.S. Lewis discussed. One starts
with a presumption, in this case that the death of Tolkien's
mother determined the depths and flaws of his whole personality for the rest of his life, and then one sets about making the
events of the life fit into the theory. Thus Tolkien's vivacious
and often rumbustious approach to life is admitted but
glossed over, while the relatively rare moments when he is
more melancholy are magnified, caricatured and pronounced
solemnly to be 'more closely related to his mother's death'.
In this way, Tolkien's faith, philosophy, personality, and his
whole outlook on life, are squeezed into the confines of an odd
sort of Oedipus complex.

Perhaps the shallowness of Carpenter's approach is best
exemplified by his claim that Tolkien was 'capable of bouts
of profound despair'. No doubt such a statement would
have elicited a wry smile from Tolkien who, on theological
grounds, would have dismissed the very notion that despair
could ever be 'profound'. Yet, in point of fact, there is precious
little evidence that Tolkien ever despaired. He accepted the

sorrows of life with patient forbearance, and his distressed disapproval of the way society was 'progressing' was tempered by sincere hope in the grace of God.

Tolkien had moments of joy and moments of melancholy, as does everybody, but he exhibited in his life and in his character a *joie de vivre* scarcely commensurate with one perpetually brooding over a lost parent. Neither is it plausible to suggest that a scholar as widely read and as perceptive as Tolkien would cling blindly to a belief throughout his entire life out of loyalty to, or as a substitute for, a mother's love. Although he began his journey through life as a Catholic due to his mother's actions, he still had to test the Catholic view of life against all the other theories he came across, many of which were in the ascendency. Decades as an Oxford don brought him into contact with every shade of opinion, but he remained convinced of the objective truth of his religious convictions. For Tolkien, Catholicism was not an opinion to which one subscribed but a reality to which one submitted. Quite simply, and pseudo-psychology aside, Tolkien remained a Catholic for the simple if disarming reason that he believed Catholicism was true.

Similarly, Tolkien's 'deep sense of impending loss' had more to do with the tenets of his faith than with memories of his mother. He believed that human history, rooted in a fallen world, was doomed to become little more than a succession of defeats and disappointments, and that even victories carried the shadows of impending loss. Yet history is temporary, locked in time as much as it is rooted in the Fall, and is itself but a shadow of eternity. Beyond the defeats of history there is always the hope of eternal joy. 'Actually I am a Christian, and indeed a Roman Catholic,' he wrote in 1956, shortly after publication of *The Lord of the Rings*, 'so that I do not expect "history" to be anything but a "long defeat" – though it contains (and in a legend may contain more clearly and movingly) some samples or glimpses of final victory.'[17]

Other critics have perceived this theocentric aspect of Tolkien's psyche with a depth which eluded Carpenter. Verlyn Flieger, in *Splintered Light: Logos and Language in Tolkien's World*, suggested that 'Carpenter's description of Tolkien as two people – one a naturally cheerful man, the other pessimistic and despairing ... may be too simple a description of the complexity of feeling which Tolkien experienced and which his work reflects. For these feelings found a Christian context in Tolkien's Catholic view of the world as fallen and of man as imperfect ... a Christian acceptance of the Fall of Man leads inevitably to the idea that imperfection is the state of things in this world, and that human actions – however hopeful – cannot rise above imperfection.'[18]

Flieger then suggests that Tolkien had placed the loss of his mother within the wider context of a larger truth: 'All this adds up to an outlook both psychological and religious in which the one can hardly be separated from the other, an outlook based on the sense of expulsion from both a private and a communal Eden ... His world is shadowed by its past as well as his past, lighted only by the vision of the white Light ... That vision of the Light remains a vision – a Grail to be sought but never grasped by fallen man in a fallen world.'[19]

Perhaps Flieger is correct to assert the futility of trying to separate the psychological and the religious, and Carpenter, for all his specious speculations and presumptions of despair, was correct to stress the importance of Mabel Tolkien's death on her son's life. Tolkien's relationship with his mother was very important, potent if not omnipotent. He owed his faith to her in the same way that he owed his life to her. She had given him both. Physically she had been taken from him early; metaphysically she accompanied him from the cradle to the grave, having a greater influence than anyone in shaping the man behind the myth.

CHAPTER 3

FATHER FRANCIS TO FATHER CHRISTMAS:
THE FATHER BEHIND THE MYTH

Father Francis Morgan became a surrogate father to the two orphaned boys in the years following their mother's death. Tolkien described the priest as 'a guardian who had been a father to me, more than most real fathers'.[1] Every summer he took them to Lyme Regis, where they stayed at the Three Cups Hotel, a favourite haunt of G.K. Chesterton in later years. During these holidays they paid visits to some of Father Francis's friends in the neighbourhood. They also talked a great deal and it was on one of these visits to Dorset that the priest discovered the two boys were not happy in the drab and loveless lodging that was provided for them by their Aunt Beatrice. Returning to Birmingham, he set about looking for somewhere more suitable. Early in 1908 the brothers moved to Duchess Road, behind the Oratory, home of a Mrs Faulkner, a friend of Father Francis who gave musical soirees which the priest and several other Oratory Fathers attended. Little did Tolkien realize that the move to Mrs Faulkner's would change the direction of his life.

Tolkien shared a room on the second floor with his brother. In the room below lived another lodger, a girl of nineteen who spent most of her time at her sewing machine. She was very pretty, small and slim, with grey eyes and short dark hair parted in the middle. Her name was Edith Bratt and Tolkien soon learned that they had much in common. She too was an orphan, her mother having died five years previously and her father, apparently, some time before that. In fact, she was illegitimate. Her mother never married and her father was not named on the birth certificate. In spite of the fact that she was three years his senior, Tolkien struck up an immediate friendship with her. By the summer of 1909 they were in love.

In a letter to Edith many years later Tolkien recalled 'my first kiss to you and your first kiss to me (which was almost accidental) – and our goodnights when sometimes you were in your little white nightgown, and our absurd long window talks; and how we watched the sun come up over town through the mist ... and our whistle-call – and our cycle-rides – and the fire talks ...'[2]

It was one of their 'cycle rides' which first landed the young couple in trouble and ended, at least temporarily, their clandestine courtship. Towards the end of the autumn term of 1909 Tolkien had arranged secretly with Edith that they should go for a bicycle ride into the countryside. Edith departed first, nominally to visit her cousin, and Tolkien left a little later on the pretext that he was going to the school sportsground. They spent the afternoon on the Worcestershire hills before taking tea in Rednal village. They returned home, arriving separately so as not to arouse suspicion. Their elaborate precautions came to naught when the woman who had given them tea at Rednal told the caretaker at Oratory House that she had seen Tolkien with an unknown girl. The gossip sealed their fate. The caretaker told the cook and the cook told Father Francis.

The priest was furious. The boy on whom he had lavished so much love and money had been caught deceiving him and was, moreover, neglecting his studies so shortly before he was due to take the scholarship exam for Oxford. He summoned

Tolkien to the Oratory and demanded that the romance with Edith come to an end. Reluctantly, Tolkien agreed to terminate the relationship and the priest made arrangements to move his ward to new lodgings away from the girl.

In the weeks ahead, Tolkien was distraught. 'Depressed and as much in dark as ever,' he recorded in his diary on New Year's Day 1910. 'God help me. Feel weak and weary.'[3] Perhaps in these circumstances it was not surprising that he found it extremely difficult to keep his promise, especially as the new lodgings to which he and his brother had been moved were not very far from Mrs Faulkner's house. The temptation was too great and Tolkien resorted to some desperate reasoning to justify his decision to see Edith again. He reasoned that his guardian's demand that their love affair be broken off did not specifically forbid him seeing her as a friend. Although he hated to deceive the priest, he resumed the clandestine meetings. During January he and Edith spent an afternoon together, taking a train into the countryside and discussing their plans. They also visited a jeweller's shop, Edith purchasing a pen for Tolkien's eighteenth birthday, and Tolkien a wrist-watch for Edith's twenty-first. None the less, they had little to celebrate and Edith, accepting the inevitability of their separation, had decided to go and live with a friend in Cheltenham. Tolkien took the news stoically, writing 'Thank God' in his diary. It seemed the only practical solution to their plight, if not a particularly palatable one.

In the meantime, however, they had been seen together yet again. This time Father Francis's ultimatum was given in no uncertain terms. Tolkien must neither meet nor write to Edith except to say goodbye on the day she left for Cheltenham. Thereafter they were not to communicate again until Tolkien was twenty-one, the age at which the priest would no longer be responsible for him. Even then the love-lorn eighteen-year-old found it hard to obey his guardian's wishes. His diary entry for 16 February illustrated the depth of his desire to see her again before she departed for her new home: 'Last night prayed would see E. by accident. Prayer answered. Saw her at 12.55 at Prince of Wales. Told her I could not write and arranged to see her off on Thursday fortnight. Happier but so much long to see her just once to cheer her up. Cannot think of anything else.'[4] On 21 February he recorded seeing 'a dejected little figure sloshing along in a mac and tweed hat and could not resist crossing and saying a word of love and cheerfulness. This cheered me up a little for a while. Prayed and thought hard.'[5] Edith was also praying and thinking hard because two days later Tolkien wrote in his diary that he had 'met her coming from the Cathedral to pray for me'.

On 26 February Tolkien received 'a dreadful letter from Fr F saying I had been seen with a girl again, calling it evil and foolish. Threatening to cut short my university career if I did not stop. Means I cannot see E. Nor write at all. God help me. Saw E. at midday but would not be with her. I owe all to Fr F and so must obey.'[6]

Edith wrote to him, lamenting that 'our hardest time of all has come', and on 2 March she set out from Duchess Road for her new home in Cheltenham. For one last time Tolkien defied Father Francis's ban and prayed that he might catch a last glimpse of her. He scoured the streets as the hour for her depar-ture approached and eventually his prayer was answered: 'At Francis Road corner she passed me on bike on way to station. I shall not see her again perhaps for three years.'[7]

Commenting on this distressing episode in Tolkien's life, Humphrey Carpenter suggests that it 'may seem strange' that

Tolkien 'did not simply disobey Father Francis and openly continue the romance' and that 'a more rebellious young man might have refused to obey'.[8] Yet, in spite of his inability to do his guardian's will initially, Tolkien was utterly obedient to the priest's strict conditions after Edith had left for Gloucestershire.

Tolkien genuinely believed that he owed everything to Father Francis 'and so must obey', but the conflict had put a strain on their previously close relationship, and it is difficult to see the priest's apparent lack of compassion as anything but reprehensible. It was not until many years later that Tolkien was able to put the whole affair into some sort of context:

> I had to choose between disobeying and grieving (or deceiving) a guardian who had been a father to me, more than most real fathers ... and 'dropping' the love-affair until I was twenty-one. I don't regret my decision, though it was very hard on my lover. But that was not my fault. She was perfectly free and under no vow to me, and I should have had no just complaint ... if she had got married to someone else. For very nearly *three* years I did not see or write to my lover. It was extremely hard, painful and bitter, especially at first. The effects were not wholly good: I fell back into folly and slackness and misspent a good deal of my first year at College. But I don't think anything else would have justified marriage on the basis of a boy's affair; and probably nothing else would have hardened the will enough to give such an affair (however genuine a case of true love) permanence.[9]

'When Father Morgan extracted that promise not to contact Edith,' suggests Charles Moseley in his study of Tolkien, 'there was no question, in his or her mind, but that it should be kept. The period of waiting, in which he passed through the years of greatest change in any man's life and might easily have transferred his affection elsewhere, seems, for Tolkien, to have been seen as almost a Romance test: he was obedient to the prohibition, the *geas*, laid on him, and proved his honour by his obedience, and by his faithfulness to Edith.'[10]

Tolkien's concern for honour, obedience and faithfulness was rooted in his fundamental Christianity, in the belief that such characteristics were virtues towards which one aspired, as opposed to their opposites, dishonour, disobedience and unfaithfulness, which were vices to be spurned. The Christianity he had learned both from his mother and from Father Francis shaped his whole view of life to such an extent that sacrifices were borne willingly, if grudgingly, when they were deemed necessary to the pursuit of virtue. Such a view had been further bolstered by his love of mediaeval literature. 'Trouthe is the hyeste thing that man may kepe,' says Chaucer's Arveragus. Tolkien digested Chaucer's words avidly from the moment his form master at King Edward's School, George Brewerton, had introduced the mediaeval master to him in the correct pronunciation and had lent him an Anglo-Saxon grammar. Thereafter Tolkien added a love of Chaucer and a love of early Anglo-Saxon literature to his love of faerie.

Moseley believes that Tolkien's taste in literature had an important effect on his attitude to the love affair with Edith:

Of course, nobody is unaffected by what he reads. If you spend your days reading books and poems from a world where women are honoured, put on a pedestal – worshipped, even – where the chief male virtues are courage, and honesty, and honour, and generosity, you will in the end come to think in those terms (and may suffer no harm).

Tolkien's intellectual diet from an early age had been just that: from George Macdonald's fantasies *The Princess and the Goblin* (1872) and *The Princess and Curdie* (1882), through stories collected in Andrew Laing's twelve *Fairy Books* to his version of the *Volsungasaga* and then, in maturity, to the riches of medieval and ancient literature, to the courts of Arthur and the halls of Asgard, to the tragedy of Deirdre and the sons of Usna and the love of Pwyll and Rhiannon.[11]

These were the roots, the archetypes, of Tolkien's view of romantic love, a view which found expression in his own self-denial during the three years of separation from Edith. They were also roots which would bear fruit eventually in the heroic love of Aragorn and Arwen, and of Beren and Lúthien, in Tolkien's mythology. 'These are the values, unfashionable, perhaps inconceivable, now, held by many in Tolkien's generation, and by not a few in later ones,' writes Moseley. 'They are the values that lie at the heart of the fictions of Middle-earth.'[12]

During the three years of exile from Edith, Tolkien returned to his studies. In 1910 he won an exhibition at Exeter College, Oxford, but by the high standards of King Edward's School the award 'was tolerable rather than praiseworthy'.[13] Certainly there was little sign of the exceptional abilities which would later mark him out as one of Oxford's *illustrissimi*. Looking back on this period of his life, Tolkien ascribed his underachievement to 'folly and slackness', describing himself as 'one of the idlest boys Gilson (the Headmaster) ever had'.[14] In fact, his lack of success had as much to do with his extracurricular interest in Gothic, Anglo-Saxon and Welsh, and with his early fascination with inventing his own languages, than with mere idleness. The same 'weakness' for private intellectual passions also affected his studies at Oxford. He was reading Classics but took only a second in Honour Moderations, the first of the two examinations that would earn him his degree, having neglected his studies in favour of 'Old Norse, festivity, and classical philology'. 'My love for the classics,' he recalled later, 'took ten years to recover from lectures on Cicero and Demosthenes.'[15]

Neglecting Latin and Greek lectures, Tolkien turned his attention to his own private language. It was during this period that he became busily engaged on the invention of Elvish. 'This was no arbitrary gibberish,' wrote his obituarist in *The Times*, 'but a really possible tongue with consistent roots, sound laws, and inflexions, into which he poured all his imaginative and philological powers; and strange as the exercise may seem it was undoubtedly the source of that unparalleled richness and concreteness which later distinguished him from all other philologists. He had been inside language. He had not gone far with his invention before he discovered that every language presupposes a mythology; and at once began to fill in the mythology presupposed by Elvish.'[16]

Tolkien's passion for sub-creating myth had been awakened and Middle Earth had been conceived, albeit only in embryonic form.

As his twenty-first birthday approached, thoughts of Edith returned, jostling Elvish, the Classics and Old Norse into the background. On the stroke of midnight, at the very beginning of 3 January 1913, Tolkien celebrated his coming of age by sitting up in bed and writing his first letter to her for almost three years. It was a renewal of his declaration of love which culminated in the question which was uppermost in his mind: 'How long will it be before we can be joined together before God and the world?'[17]

Edith's reply was devastating. She was engaged to marry the brother of an old schoolfriend.

Overcoming the initial shock, Tolkien detected hints in her letter that gave him the hope of winning her back. She had only become engaged to her fiancé because he had been kind to her. She felt 'on the shelf' and had given up believing that Tolkien would still want to see her when the three years had elapsed. 'I began to doubt you, Ronald,' she had written, 'and to think you would cease to care for me.'[18]

On 8 January Tolkien travelled by train to Cheltenham. Edith met him on the platform and they walked out into the surrounding countryside. By the end of the day she had decided to break off her engagement so that she could marry Tolkien. He returned to the new term at Oxford in 'a bursting happiness'.[19]

Dutifully he wrote to Father Francis informing him that he and Edith were intending to be married. He awaited the priest's reply with trepidation, partly because he still relied on his continuing financial support, but also because he genuinely desired his blessing. Father Francis replied in a spirit of calm, if unenthusiastic, resignation, indicating his acceptance of the inevitable. This was hardly a wholehearted blessing and Tolkien realized that he was not likely to receive the priest's blessing, or indeed the blessing of the Church, until or unless his future wife became a Catholic. This then became one of the most pressing concerns in the months following their reunion.

In theory Edith was quite happy to become a Catholic, but in practice there were several difficulties attached to her doing so. In the three years of her separation from Tolkien she had become a very active member of the Church of England. Consequently, she had made many friends at the local Anglican church, she enjoyed a certain status in the parish and the routines of local parish life had become interwoven with the very fabric of her existence. To renounce all this would not be easy. Furthermore, the house in which she lived was owned by a friend who was strongly anti-Catholic. Would she still have a roof over her head if she 'poped'? She was in a difficult situation and suggested to Tolkien that it would be easier if her conversion could be delayed, at least until they were officially engaged or until their marriage was near. Tolkien would hear nothing of this and insisted that she act quickly and decisively.

His insistence, and her hesitation, amounted to their first major disagreement, but Tolkien was not prepared to compromise what he perceived to be the truth. He held the Church of England in contempt, declaring it 'a pathetic and shadowy medley of half-remembered traditions and mutilated beliefs'.[20] Neither did he have much sympathy for Edith's fear of being persecuted or ostracized. Memories of his mother's sacrifices were still too fresh in his mind for such 'cowardice' to be countenanced. 'I do so dearly believe,' he wrote to Edith, 'that no half-heartedness and no worldly fear must turn us aside from following the light unflinchingly.'[21] For Tolkien, Edith's conversion would be an act of heroism, a worthy sacrifice on the altar of truth. Perhaps, as Humphrey Carpenter suggests, 'it was also in part, though he would not have admitted it, a test of her love after her unfaithfulness' in becoming engaged to another man. Whatever the reason, Tolkien's impatience bore bitter fruit. Edith entered the Church with more mixed feelings than may have been the case if he had been prepared to wait. The residue of resentment, the result of her being rushed into a decision before she was ready, remained with Edith for many years, possibly for the remainder of her days. It is, of course, speculative to draw conclusions, but it is at least possible that had Tolkien been a better Catholic in 1913, Edith may have been a better Catholic in the years that followed.

Edith did what Tolkien wanted, but in proving her love and 'passing the test' she also paid the price she had feared. Her friend reacted angrily when Edith announced her intention to become a Catholic and ordered her to leave the house as soon as she could find alternative accommodation. In desperation she found temporary rooms in Warwick.

Tolkien paid his first visit in June 1913 and his initial impressions of the town were unreservedly favourable. He admired its trees, its hill and its castle. He and Edith went punting on the river Avon, making the most of the hot weather, and they attended Benediction in the Roman Catholic church. Tolkien wrote that he and Edith 'came away serenely happy, for it was the first time that we had ever been able to go calmly side by side to church'.[22] Possibly this experience helped allay Edith's fears because she returned to the same church a few weeks afterwards to ask Father Murphy, the parish priest, to instruct her in the Catholic faith.

On 8 January 1914 Edith was received into the Church. It was exactly a year since she had been reunited with Tolkien. Shortly after her reception the couple were formally betrothed in church by Father Murphy. Edith made her first confession and first communion, which she found to be 'a great and wonderful happiness'.[23] Unfortunately the initial happiness would not be sustained. She slipped into a lukewarm acceptance of her adopted creed which contrasted starkly with the passion and depth of Tolkien's faith.

While Edith languished unhappily in Warwick, Tolkien returned to Oxford. He had long since abandoned Classics in favour of the 'English' school where the strongly historical and philological emphasis was more to his liking and more in keeping with his enthusiasm for the study of the northern tongues of Europe as opposed to Latin or Greek. Having found his intellectual niche he was now beginning to excel in his studies. When war was declared he still had a year to go and, unlike many of his contemporaries, decided to stay on at Oxford rather than enlist. 'In those days chaps joined up, or were scorned publicly,' he recalled in a letter to one of his sons many years later. 'It was a nasty cleft to be in, especially for a young man with too much imagination and little physical courage. No degree: no money: fiancée. I endured the obloquy, and hints becoming outspoken from relatives, stayed up and produced a First in Finals in 1915. Bolted into the army: July 1915. I found the situation intolerable and married on March 22, 1916. May found me crossing the Channel (I still have the verse I wrote on the occasion!) for the carnage of the Somme.'[24]

A First in Finals ... marriage ... the carnage of the Somme. With the comfort and complacency of hindsight, Tolkien was able to pass over possibly the most crucial year of his life in a few glib, shorthand sentences. In fact, of course, all three events would affect him irrevocably. Tolkien's triumph during the second week of June 1915, achieving First Class Honours in his final examination in English Language and Literature, virtually ensured him an academic career when the war was over. He 'bolted into the army' in the following month fearing that his triumph in Oxford could soon turn into tragedy in France. He took up his commission as a second lieutenant in the Lancashire Fusiliers and endured the calm before the inevitable storm. His training took place in Bedford and Staffordshire where he learned to drill a platoon and attended military lectures.

By the beginning of 1916 embarkation for the killing fields of France seemed imminent. Fearing that he may never return, he and Edith decided to get married before he left. It was eight years since their teenage love affair had begun. In the grim reality of 1916 there was every prospect that their marriage would not last the number of months that their courtship had lasted in years. It seemed that it was now or never if, as Tolkien had put it three years earlier, they were to 'be joined together before God and the world'.

He was now twenty-four and she twenty-seven. They had little money apart from his army pay and Tolkien decided to ask Father Francis to transfer the remainder of his modest share capital to his own name. With this in mind he travelled to Birmingham to see Father Francis, intending at the same time to tell him of his wedding plans. He arranged the financial matters satisfactorily but could not bring himself to mention the marriage. It was not until a fortnight before the wedding that he finally found the courage to write. Father Francis's reply was full of kindness and he wished them both 'every blessing and happiness'. As a final gesture of reconciliation he offered to conduct the ceremony himself in the Oratory Church. If Tolkien had been able to broach the subject during his visit, all may have worked out as the priest intended and their marriage could have served also as a symbolic reconciliation between the previously warring parties. As it was, arrangements had been finalized already for the wedding to take place at the Catholic church in Warwick and the couple were married by Father Murphy after early Mass on 22 March 1916. After the wedding they enjoyed a week's honeymoon in Somerset but, as expected, their bliss was blistered within weeks by news that Tolkien's battalion was bound 'for the carnage of the Somme'.

'Think of your mother!' Tolkien wrote to his son Michael in 1941:

> Yet I do not now for a moment feel that she was doing more than she should have been asked to do – not that that detracts from the credit of it. I was a young fellow, with a moderate degree, and apt to write verse, a few dwindling pounds p.a. (£20–40), and no prospects, a Second Lieut. on 7/6 a day in the infantry where the chances of survival were against you heavily (as a subaltern). She married me in 1916 and John was born in 1917 (conceived and carried during the starvation-year of 1917 and the great U-Boat campaign) round about the battle of Cambrai, when the end of the war seemed as far-off as it does now.[25]

However, if Tolkien's departure for the trenches was hard on his newly wedded wife, it was scarcely any easier for himself. His first impressions of the horrors of the front line were described graphically by Humphrey Carpenter in his biography: 'Worst of all were the dead men, for corpses lay in every corner, horribly torn by shells. Those that still had faces stared with dreadful eyes. Beyond the trenches no-man's-land was littered with bloated and decaying bodies. All around was desolation. Grass and corn had vanished into a sea of mud. Trees, stripped of leaf and branch, stood as mere mutilated and blackened trunks. Tolkien never forgot what he called the "animal horror" of trench warfare.'[26]

Tolkien was rescued from the 'animal horror' by 'pyrexia of unknown origin', as the medical officers called it. To the troops it was simply 'trench fever'. He was invalided home, grateful to have escaped the nightmare. Many of his friends were not so lucky, joining the ranks of the bodies littering no-man's-land.

Amidst the enduring negative images which continued to haunt him, Tolkien retained at least one positive image which inspired one of the most lovable characters in *The Lord of the Rings*. 'My "Sam Gamgee",' he wrote many years later, 'is indeed a reflexion of the English soldier, of the privates and batmen I knew in the 1914 war, and recognised as so far superior to myself.'[27]

John, the first of the four Tolkien children, was born on 16 November 1917 in a Cheltenham nursing home. Their second son, Michael, followed in October 1920, Christopher in November 1924, and Priscilla, their first daughter and final child, in 1929. The importance of these four events in Tolkien's life cannot be overstated. Certainly, their importance should never be understated or, worse, ignored. Sadly, all too often, it is.

Charles Moseley, in his study of Tolkien, discusses the aspects of Tolkien's life 'which can illuminate his published narratives'. Of these, he writes, 'three things are especially important: Tolkien's religion, the experience of the 1914–18 War, and the nature of Oxford academic life and society'.[28] Without denigrating any of these, all of which influenced his work to a greater or lesser degree, his role as storyteller and *paterfamilias* to his children was equally important, at least initially. When Tolkien scrawled 'in a hole in the ground there lived a hobbit', the opening sentence of *The Hobbit* in around 1930, he was writing for the amusement of his children as well as for the amusement of himself. Indeed, it is fair to assume that if Tolkien had remained a bachelor and had not been blessed with children he would never have written either *The Hobbit* or *The Lord of the Rings*. Perhaps he would have written *The Silmarillion*, but in all probability it would never have been published.

Soon after he began his first tentative sketches for what became *The Silmarillion* and long before he had even thought about hobbits, Tolkien amused himself and his children by becoming Father Christmas once a year. He was a talented artist as well as a gifted storyteller and he used both to great effect every Christmas in what became the 'Father Christmas Letters'. The first letter was written in 1920 when John was three years old and the family was on the point of moving to Leeds, where Tolkien had been appointed Reader in English Language at Leeds University. One wonders whether his son was able to read the English language at the time or whether he needed his parents' assistance to decipher Father Christmas's handwriting:

Christmas House
North Pole
1920

Dear John,

I heard you ask daddy what I was like and where I lived. I have drawn ME and My House for you. Take care of the picture. I am just off now for Oxford with my bundle of toys – some for you. Hope I shall arrive in time: the snow is very thick at the NORTH POLE tonight.

On each subsequent Christmas, as John grew older and other children were born, the Father Christmas Letters became more and more elaborate and imaginative. From the first short note signed 'Yr loving Fr. Chr.', there emerged new characters with every passing year. There was the Polar Bear, Father Christmas's helper who was, more often than not, more of a hindrance than a help; there was the Snow Man, Father Christmas's gardener; Ilbereth the elf, his secretary;

and a host of other minor characters including snow-elves, gnomes and evil goblins.

Every Christmas Tolkien would write a letter addressed to his children in Father Christmas's shaky handwriting, or the Polar Bear's rune-like capitals, or Ilbereth's flowing script, giving the latest news from the North Pole. In 1925 disaster struck when the Polar Bear climbed to the top of the North Pole to retrieve Father Christmas's hood. The pole broke in the middle and landed on the roof of Father Christmas's house with catastrophic results. The Polar Bear was also to blame the following year, turning on all the Northern Lights for two years in one go, which shook all the stars out of place and caused the Man in the Moon to fall into Father Christmas's back garden.

Tolkien would go to elaborate lengths to add 'realism' to the letters. He added drawings, painstakingly coloured and sketched. He wrote out an envelope on which he stuck a hand-painted North Polar postage stamp, and across the envelope he wrote 'By gnome-carrier. Immediate haste!' to give it added importance. Elaborate lengths were also taken to add 'realism' to the way in which the letter was delivered. In the early years it was left in the fireplace so that it looked as if it had been put down the chimney. On another occasion a snowy footprint was left ostentatiously on the carpet, irrefutable evidence that Father Christmas had delivered the letter personally. In later years the local postman became an accomplice and delivered the letters himself.

The Father Christmas Letters were published posthumously by his family in 1976, half a century after they were written. Their considerable charm is accentuated by the fact that they were composed solely by a father for his children and were never intended for publication. They also represent a cosy fireside foreshadowing of the familiar foundations upon which the edifice of Middle Earth was built. 'Those lovely letters,' wrote Simonne d'Ardenne, a fellow philologist and family friend, 'were the origin of *The Hobbit*, which soon made Tolkien famous, and the starting point of the later "fairy tale for grown-ups", the great trilogy of *The Lord of the Rings*.'[29]

Although d'Ardenne mistakenly believed, or erroneously remembered, that Tolkien had introduced hobbits into the Father Christmas Letters, her opinions are of considerable value. She was one of relatively few people who successfully bridged the gap between being both an academic colleague and a family friend. She was at Oxford before becoming a professor at the University of Liège, and Tolkien contributed much to her edition of *The Life and Passion of St Julienne*, a mediaeval religious work written in the *Ancrene Wisse* dialect. At the same time she became a close friend of the family, as close to Edith as she was to Tolkien. When she was asked to contribute to a memorial volume of essays following Tolkien's death, she based it 'on the vivid memories I have kept of several visits I paid to his house, and on a friendship which extended over forty years ... During these visits I gained firsthand knowledge of the man and the scholar.'[30] Of all the 'many aspects of him' that she came to know, the facet of his 'humanity' which she chose to focus on was his role as father to his children:

Among the different aspects of Tolkien's *humanity*, there is one which deserves special attention, that of the *paterfamilias*. All his letters, extending over about forty years, tell of his concern about his children's health, their comfort, their future; how best he could help them to succeed in life, and how to make their lives as perfect as possible. He started by giving them a most pleasant childhood, creating for them the deep sense of home, which had been denied to him, as he lost his father when he was a small child, and his splendid mother a few years later. And to provide all this Tolkien accepted the heavy and tedious burden of examining in several English universities, which, of course, took up much time that he might have devoted to his research. But, however busy he was, he always found time to rush home and kiss his younger children goodnight.

And it was this great love of his children that prompted him to invent and create the delightful hobbits and their mythology. They were wildly discussed at the breakfast table and in the nursery.[31]

Tolkien was, therefore, the father of the myth he created in a literal as well as in a literary sense. His sub-creation was rooted in the familiar, again in its literal as well as in its literary sense: in the very heart of the family he loved.

CHAPTER 4

TRUE MYTH:
TOLKIEN AND THE CONVERSION
OF C. S. LEWIS

'Not Facts first Truth first.'[1]

'Tolkien was immensely kind and understanding as a father,' wrote Humphrey Carpenter, 'never shy of kissing his sons in public even when they were grown men, and never reserved in his display of warmth and love.'[2] This being so, it is scarcely surprising that his children recalled their lives with their father with evident fondness. There were hot summer afternoons punting up the river Cherwell towards Water Eaton and Islip, where picnics could be spread on the bank; walks in the countryside when their father's knowledge of trees and plants seemed boundless; and summer holidays by the sea at Lyme Regis when the aging Father Francis Morgan would come down from Birmingham to join them. The children remembered being as embarrassed by the priest's loud and boisterous ways as had their father and his brother during holidays in Dorset twenty-five years earlier. They also retained vivid memories of bicycling to early Mass at St Aloysius', or at St Gregory's up the Woodstock Road, or at the Carmelite convent nearby. There were memories of the barrel of beer in the coal-hole behind the kitchen which dripped regularly, and their mother's complaints that it made the house smell like a brewery. The children also recalled that their mother and father were keen gardeners, cultivating a large vegetable plot, and that their father was particularly fond of the roses.

These visions of halcyon days may give the impression that the Tolkien marriage was itself a bed of roses. Perhaps it was, at least when seen in relation to other marriages. Yet every bed of roses contains a crown of thorns, and the marriage had its sorrows as well as its joys. Unfortunately, it is the peculiar modern obsession to focus on the thorns to the exclusion of the roses. Far from being objective, such a jaundiced view often neglects or even fails to recognize the positive and most important facets of a subject's character, preferring instead the blind pursuit of lurid fantasy.

Tolkien's marriage has not escaped this cynical scrutiny. One of the worst examples was the distorted view projected by John Carey in a review of Humphrey Carpenter's biography in *The Listener*. Carpenter records that Edith Tolkien 'had almost given up going to mass' in the years following the marriage: 'In the second decade of marriage her anti-Catholic feelings hardened, and by the time the family returned to Oxford in 1925 she was showing resentment of Ronald taking the children to church.'[3] Carpenter suggests that Edith's resentment was rooted in part to her dislike of confession. She 'had always hated confessing her sins to a priest', whereas her husband made frequent use of the sacrament. From these facts Carey composed what the critic Brian Rosebury called a 'pharisaic fantasy'. Tolkien, Carey wrote, 'retained something of Father Francis's view of sex. Even marital relations had to be atoned for by frequent confession – a requirement Mrs Tolkien found distasteful, and hotly contested.'[4] This 'pharisaic fantasy' of Carey's was itself considered distasteful and was hotly contested by Rosebury in his critical study of Tolkien:

The implication (shielded by a theoretical ambiguity in Carey's sentence) is that what Mrs Tolkien contested, with understandable heat, was not confession *per se*, but confession of, or prompted by, 'marital relations'. Those readers of *The Listener* who had not already read Carpenter's book – i.e. virtually all of them – would naturally suppose that this bizarre insinuation is supported by the biography, which it is not: Carey, with an ingenuity familiar to connoisseurs of his biography reviews, has introduced it himself. His innuendo is that Tolkien – a father of four, and 'past master of bawdy in several languages' (Carpenter, *The Inklings*, p55) – was preoccupied by guilt about sex; but here it is Carey, not Tolkien, who takes it for granted that the mere practice of sexual intercourse may be a Catholic's motive for confession.[5]

The sheer fantasy of Carey's innuendo is best exposed by quoting Tolkien himself. In a letter to C.S. Lewis, Tolkien wrote: 'Christian marriage is not a prohibition of sexual intercourse, but the correct way of sexual temperance – in fact probably the best way of getting the most satisfying *sexual pleasure*, as alcoholic temperance is the best way of enjoying beer and wine.'[6]

In this, Tolkien was merely echoing the teaching of the Church, as distilled via St Thomas Aquinas from Aristotle's *Ethics*. Sexual pleasure was good and God-given, but sexual temperance was necessary because man does not live on sex alone. Temperance was the moderate path between prudishness and prurience, the two extremes of sexual obsession. In falsely accusing Tolkien of the former, Carey was guilty of the latter.

In the same review, Carey betrayed a similarly contorted view when he described the women in Tolkien's mythology as

'perfectly sexless'. Perhaps it says something of Carey's prurience that he neglects to mention that the men in Tolkien's
mythology are also 'perfectly sexless', at least in the sense
that Carey intends. Tolkien's characters are certainly not
sexless in the sense of being asexual but, on the contrary, are
archetypally and stereotypically sexual. There are, however,
no descriptions of sexual activity, or what modern material-
ists refer to as 'sexual chemistry', and an absence of implicit
or explicit sexual activity is seen by some modern critics as
itself sinful. None the less, the omission reveals nothing of
Tolkien's subconscious view of sex, as implied by Carey and
others, but displays his conscious intention to concentrate on
those aspects of life which are more important than sexual
activity. As a writer he was aware that the introduction of
sexual carnality within Middle Earth would detract from the
greater issues on which he was intent on focusing. His
'perfectly sexless' characterization was a necessary literary
device and nothing more.

For a greater understanding of Tolkien's view of marriage
and the relations between the sexes one need not scavenge for
tantalizing titbits within the pages of *The Lord of the Rings*,
especially as such scavenging is likely to lead to erroneous
conclusions. One need look no further than a long letter he
wrote to his son in March 1941:

There is in our Western culture the romantic chivalric tradition still strong, though as a product of Christendom (yet by
no means the same as Christian ethics) the times are inimical
to it. It idealizes 'love' – and as far as it goes can be very good,
since it takes in far more than physical pleasure, and enjoins
if not purity, at least fidelity, and so self-denial, 'service',
courtesy, honour, and courage. Its weakness is, of course, that

it began as an artificial courtly game, a way of enjoying love for its own sake without reference to (and indeed contrary to) matrimony. Its centre was not God, but imaginary Deities, Love and the Lady. It still tends to make the Lady a kind of guiding star or divinity ... This is, of course, false and at best make-believe. The woman is another fallen human-being with a soul in peril. But combined and harmonized with religion ... it can be very noble. Then it produces what I suppose is still felt, among those who retain even vestigiary Christianity, to be the highest ideal of love between man and woman. Yet I still think it has dangers. It is not wholly true, and it is not perfectly 'theocentric'. It takes, or at any rate has in the past taken, the young man's eyes off women as they are, as companions in shipwreck not guiding stars. (One result is for observation of the actual to make the young man turn cynical.) ... It inculcates exaggerated notions of 'true love', as a fire from without, a permanent exaltation, unre-lated to age, childbearing, and plain life, and unrelated to will and purpose. (One result of that is to make young folk look for a 'love' that will keep them always nice and warm in a cold world, without any effort of theirs; and the incurably romantic go on looking even in the squalor of the divorce courts.)[7]

Having discoursed in general about the relations between the sexes, Tolkien progressed to a discussion of sacrifice within marriage:

However, the essence of a *fallen* world is that the *best* cannot be attained by free enjoyment, or by what is called 'self-realization' (usually a nice name for self-indulgence, wholly inimical to the realization of other selves); but by denial, by suffering. Faithfulness in Christian marriage entails that: great mortification ... No man, however truly he loved his betrothed and bride as a young man, has lived faithful to her as a wife in mind and body without deliberate conscious exercise of the *will*, without self-denial. Too few are told that – even those brought up 'in the Church'. Those outside seem seldom to have heard it. When the glamour wears off, or merely works a bit thin, they think they have made a mistake, and that the real soul-mate is still to find. The real soul-mate too often proves to be the next sexually attractive person that comes along. Someone whom they might indeed very profitably have married, if only—. Hence divorce, to provide the 'if only' ... But the 'real soul-mate' is the one you are actually married to ... only the rarest good fortune brings together the man and woman who are really as it were 'destined' for one another, and capable of a very great and splendid love. The idea still dazzles us, catches us by the throat: poems and stories in multitudes have been written on the theme, more, probably, than the total of such loves in real life (yet the greatest of these tales do not tell of the happy marriage of such great lovers, but of their tragic separation; as if even in this sphere the truly great and splendid in this fallen world is more nearly achieved by 'failure' and suffering). In such great inevitable love, often love at first sight, we catch a vision, I suppose, of marriage as it should have been in an unfallen world. In this fallen world we have as our only guides, prudence, wisdom (rare in youth, too late in age), a clean heart, and fidelity of *will* ...[8]

This letter contains much of crucial importance to anyone wishing to understand Tolkien. It illuminates his own marriage, and his attitude towards it, and illustrates many of the virtues and much of the philosophy which underpins his creation of Middle Earth. The influence of Tolkien's marriage upon his work was discussed perceptively by Brian Rosebury:

> Their marriage, though at times troubled, was to last fifty-five years, from 1916 until her death in 1971. If its difficulties are dimly discernible in his work, in a recurring theme of estrangement of interests between husband and wife (the Ents and Entwives in *The Lord of the Rings*; the late, bleak, unfinished tale 'Aldarion and Erendis'), the romance in which it was founded is also commemorated, in the tale of Beren and Lúthien (whose names appear on the Tolkiens' tombstone), and in a number of shorter works, from early poems such as 'You & Me' to the last story, *Smith of Wootton Major*. It undoubtedly surfaces also in *The Lord of the Rings*, where Elrond (in the Father Francis role) forbids Aragorn to marry Arwen unless and until he achieves the kingship: Sam Gamgee's delayed marriage to Rosie Cotton duplicates the theme at a homely level.[9]

For Tolkien, drawing on a profound understanding of orthodox theology and the depth of his own Christian mysticism, the rose of Christian marriage was inextricably linked with the thorns of mortification. The joys and sorrows of life, as in the Joyful and Sorrowful mysteries of the Rosary, were not to be seen in isolation but were light and dark threads interwoven in a richer fabric. 'Christian joy,' Tolkien wrote in a letter to one of his sons, 'produces tears because it is qualitatively so like sorrow, because it comes from those places where Joy and Sorrow are at one, reconciled, as selfishness and altruism are lost in Love.'[10] For his wife, who never attained these theological or mystical depths, the sorrows of married life could not be accepted with such philosophical resignation. Rather, they were the occasion of frustration and resentment.

In the first years of their marriage, and particularly during the four years that they lived in Leeds, Edith was fairly happy and settled. It was following their return to Oxford in 1925, after Tolkien had succeeded Sir William Craigie as Rawlinson and Bosworth Professor of Anglo-Saxon, that Edith's loneliness and sense of isolation began. She never felt comfortable in academic circles and initially made few friends among the families of other dons. Her husband, on the other hand, was entirely at home in Oxford and relished its heightened intellectual atmosphere. Edith began to feel that she was being ignored, even though Tolkien was in the house for much of the time and did much of his teaching from home. He was not often out for more than one or two evenings a week, and was always 'very loving and considerate to her, greatly concerned about her health (as she was about his) and solicitous about domestic matters'.[11] None the less, she still felt that his affections were elsewhere and that there were needs in his life that she was unable to satisfy. Sadly she began to realize that there was one side of her husband's character that only came alive when he was in the company of men of his own kind. She became resentful of the time he spent with male friends. Her view has been echoed and supported by some later critics of Tolkien such as, for example, Valentine Cunningham who claimed that Tolkien 'openly neglected' his wife by attending twice-weekly meetings with friends – or 'chums' as Cunningham preferred to call them.[12]

In particular, Edith resented her husband's friendship with a young don named C.S. Lewis, a Fellow of Magdalen College. Lewis was popular with the Tolkien children, never talking condescendingly to them and giving them books by E. Nesbit which they enjoyed, but he was shy and ill at ease with Edith. His awkwardness with her added to her incomprehension of the evident delight that her husband took in Lewis's company and this, in turn, added to the jealousy she felt towards their friendship. Tolkien was aware of, and regretted, his wife's resentment but insisted on the legitimacy of male companionship. Years later, when one of his sons was contemplating marriage, he endeavoured to explain the difficulties:

> There are many things that a man feels are legitimate even though they cause a fuss. Let him not lie about them to his wife or lover! Cut them out – or if worth a fight: just insist. Such matters may arise frequently – the glass of beer, the pipe, the non writing of letters, the other friend, etc., etc. If the other side's claims really are unreasonable (as they are at times between the dearest lovers and most loving married folk) they are much better met by above board refusal and 'fuss' than subterfuge.[13]

Years later C.S. Lewis tried to explain the differences between married love and friendship in his book, *The Four Loves*. Whereas the 'importance and beauty' of sexual love had been 'stressed and almost exaggerated again and again', he wrote, 'very few modern people think Friendship a love of comparable value or even a love at all.'

> To the Ancients, Friendship seemed the happiest and most fully human of all loves; the crown of life and the school of virtue. The modern world, in comparison, ignores it. We admit of course that besides a wife and family a man needs a few 'friends'. But the very tone of the admission, and the sort of acquaintanceships which those who make it would

describe as 'friendships', show clearly that what they are talking about has very little to do with that *Philia* which Aristotle classified among the virtues or that *Amicitia* on which Cicero wrote a book.[14]

Predictably perhaps, considering the spirit of the age – or rather its lack of spirit – at least one critic has suggested that the friendship between Lewis and Tolkien was sexual. Brenda Partridge, in her feminist critique, 'The Construction of Female Sexuality in *The Lord of the Rings*',[15] implies, in a woeful and wishful flight of fancy, that Lewis and Tolkien carried on a homosexual relationship. The best riposte to such a viewpoint was given by Lewis himself in his essay on 'Friendship' in *The Four Loves*:

> It has actually become necessary in our time to rebut the theory that every firm and serious friendship is really homosexual.
>
> The dangerous word *really* is here important. To say that every Friendship is consciously and explicitly homosexual would be too obviously false; the wiseacres take refuge in the less palpable charge that it is *really* – unconsciously, cryptically, in some Pickwickian sense – homosexual. And this, though it cannot be proved, can never of course be refuted. The fact that no positive evidence of homosexuality can be discovered in the behaviour of two Friends does not disconcert the wiseacres at all: 'That,' they say gravely, 'is just what we should expect.' The very lack of evidence is thus treated as evidence; the absence of smoke proves that the fire is very carefully hidden. Yes – if it exists at all. But we must first prove its existence. Otherwise we are arguing like a man who should say 'If there were an invisible cat in that chair, the chair would look empty; but the

chair does look empty; therefore there is an invisible cat in it.'[16]

Tolkien had first come to Lewis's attention on 11 May 1926 during a discussion of faculty business at an 'English Tea' at Merton College. 'I had a talk with him afterwards,' Lewis recorded in his diary. 'He is a smooth, pale, fluent little chap ... No harm in him: only needs a smack or so.'[17] From these indifferent and inauspicious beginnings, a friendship soon developed which would become increasingly important to both men.

Shortly before Tolkien and Lewis had first met, Tolkien had formed the Coalbiters, a club among the dons dedicated to the reading of Icelandic sagas and myths. Its name derived from the Icelandic *Kolbítar*, a lighthearted term for those who lounge so close to the fire in winter that they bite the coal. Initially its members were confined primarily to those with a reasonable knowledge of Icelandic, but soon the club's numbers were augmented by enthusiastic beginners, one of whom was C.S. Lewis. By January 1927 Lewis was attending the *Kolbítar* regularly and finding it invigorating. The influential friendship between Lewis and Tolkien had begun.

Like Tolkien, Lewis had been excited by Norse mythology and 'Northernness' since his childhood. He had always been enthralled by what Tolkien referred to mystically as 'the nameless North' and now, in the person of the Professor of Anglo-Saxon, he had found not only a kindred spirit but a mentor. On 3 December 1929 Lewis wrote to his friend Arthur Greeves: 'I was up till 2.30 on Monday, talking to the Anglo Saxon professor Tolkien, who came back with me to College from a society and sat discoursing of the gods and giants of Asgard for three hours, then departing in the wind and rain – who could turn him out, for the fire was bright and the talk was good.'[18]

A few days after this late-night conversation, Tolkien decided to show his Beren and Lúthien poem to Lewis. On 7 December Lewis wrote to Tolkien, expressing his enthusiasm:

> I can quite honestly say that it is ages since I have had an evening of such delight: and the personal interest of reading a friend's work had very little to do with it – I should have enjoyed it just as well if I'd picked it up in a bookshop, by an unknown author. The two things that come out clearly are the sense of reality in the background and the mythical value: the essence of a myth being that it should have no taint of allegory to the maker and yet should *suggest* incipient allegories to the reader.[19]

At last, Tolkien had found an appreciative and sympathetic audience and he began to read more of *The Silmarillion* aloud to Lewis in the weeks and months ahead. 'The unpayable debt that I owe to him,' Tolkien wrote of Lewis years later, 'was not "influence" as it is ordinarily understood, but sheer encouragement. He was for long my only audience. Only from him did I ever get the idea that my "stuff" could be more than a private hobby.'[20]

If Tolkien's debt to Lewis was due to the latter's encouragement and enthusiasm, Lewis's debt to Tolkien was to be much more profound. Friendship with Tolkien, wrote Lewis in *Surprised by Joy*, 'marked the breakdown of two old prejudices. At my first coming into the world I had been (implicitly) warned never to trust a Papist, and at my first coming into the English Faculty (explicitly) never to trust a philologist. Tolkien was both.'[21]

It did not take Tolkien long to win Lewis over to philology, and it was partly due to Lewis's support that Tolkien succeeded in getting his reformed syllabus accepted in 1931, yet Lewis's prejudice against Catholicism was deeply ingrained, rooted in his sectarian upbringing in Ulster.

When they had first met, Lewis was beginning to perceive the inadequacy of the agnosticism into which he had lapsed, having previously discarded any remaining remnants of childhood Christianity. By the summer of 1929 he had renounced agnosticism and professed himself a theist, believing in the existence of God but renouncing the claims of Christianity. According to Walter Hooper, Lewis's friend and biographer, 'a realisation of the truth in mythologies triggered Lewis's conversion' to Christianity:

> This came about after a long discussion in 1931 with Tolkien and Hugo Dyson which continued until four o'clock in the morning. At the end of this marathon discussion Lewis believed that myths were real and that facts took the shine off truth, emptying truth of its glory. Thereafter he became an excellent Christian apologist.[22]

This meeting, which was to have such a revolutionary impact on Lewis's life, took place on 19 September 1931 after Lewis had invited Tolkien and Dyson to dine at Magdalen. Dyson, who was Lecturer in English Literature at Reading University, was a good friend of Lewis, visiting Oxford frequently, and was also known by Tolkien who had first met him at Exeter College in 1919. After dinner the three men went for a walk beside the river and discussed the nature and purpose of myth. Lewis explained that he felt the power of myths but that they were ultimately untrue. As he expressed it to Tolkien, myths are 'lies and therefore worthless, even though breathed through silver'.

'No,' said Tolkien. 'They are not lies.'

At that moment, Lewis later recalled, there was 'a rush of wind which came so suddenly on the still, warm evening and sent so many leaves pattering down that we thought it was raining. We held our breath.'

Tolkien resumed, arguing that myths, far from being lies, were the best way of conveying truths which would otherwise be inexpressible. We have come from God, Tolkien argued, and inevitably the myths woven by us, though they contain error, reflect a splintered fragment of the true light, the eternal truth that is with God. Myths may be misguided, but they steer however shakily towards the true harbour, whereas materialistic 'progress' leads only to the abyss and to the power of evil.

'In expounding this belief in the inherent *truth* of mythology,' wrote Humphrey Carpenter, 'Tolkien had laid bare the centre of his philosophy as a writer, the creed that is at the heart of *The Silmarillion*.'[23]

Lewis listened as Dyson reiterated in his own way what Tolkien had said.

Building on this philosophy of myth, Tolkien and Dyson went on to express their belief that the story of Christ is simply a true myth, a myth that works in the same way as the others, but a myth that really happened. This revelation changed Lewis's whole conception of Christianity.

In fact, such a line of reasoning struck a particular note of poignancy with Lewis because he had examined the historicity of the Gospels and had come to the almost reluctant conclusion that he was '*nearly* certain that it really happened'.[24] Indeed the discussion with Tolkien and Dyson had been foreshadowed by a previous conversation five years earlier. At the time, Lewis had just read Chesterton's *The Everlasting Man*, 'and for the first time saw the whole Christian outline of history set out in a form that seemed to me to make sense', a revelation that had shaken his agnosticism to its foundations.

> I had not long finished *The Everlasting Man* when something far more alarming happened to me. Early in 1926 the hardest boiled of all the atheists I ever knew sat in my room on the other side of the fire and remarked that the evidence for the historicity of the Gospels was really surprisingly good. 'Rum thing,' he went on. 'All that stuff of Frazer's about the Dying God. Rum thing. It almost looks as if it had really happened once.'[25]

'To understand the shattering impact' of the atheist's admission, Lewis wrote, 'you would need to know the man (who has certainly never since shown any interest in Christianity).' He was 'the cynic of cynics, the toughest of toughs'.

Now, five years later, it seemed that Tolkien was making sense of it all. He had shown that pagan myths were, in fact, God expressing Himself through the minds of poets, using the images of their 'mythopoeia' to reveal fragments of His eternal truth. Yet, most astonishing of all, Tolkien maintained that Christianity was exactly the same except for the enormous difference that the poet who invented it was God Himself, and the images He used were real men and actual history. The death and resurrection of Christ was the old 'dying god' myth except that Christ was the *real* Dying God, with a precise and verifiable location in history and definite historical consequences. The old myth had become a fact while still retaining the character of a myth.

Tolkien's arguments had an indelible effect on Lewis. The edifice of his unbelief crumbled and the foundations of his Christianity were laid. Twelve days later Lewis wrote to

Arthur Greeves: 'I have just passed on from believing in God to definitely believing in Christ – in Christianity. I will try to explain this another time. My long night talk with Dyson and Tolkien had a good deal to do with it.'[26]

The full extent of Tolkien's influence can be gauged from Lewis's letter to Greeves on 18 October:

Now the story of Christ is simply a true myth: a myth working on us in the same way as the others, but with this tremendous difference that *it really happened*: and one must be content to accept it in the same way, remembering that it is God's myth where the others are men's myths: i.e. the Pagan stories are God expressing Himself through the minds of poets, using such images as He found there, while Christianity is God expressing Himself through what we call 'real things'. Therefore it is *true*, not in the sense of being a 'description' of God (that no finite mind could take in) but in the sense of being the way in which God chooses to (or can) appear to our faculties. The 'doctrines' we get out of the true myth are of course *less* true: they are translations into our *concepts* and *ideas* of that which God has already expressed in a language more adequate, namely the actual incarnation, crucifixion, and resurrection.[27]

Now that Lewis and Tolkien had found agreement and shared the same philosophy, their friendship flourished as never before. In October 1933 Tolkien recorded the following entry in his diary: 'Friendship with Lewis compensates for much, and besides giving constant pleasure and comfort has done me much good from the contact with a man at once honest, brave, intellectual – a scholar, a poet, and a philosopher – and a lover, at least after a long pilgrimage, of Our Lord.'[28]

CHAPTER 5

A Ring of Fellowship:
Tolkien, Lewis and the Inklings

We were born in a dark age out of due time (for us). But there
is this comfort: otherwise we should not *know*, or so much
love, what we do love. I imagine the fish out of water is the
only fish to have an inkling of water.[1]

Tolkien's long discussion with Lewis inspired him to
distill his own ideas about the nature of myth. He
composed a poem, 'Mythopoeia', in which he elaborated his
philosophy more eloquently and powerfully than in almost
anything else he ever wrote. Stratford Caldecott, director of
the Centre for Faith and Culture at Westminster College,
Oxford, discussed Tolkien's philosophy in his essay, 'Tolkien,
Lewis, and Christian Myth':

Tolkien once wrote that 'legends and myths are largely made
of "truth", and indeed present aspects of it that can only be
received in this mode' (*The Letters of J.R.R. Tolkien*, ed. H.
Carpenter, London, 1981, no. 131). In one popular meaning of
the word, as we all know, a 'myth' is simply a story that is *not
true*. Like Tolkien, however, I will be using the word in almost
an opposite sense, to designate the kind of symbolic story
that is intended to *express truth*. The truth that myths are
designed to express concerns not only the world around us,
but the world within us; not so much its surface appearance,

but its inner form. For a myth is a way of describing the rules by which the world is made – 'deep magic from before the dawn of time'.[2]

Although Tolkien's philosophy of myth was pivotal to Lewis's conversion to Christianity, its cardinal importance should not obscure the role that other people played. The importance of Chesterton's writing has been noted already, but Lewis's steady progress towards Christian faith had as much to do with discussions with friends as with anything he read.

Long before Chesterton's *The Everlasting Man* had made an impression, Lewis had fallen under the benign influence of Owen Barfield, later described by Lewis as the wisest and best of his unofficial teachers. Barfield's theories on myth, poetic language and the nature of knowledge influenced Tolkien as profoundly as they had Lewis and, through them, he has exerted a major influence on the direction of twentieth-century literature. 'Lewis was very much influenced by Chesterton,' Barfield remembered, 'especially *The Everlasting Man*, but he didn't mention anybody else really. We didn't always talk about philosophy. We used to read together. We read the whole of the *Iliad*, the whole of the *Odyssey* and the whole of the *Divine Comedy*. We considered the *Divine Comedy* great poetry and we appreciated the total outlook but we never argued from a doctrinal point of view.'[3]

It was a discussion between Barfield, Lewis and Alan Griffiths, one of Lewis's pupils, which was to prove instrumental in edging Lewis closer to conversion. Barfield and Griffiths were lunching in Lewis's room when Lewis happened to refer to philosophy as 'a subject'. 'It wasn't a *subject* to Plato,' Barfield retorted, 'it was a way.'

The quiet but fervent agreement of Griffiths, and the quick glance of understanding between these two, revealed to me my own frivolity. Enough had been thought, and said, and felt, and imagined. It was about time that something should be done.[4]

Even though they unwittingly played such a crucial role in the *coup de grâce* of Lewis's conversion, neither Barfield nor Griffiths were Christians at the time of this providential conversation. Griffiths, however, was destined to play a key role in Lewis's progress. In *Surprised by Joy* Lewis described Griffiths as his 'chief companion' during his final approach to Christianity.[5] By a strange coincidence they both received their respective first Communions within a day of each other at Christmas 1931, Griffiths as a Catholic on Christmas Eve and Lewis as an Anglican on Christmas Day.

A few months after his reception Griffiths decided to try his vocation as a monk at Prinknash, the Benedictine priory at Winchcombe, and on 20 December 1932 he was clothed as a novice. It was at this point that he changed his name to Bede, after which he was known as Dom Bede Griffiths. He made his solemn vows on 21 December 1936 and wrote of his own conversion in his autobiography, *The Golden String*, published in 1954.

From the time of their conversions Griffiths began trying to discuss with Lewis the merits of their respective positions. Lewis, however, was reticent, refusing to discuss the doctrinal differences between Catholicism and Anglicanism. 'The result,' wrote Griffiths, 'was that we agreed not to discuss our differences any more, and this was perfectly satisfactory to Lewis; for me it was a great embarrassment. It meant that I could never really touch on much that meant more to me than anything else, and there was always a certain reserve therefore afterward in our friendship.'[6]

Though reserved, their friendship remained, as did their respective friendships with Owen Barfield, the only one of the original trio who was still resisting conversion. Sixty years later, Barfield remembered their friendship with nostalgic affection:

> Lewis, Griffiths and I went for long walks together. We talked a good deal about theology. I was at the time an agnostic, I suppose, and when three people go off to walk together times come when two go off to talk to each other. I was with Griffiths and I told him I was an agnostic and we got talking about being damned and some remark he made elicited the reply from me that 'in that case I suppose that I am damned'. And I'll never forget the calm, collected way he turned round and said 'but of course you are'. This amused Lewis very much of course when I told him afterwards.[7]

Griffiths' vocation as a monk effectively excluded him from the intellectual rough and tumble of Oxford life, although he and Lewis continued to correspond regularly. Barfield, on the other hand, played an important part in the intellectual circle surrounding Lewis and Tolkien at Oxford. This group of essentially like-minded people became known as the Inklings.

In *The Four Loves* Lewis had stated that 'two, far from being the necessary number for Friendship, is not even the best',[8] and he suggested that each friend added to a group brought out some special characteristic in the others. For Lewis, and for Tolkien, the Inklings soon came to embody this ideal of Friendship.

The Inklings began to form itself in the early 1930s, at about the time the Coalbiters ceased to meet. The latter came to a natural end after its reason for existence, the reading of all the principal Icelandic sagas culminating in the Elder Edda, had been achieved. The Inklings therefore filled a vacuum as well as fulfilling a need. Whereas the Coalbiters had been formed by Tolkien with a specific purpose, however, the Inklings centred on Lewis and had no specific agenda beyond a vague shared interest in literature amongst its members. Lewis was the invariable nucleus, without whom any gathering would have been inconceivable, but Tolkien was also almost always present. Barfield was considered a key member of the group even though his job as a London solicitor kept him from attending regularly. Other members included Major Warren 'Warnie' Lewis, C.S. Lewis's brother, who had returned to the practice of his Anglican faith at the same time as his brother on Christmas Day 1931; R.E. Havard, a Catholic convert and Oxford doctor who attended the Lewis and Tolkien households; and Hugo Dyson, Lecturer in English at Reading University, who along with Tolkien had been so instrumental in Lewis's conversion.

Typically, the Inklings met twice a week. On a weekday morning they would meet in a pub, normally on a Tuesday at the Eagle and Child, known familiarly by members as the 'Bird and Baby'. On Thursday nights they would meet in the spacious surroundings of Lewis's large sitting room in Magdalen College. The group would congregate soon after nine o'clock and one of its members would produce a manuscript – a poem, a story or a chapter – and begin to read it aloud. This would be followed by criticism by the other members. After this there might be more reading before the proceedings drifted into general discussion and often heated debate on almost any subject that happened to arise.

It was at the early meetings of the Inklings that Tolkien had read his manuscript of *The Hobbit*, a book he had written principally for the amusement of his own children. He had shown an early typescript of it to C.S. Lewis in 1932 and, as ever, he found in Lewis a ready and vociferous admirer. Following its publication in 1937 Lewis was one of *The Hobbit's* most vocal champions:

> It must be understood that this is a children's book only in the sense that the first of many readings can be undertaken in the nursery. *Alice* is read gravely by children and with laughter by grown-ups; *The Hobbit*, on the other hand, will be funniest to its youngest readers, and only years later, at a tenth or a twentieth reading, will they begin to realise what deft scholarship and profound reflection have gone to make everything in it so ripe, so friendly, and in its own way so true. Prediction is dangerous: but *The Hobbit* may well prove a classic.[9]

Lewis did not modify this view as time went on. A decade later, in his essay 'On Stories', he wrote: '*The Hobbit* escapes the danger of degenerating into mere plot and excitement by a very curious shift of tone. As the humour and homeliness of the early chapters, the sheer 'Hobbitry', dies away we pass insensibly into the world of epic.'[10]

At around the time that Tolkien had first shown Lewis an early draft of *The Hobbit*, Lewis was busy working on his first book. *The Pilgrim's Regress*, which was subtitled 'An Allegorical Apology for Christianity, Reason, and Romanticism', signalled Lewis's entry into the literary fray as a forthrightly outspoken Christian apologist. Published in 1933, the book caused anger and controversy because of its broadsides against both the High Anglicans and the Broad Churchmen within the Church of England. To many of those in both camps, Lewis became a new and unwelcome 'enemy within'. His attacks on the Broad Church were based on orthodox theological objections to modernism. The Broad Church, Lewis believed, suffered from a 'confusion between mere natural goodness and Grace which is non-Christian' and is 'what I most hate and fear in the world'.[11] Meanwhile, the High Anglicans he singled out for scorn were 'a set of people who seem to me ... to be trying to make of Christianity itself one more high-brow, Chelsea, bourgeois-baiting fad.'[12]

This increasingly awkward positioning of himself on a self-styled 'centre ground' of 'mere Christianity' was to remain the hallmark of Lewis's writing and was probably the result of a personal psychological compromise, emanating from his roots. At least this was the view of Tolkien: 'It was not for some time that I realized that there was more in the title *Pilgrim's Regress* than I had understood (or the author either, maybe). Lewis would regress. He would not enter Christianity by a new door, but by the old one; at least in the sense that in taking it up again he would also take up, or reawaken, the prejudices so sedulously planted in boyhood. He would become again a Northern Ireland Protestant.'[13] Perhaps one is tempted to see elements of Tolkien's own boyhood prejudices in this bitter assessment of Lewis's Christianity. None the less, Tolkien does seem justified in his complaints about Lewis's anti-Catholic prejudice and the duplicity it caused. If a Lutheran is put in jail, Tolkien observed, Lewis 'is up in arms; but if Catholic priests are slaughtered – he disbelieves it, and I daresay really thinks they asked for it. There is a good deal of Ulster still left in C.S.L., if hidden from himself.'[14] The matter was put poignantly and humorously by Christopher Derrick, a friend and pupil of Lewis and author of *C.S. Lewis and the Church of Rome*: 'If a man is brought up in Belfast in a full Orange Order *Sash My Father Wore* paranoia, and then has his first formation in the great school at Oxford, divine grace has a hell of a nut to crack!'[15]

Certainly Lewis would have denied vehemently that he suffered from any Orange paranoia, but there is little doubt that he retained more than a trace of Belfast Protestant bigotry. In unguarded moments he and his brother Warnie would refer to Irish Catholics as 'bog-trotters' or 'bog-rats' and the fact that these negative stereotypes, deeply ingrained, derived from their earliest youth can be gauged from an entry Lewis made in his diary as a ten-year-old schoolboy:

> We were obliged to go to St John's (Watford), a church which wanted to be Roman Catholic, but was afraid to say so. A kind of church abhorred by respectful [*sic*] Irish Protestants. In this abominable place of Romish hypocrites and English liars, the people cross themselves, bow to the Lord's Table (which they have the vanity to call an altar), and pray to the Virgin.[16]

Walter Hooper, Lewis's biographer, concedes that Lewis's Ulster background was 'probably important' as a factor in his attitude to Catholicism, but believes other factors also played a part: 'After Lewis started broadcasting for the BBC he became trapped by his own success ... He suddenly became everyman's Christian apologist. Thereafter Mere Christianity became a ring fence and he preferred to stay out of theological dog-fights.'[17] This desire to avoid controversy in order to please most of the people most of the time did not please Tolkien, who referred to Lewis disparagingly as 'Everyman's Theologian'.[18]

Although the ingrained prejudices of a Belfast upbringing may have given Lewis a jaundiced view of the Catholic

Church, one suspects that Tolkien may have overstated the case. Lewis's practice of going to weekly confession, which he commenced at the end of 1940, was hardly the sort of behaviour one would expect from an Ulster Protestant. He also had a deeply sacramental approach to Christianity, and even Tolkien admitted that Lewis 'reveres the Blessed Sacrament, and admires nuns!'[19] Furthermore, if Lewis is to be judged by the fruit of his labour, there can be little doubt that he brought in a more bountiful harvest of converts to Christianity, both during and after the war, than any other writer of his generation.

If Tolkien was wrong to overstate the extent of Lewis's antagonism towards the Catholic Church, it would be wrong also to overstate the extent of the antagonism which Tolkien felt towards Lewis. Most of Tolkien's adverse references to Lewis date from much later, from after their partial estrangement in the 1950s, and there is no doubt that the first twenty years of their friendship were a great joy to both men. By the late 1930s the meetings of the Inklings were an important and integral part of their lives, a source of enjoyment and inspiration, as well as being a catalyst that assisted the fruitful cross-fertilization of ideas.

When war broke out in 1939 the Inklings welcomed a new member. This was Charles Williams, who worked for the Oxford University Press at their London office but who had been transferred to Oxford with the rest of the publishers' staff after war was declared. Williams was in his fifties, older than Tolkien and Lewis, and was known as a novelist, poet, theologian, and critic. Like Lewis he was an Anglican and his 'spiritual thrillers' commanded a small but enthusiastic following. Lewis had known and admired Williams for some time before he joined the Inklings, but Tolkien had only met him once or twice and he failed to share Lewis's enthusiasm for his work. 'We liked one another,' Tolkien recalled twenty years later, 'and enjoyed talking (mostly in jest).' Yet, significantly, he added: 'We had nothing to say to one another at deeper (or higher) levels.'[20]

Although Williams enjoyed and admired the chapters from *The Lord of the Rings* that were being read to the Inklings during the war years, Tolkien neither enjoyed nor admired Williams's books, declaring that he found them 'wholly alien, and sometimes very distasteful, occasionally ridiculous'.[21] Perhaps it was not surprising, therefore, that Tolkien objected to the 'dominant influence' that he believed Williams was beginning to exercise over Lewis, and especially over Lewis's third novel, *That Hideous Strength*.

Williams was not, however, the only person exercising an influence on Lewis's novels. *That Hideous Strength* was the final part of a trilogy of science fiction novels featuring the character of Ransom as the philologist hero. Ransom was certainly modelled in part on Tolkien, and Tolkien wrote to his son Christopher in 1944 of his unwittingly benign influence on Lewis's characterization of Ransom: 'As a philologist I may have some part in him, and recognize some of my opinions and ideas Lewisified in him.'[22] Lewis, in turn, would influence Tolkien's characterization of Treebeard in *The Lord of the Rings*, which Tolkien was writing throughout the war years. Tolkien told Nevill Coghill, a fellow Inkling and Fellow of Exeter College, that he had modelled Treebeard's way of speaking, '*Hrum, Hroom*', on the booming voice of C.S. Lewis.[23] Tolkien also told Walter Hooper that 'I wrote *The Lord of the Rings* to make Lewis a story out of *The Silmarillion*.' Hooper admits that Tolkien was 'probably exaggerating light-heartedly', knowing that Lewis 'had a huge appetite for stories', but he did consider Lewis 'a great encourager'.[24]

During the war years Tolkien, Lewis and the other Inklings continued to meet, their gatherings representing a network of minds energizing each other into creativity. Towards the end of the war, in November 1944, Tolkien wrote of a meeting with Lewis and Williams, stating that he could 'recollect little of the feast of reason and flow of soul, partly because we all agree so'.[25] Later in the same month, in a letter to his son Christopher, Tolkien wrote of 'a great event: an evening Inklings'. On this occasion Tolkien had been joined by Charles Williams and R.E. Havard in the Mitre public house, where they enjoyed a pint before joining Lewis and Owen Barfield in Magdalen College. Lewis 'was highly flown, but we were also in good fettle'. Barfield, Tolkien wrote, was

> the only man who can tackle C.S.L. making him define everything and interrupting his most dogmatic pronouncements with subtle *distinguo*'s. The result was a most amusing and highly contentious evening, on which (had an outsider eavesdropped) he would have thought it a meeting of fell enemies hurling deadly insults before drawing their guns. Warnie was in excellent majoral form. On one occasion when the audience had flatly refused to hear Jack discourse on and define 'Chance', Jack said: 'Very well, some other time, but if you die tonight you'll be cut off knowing a great deal less about Chance than you might have.' Warnie: 'That only illustrates what I've always said: every cloud has a silver lining.' But there was some quite interesting stuff. A short play on Jason and Medea by Barfield, two excellent sonnets sent by a young poet to C.S.L.; and some illuminating discussion of 'ghosts', and of the special nature of Hymns (CSL has been on the Committee revising Ancient and Modern). I did not leave till 12.30, and reached my bed about 1 a.m. this morn ...[26]

One of Tolkien's most interesting and illuminating accounts of an Inklings gathering was given in another letter to his son six weeks earlier. Tolkien had called in at the Eagle and Child with Charles Williams on 3 October and was surprised to find Lewis and his brother 'already ensconced'. The conversation was 'pretty lively' and Tolkien noticed 'a strange tall gaunt man half in khaki half in mufti with a large wide-awake hat, bright eyes and a hooked nose sitting in the corner. The others had their back to him, but I could see in his eye that he was taking an interest in the conversation quite unlike the ordinary pained astonishment of the British (and American) public at the presence of the Lewises (and myself) in a pub.'[27] The stranger reminded Tolkien of Strider in *The Lord of the Rings*, the mysterious Ranger who eavesdropped on the conversation of the hobbits at the Prancing Pony at Bree. All of a sudden the stranger 'butted in, in a strange unplaceable accent, taking up some point about Wordsworth'. He was revealed as Roy Campbell, and Tolkien was gratified to learn that 'this powerful poet and soldier desired in Oxford chiefly to see Lewis (and myself)' and had been told where to find them by the Jesuit, Father Martin D'Arcy. After the stranger's identity became known, the conversation became 'fast and furious', not least because Lewis had violently lampooned Campbell in a recent issue of the *Oxford Magazine*. Lewis and Tolkien invited Campbell to a meeting of the Inklings two days later, on the evening of 5 October. This time the venue was Lewis's room at Magdalen. Tolkien reported that Lewis 'had taken a fair deal of port and was a little belligerent' and insisted on reading out his lampoon while Campbell laughed at him.

If Lewis was belligerent towards Campbell, Tolkien was transfixed by him, listening intently as the assembled

company 'were mostly obliged to listen to the guest'.
Paradoxically, he felt that Campbell was 'gentle, modest, and
compassionate', even though he spent most of the evening
listening to Campbell's embellished and highly romanticized
account of his own life:

> What he has done ... beggars description. Here is a scion of
> an Ulster prot. family resident in S. Africa, most of whom
> fought in both wars, who became a Catholic after sheltering
> the Carmelite fathers in Barcelona – in vain, they are caught
> & butchered, and R.C. nearly lost his life. But he got the
> Carmelite archives from the burning library and took them
> through the Red country. He speaks Spanish fluently (he has
> been a professional bullfighter). As you know he then fought
> through the war on Franco's side, and among other things
> was in the van of the company that chased the Reds out of
> Malaga ... But he is a patriotic man, and has fought for the
> B. Army since ... However, it is not possible to convey an
> impression of such a rare character, both a soldier and a poet,
> and a Christian convert. How unlike the Left – the 'corduroy
> panzers' who fled to America.[28]

As well as displaying a somewhat reactionary side to his character, Tolkien's meeting with Roy Campbell highlighted
further differences with Lewis. Tolkien was puzzled by his
friend's hostility to Campbell, describing his reactions as 'odd'.
'Nothing is a greater tribute to red propaganda than the fact that
he (who knows they are in all other subjects liars and traducers)
believes all that is said against Franco, and nothing that is said
for him.' In fact, following the meeting with Campbell, Lewis
had stated that 'I loathed and loathe Roy Campbell's particular
blend of Catholicism and Fascism, and told him so.'[29]

Lewis's judgement was unfair. Campbell never considered himself a Fascist, and his decision to fight for Franco's Nationalists when the Spanish Civil War began in 1936 was based on a desire to defend traditional Catholic culture from the destructive atheism of the communists. He was living in Spain at the outbreak of hostilities, having become a Catholic along with his wife the previous year, and was sucked into the vortex. Believing that his duty was to fight for the culture and traditions he had recently discovered and embraced, Campbell saw his part in the conflict as a straightforward defence of hearth and home.

Back in England the choice had not seemed so cut and dried. In 1936 Nazism was considered a far greater threat than communism and even those who had no time for the communists were worried about Hitler's support for Franco. The *Anschluss*, Hitler's annexation of Austria, had taken place in March of that year and the Nazis were demanding territory in Czechoslovakia. War, it seemed, could engulf far more than Spain and, if it did, Hitler and not Stalin would be Britain's enemy. Yet Catholics throughout the world were horrified by news of atrocities carried out against priests and nuns by the communists and anarchists in Spain. Before the war was over twelve bishops, 4,184 priests, 2,365 monks and about 300 nuns were killed. Churches were burned and George Orwell recorded of Barcelona that 'almost every church had been gutted and its images burned'. Priests had their ears cut off, monks had their eardrums perforated by rosary beads being forced into them and the mother of two Jesuit priests had a rosary forced down her throat. For all Franco's faults, many considered anything preferable to the brutal anti-Catholic atheism of his opponents. Evelyn Waugh had spoken for many Catholics when, in 1937, he replied to a questionnaire sent to writers in the British Isles asking them to state their attitude towards the war in Spain: 'If I were a Spaniard I should be fighting for General Franco. As an Englishman I am not in the predicament of choosing between two evils.'[30] Similar sentiments were expressed at the time by other members of the Catholic *literati*, including Arnold Lunn, Alfred Noyes, Ronald Knox, Christopher Hollis and Christopher Dawson, and their views were reflected by Tolkien. None of these men, by any stretch of the imagination, could be described as 'Fascists'. Neither was Campbell. The only difference between his position and those of his literary peers was that he happened to be living in Spain and so had become embroiled in the grim reality. His friend, the Carmelite prior of Toledo, had been murdered along with many of the other monks under his charge in spite of Campbell's efforts to hide them in his house. Having witnessed the horrors at first hand, it is scarcely surprising that Campbell was somewhat vociferous in his attacks on communism.

He was, however, equally opposed to Nazism. Before the Spanish war had started he had made the acquaintance of fellow foreigners in the neighbourhood of Altea. These included two Norwegians, Helge Krog and Erling Winsness: 'Helge was a Communist and Erling was a Nazi,' Campbell observed, 'but they were both staunchly united in their hate of Christ and Christianity.'[31] One can imagine the heated discussions which ensued when Campbell met up with these two Scandinavians. Their religious and political arguments must have been a foretaste in microcosm of the struggles about to explode into violence on a worldwide scale. 'From the very beginning my wife and I understood the real issues in Spain,' Campbell had written, '... now was the time to decide whether ... to remain half-apathetic to the great fight which was obviously approaching – or whether we should step into the front ranks of the Regular Army of Christ. Hitler himself had said, even by then, how much more easy the Protestants were to enslave and bamboozle than the Catholics.'[32]

Tolkien suspected that the real root of Lewis's antagonism towards Campbell was not his alleged Fascism but his outspoken Catholicism. It was in the context of the angry exchange between Lewis and Campbell that Tolkien had made his complaint of duplicity on Lewis's part: 'If a Lutheran is put in jail he is up in arms; but if Catholic priests are slaughtered – he disbelieves it (and I daresay really thinks they asked for it).' These are strong and even bitter words, signifying perhaps that Tolkien had over-reacted to Lewis's alleged anti-Catholicism, as Lewis had over-reacted to Campbell's alleged Fascism.

Campbell made one or two more appearances at the Eagle and Child, and came to the Inklings once more in 1946, but the enmity with Lewis ensured that he was never really admitted to the group's inner sanctum.

If Tolkien's siding with Campbell during the altercation with Lewis hinted at a growing estrangement of interests between Lewis and Tolkien, it did not affect their friendship unduly at this stage and Lewis continued to act as a great encourager of Tolkien as the latter struggled to finish *The Lord of the Rings*. 'I do not seem to have any mental energy or invention,' Tolkien had written at the beginning of 1944, his work on *The Lord of the Rings* having lain untouched for many months. Lewis, noticing his friend's lack of progress, urged him to resume work. 'I needed some pressure,' said Tolkien, 'and shall probably respond.'[33] By April he was writing again, and reading the newly completed chapters to the Lewis brothers and Charles Williams. He reported in a letter to his son that the 'recent chapter' had 'received approbation' from his fellow Inklings.[34]

On 15 May 1945, only six days after the end of the war in Europe, the group of friends was shaken by the sudden and unexpected death of Charles Williams. As soon as he heard the news Tolkien wrote to Williams's widow: 'My heart goes out to you in sympathy, and I can say no more. I share a little in your loss, for in the (far too brief) years since I first met him I had grown to admire and love your husband deeply, and I am more grieved than I can express ... Fr. Gervase Mathew is saying Mass at Blackfriars on Saturday at 8 a.m., and I shall serve him; but of course I shall have you all in my prayers immediately and continually.'[35] The genuine warmth of this letter should be borne in mind when considering the nature of Tolkien's relationship with Williams. It is true that he was never a great admirer of Williams's novels, and that he complained of the 'dominant influence' that Williams came to exert on C.S. Lewis, but Williams was still one of his closest friends throughout the war years and he felt the loss immensely. Along with both Lewis brothers, Dorothy L. Sayers, Owen Barfield and Father Gervase Mathew, Tolkien contributed to *Essays Presented to Charles Williams*, which was published in 1947 as a posthumous tribute to Williams by some of his friends and admirers.

Meanwhile, Tolkien's friendship with C.S. Lewis continued, but on a somewhat cooler level than in the early years of their relationship. Indeed, it is significant that Tolkien would write later that Lewis 'was my closest friend from about 1927 to 1940, and remained very dear to me'.[36] Yet the cooling of their relationship in the years after 1940 was very gradual and, to Lewis at least, probably imperceptible. Outwardly, the friendship seemed the same as ever. Both attended the regular Inklings meetings and both could be seen together in the Eagle and Child or the White Horse, drinking and discussing as they had done for the previous twenty years. In 1949 Lewis began to read the first of his 'Narnia' stories to the Inklings. This was *The Lion, the Witch and the Wardrobe*, destined to become one of the most popular children's books ever written. Tolkien, however, was unimpressed. 'It really won't do!' he exclaimed to Roger Lancelyn Green, a mutual friend who would later become Lewis's biographer. 'I mean to say: "Nymphs and their Ways, The Love-Life of a Faun"!'[37] Fifteen years later, Tolkien would write that it was 'sad that "Narnia" and all that part of C.S.L.'s work should remain outside the range of my sympathy'.[38] Yet if Tolkien was unable to enjoy Lewis's work, Lewis continued to be full of praise for *The Lord of the Rings*. Tolkien had finally finished it in the autumn of 1949, lending the completed typescript to Lewis, who reported back in laudatory tones:

My dear Tollers,

Uton herian holbytlas indeed. I have drained the rich cup and satisfied a long thirst. Once it really gets under weigh the steady upward slope of grandeur and terror (not unrelieved by green dells, without which it would indeed be intolerable) is almost unequalled in the whole range of narrative art known to me. In two virtues I think it excels: sheer sub-creation – Bombadil, Barrow Wights, Elves, Ents – as if from inexhaustible resources, and construction. Also in *gravitas*. No romance can repel the charge of 'escapism' with such confidence. If it errs, it errs in precisely the opposite direction: all victories of hope deferred and the merciless piling up of odds against the hero are near to being too painful. And the long *coda* after the eucatastrophe, whether you intended it or no, has the effect of reminding us that victory is as transitory as conflict, that (as Byron says) 'there's no sterner moralist than pleasure', and so leaving a final impression of profound melancholy...

I congratulate you. All the long years you have spent on it are justified.[39]

Lewis's enthusiasm for *The Lord of the Rings* spilled over into letters to his friends. 'Wouldn't it be wonderful,' he wrote to Katherine Farrer on 4 December 1953, 'if it really succeeded (in selling I mean)? It would inaugurate a new age. Dare we hope?'[40]

This private praise became public knowledge when Lewis reviewed *The Fellowship of the Ring*, the first volume of *The Lord of the Rings*, after its publication in 1954:

This book is like lightning from a clear sky; as sharply different, as unpredictable in our age as *Songs of Innocence* were in theirs. To say that in it heroic romance, gorgeous, eloquent, and unashamed, has suddenly returned at a period almost pathological in its anti-romanticism is inadequate. To us, who live in that odd period, the return – and the sheer relief of it – is doubtless the important thing. But in the history of Romance itself – a history which stretches back to the *Odyssey* and beyond – it makes not a return but an advance or revolution: the conquest of new territory.[41]

If Lewis's immense admiration for Tolkien is evident, so is the influence of Tolkien's work on Lewis's own literary efforts. Lewis's creation of Narnia was all too obviously a reflection, albeit a pale reflection in shallower creative waters, of Tolkien's Middle Earth and at least one critic has suggested that the germ of Lewis's *The Great Divorce* was provided by the purgatorial peripatetics of Tolkien's *Leaf by Niggle*.[42]

Yet, in spite of Tolkien's criticism of Lewis's work, it would be woefully wrong and unjust to suggest that the influence only flowed in one direction. Tolkien gained a great deal from his friendship with Lewis, benefiting from Lewis's enthusiasm, his encouragement and his comradeship. Tolkien's daughter Priscilla believed that her father owed an 'enormous debt' to Lewis,[43] and his son, Christopher, was even more emphatic in his insistence that his father's relationship with Lewis was crucial to his creative vision. 'The profound attachment and imaginative intimacy between him and Lewis were in some ways the core of it,' he said, adding that their friendship was of 'profound importance ... to both of them'.[44]

Their friendship with the other members of the Inklings was also of profound importance and they derived more than mere pleasure from the twice-weekly meetings. Over the years, the network of minds and cross-fertilization of ideas that the Inklings facilitated allowed both men to develop their creativity in a critically sympathetic and intellectually stimulating atmosphere. The appearance of Tolkien's *The Lord of the Rings* and *The Hobbit*, and Lewis's *The Lion, the Witch and the Wardrobe*, in the top thirty 'greatest books of the century' was a vindication of the Inklings as much as it was of the authors themselves. This was admitted by Nigel Reynolds, an arts correspondent with the *Daily Telegraph*, who wrote that the results of the Waterstone's poll 'suggests that The Inklings, a 1930s Oxford drinking club, has been a more powerful force than the Bloomsbury Group, the Algonquin set in New York, Hemingway's Paris set or the W.H. Auden/Christopher Isherwood group of writers in the 1930s'.[45]

Other writers have also stressed the importance of the Inklings. Chad Walsh wrote in the *New York Times Book Review* that Tolkien, Lewis and Charles Williams had 'renewed the sense of magic and enchantment and assimilated it into the contemporary Christian sensibility'.[46] Meanwhile, Sister Mary Anthony Weinig wrote from a specifically Christian viewpoint in the *University of Portland Review*:

> Bedrock reality of human values and spiritual truth comes to light under the probing of rays beyond the ordinary spectrum of the naturalistic novel, and a vision emerges whose depth and wholeness stagger an imagination fed on fragments [in] the symbolic situation of Charles Williams, the allegorical narrative of C.S. Lewis, and the mythic rendering of J.R.R. Tolkien.[47]

Perhaps the final word on the enduring influence of Tolkien, Lewis and the Inklings should be left to Stephen R. Lawhead, the bestselling fantasy writer:

> I discovered the Inklings – quite by accident, as it happens. While researching an article about Tolkien for *Campus Life*, I picked up a copy of Humphrey Carpenter's biography of the professor. The author described the importance in Tolkien's life of his literary friends, a fairly informal group of Oxford academics of one sort or another who went by the name of the Inklings.
>
> Having enjoyed Tolkien's books, I tracked down and read some of the work of some of the other Inklings – C.S. Lewis and Charles Williams especially. I enjoyed the books, but in the end it wasn't the Inklings' work that moved me. It was the informing spirit of their work, a spirit which I began to sense they all shared.
>
> ...the lessons I learned from Lewis and Tolkien penetrated deep into my psyche – deeper than emulation, deeper than

imitation. In short, it was not Tolkien's style or subject matter that influenced me; it was the integrity of the work itself.

I found this same integrity in Lewis's space tales. Taken together, these books possessed an inner worth that far exceeded the narrative skills of their authors. *Perelandra* and *The Lord of the Rings* seemed to me more in total than the simple sum of their parts. These books, I concluded, derived their value chiefly from this inner worth, this integrity that lay behind the stories themselves. But what was it?

It was, of course, the Christian faith of the authors shining through the fabric of their work. I saw that faith informed the story, and infused it with value and meaning, lifting the tale above the ordinary expressions of the genre. Even though the stories of Lewis, Tolkien, or other Inklings like Charles Williams, were not explicitly promoting Christianity, nevertheless the books were ripe with it.

What an extraordinary thing, I thought; though Tolkien makes never so much as a glancing reference to Jesus Christ in a single paragraph of all *The Lord of the Rings'* thick volumes, His face is glimpsed on virtually every page. *The Lion, the Witch and the Wardrobe* is the furthest thing from a religious tract, yet it proclaims a clear and winning gospel. In my narrow experience, I had never before encountered such a thing.[48]

CHAPTER 6

THE CREATION OF MIDDLE EARTH:
THE MYTH BEHIND THE MAN

Probably no book yet written in the world is quite such a radical instance of what its author has elsewhere called 'sub-creation'. The direct debt (there are of course subtler kinds of debt) which every author must owe to the actual universe is here deliberately reduced to the minimum. Not content to create his own story, he creates, with an almost insolent prodigality, the whole world in which it is to move, with its own theology, myths, geography, history, palaeography, languages, and orders of beings – a world 'full of strange creatures beyond count'.[1]

These words were written in 1954 by C.S. Lewis in his review of *The Fellowship of the Ring*, the first volume of *The Lord of the Rings*. Yet the 'theology, myths, geography, history, palaeography, languages, and orders of beings' did not originate in *The Lord of the Rings* but in an earlier work which was not actually published until after Tolkien's death. This was *The Silmarillion*, the earliest versions of which dated back to 1917.

The Silmarillion delved deep into the past of Middle Earth, Tolkien's sub-created world, and the legends recounted in its pages formed the vast landscape of myth within which *The Lord of the Rings* was born. Indeed, Tolkien's *magnum opus* would not have been born at all if he had not first created, in *The Silmarillion*, the world, the womb, in which it was conceived.

The most important part of *The Silmarillion* is its account of the Creation of Middle Earth by the One. This Creation myth is perhaps the most significant, and the most beautiful, of all Tolkien's work. It goes to the very roots of his creative vision and says much about Tolkien himself. Somewhere within the early pages of *The Silmarillion* is to be found both the man behind the myth and the myth behind the man.

The 'myth' behind Tolkien was, of course, Catholic Christianity, the 'True Myth', and it is scarcely surprising that Tolkien's own version of the Creation in *The Silmarillion* bears a remarkable similarity to the Creation story in the book of Genesis.

According to T.A. Shippey in *The Road to Middle Earth*, a similarity with 'the history of Genesis' was the 'most obvious fact about the design of *The Silmarillion*'.[2] Shippey compares Tolkien's Creation myth with 'a summary list of doctrines of the Fall of Man common to Milton, to St Augustine, and to the Church as a whole' which C.S. Lewis had given in chapter ten of *A Preface to Paradise Lost*. Most of these reappeared with little change in *The Silmarillion*:

Thus Lewis asserts that 'God created all things without exception good'; in Tolkien even Melkor begins with good intentions (p. 18). 'What we call bad things are good things perverted ... This perversion arises when a conscious creature becomes more interested in itself than in God ... the sin of Pride'; compare Melkor in the music of the Ainur seeking 'to increase the power and glory of the part assigned to himself'. Lewis again, 'whoever tries to rebel against God produces the result opposite to his intention ... those who will not be God's sons become his tools': and Ilúvatar to Melkor, 'no theme may be played that hath not its uttermost source in me ... he that attempteth this shall prove but mine *instrument* in the devising of things more wonderful, which he himself hath not imagined'.[3]

Shippey concludes that the remarkable similarity between Lewis's and Tolkien's approach suggests that they probably 'collaborated in their analysis of Christian essentials'. This is not the case. Not only did Tolkien compose his Creation myth before Lewis wrote *A Preface to Paradise Lost*, but the doctrines present in *The Silmarillion* were merely an expression of the orthodox Christian theology on which Tolkien had been reared since childhood. He had no need to collaborate with Lewis in order to incorporate Catholic teaching into his writing.

Shippey was more perceptive in his belief that Tolkien was careful to ensure that his own Creation myth did not contradict the account in Genesis:

Is it a *rival* to Christian story? The thought clearly occurred to Tolkien, if only to be repudiated. Significantly he left a gap in *The Silmarillion*, or designed a dovetail, for the Fall of Man as described in the Old Testament. In his work the human race does not originate 'on stage' in Beleriand, but drifts into it, already sundered in speech, from the East. There something terrible has happened to them of which they will not speak: 'A darkness lies behind us ... and we have turned our backs on it' (p. 141). Furthermore they have met 'the Lord of the Dark' before they meet the Elves; Morgoth went to them before they were created, to 'corrupt or destroy'. Clearly one can, if one wishes, assume that the exploit of Morgoth of which the Eldar never learnt was the traditional seduction of Adam and Eve by the serpent, while the incoming Edain and Easterlings are all sons of Adam flying from Eden and subject to the curse of Babel. *The Silmarillion*, then, tells the story of the fall and partial redemption of the elves, without contradicting the story of the Fall and Redemption of Man.[4]

Tolkien's totally orthodox understanding of the Fall and Redemption of Man was deeply coloured by his philosophy of myth. This was evident in the poignancy of his view of Genesis in general and Eden in particular in a letter to his son Christopher on 30 January 1945:

As for Eden. I think most Christians ... have been rather bustled and hustled now for some generations by the self-styled scientists, and they've sort of tucked Genesis into a lumber-room of their mind as not very fashionable furniture, a bit ashamed to have it about the house, don't you know, when the bright clever young people called: I mean, of course, even the *fideles* who did not sell it secondhand or burn it as soon as modern taste began to sneer. In consequence they have ... forgotten the beauty of the matter even 'as a story'. Lewis recently wrote a most interesting essay ... showing of what great value the 'story-value' was, as mental nourishment ... It was a defence of that kind of attitude which we tend to sneer at: the fainthearted that loses faith, but clings at least to the beauty of 'the story' as having some permanent value. His point was that they do still in that way get some nourishment and are not cut off wholly from the sap of life: for the beauty of the story while not necessarily a guarantee of its truth is a concomitant of it, and a *fidelis* is meant to draw nourishment from the beauty as well as the truth ... But partly as a development of my own thought on my lines of work (technical and literary), partly in contact with C.S.L., and in various ways not least the firm guiding hand of Alma Mater Ecclesia, I do not now feel either ashamed or dubious on the Eden 'myth'. It has not, of course, historicity of the same kind as the NT, which are virtually contemporary documents, while Genesis is separated by we do not know how many sad exiled generations from the Fall, but certainly there was an Eden on this very unhappy earth. We all long for it, and we are constantly glimpsing it: our whole nature at its best and least corrupted, its gentlest and most humane, is still soaked with the sense of 'exile'.[5]

The Eden 'myth' was at the very heart of Tolkien's creation of *The Silmarillion*, as well as being at the very heart of the Creation myth contained within it. Tolkien's longing for this lost Eden and his mystical glimpses of it, inspired and motivated by his sense of 'exile' from the fullness of truth, was the source of his creativity. At the core of *The Silmarillion*, indeed at the core of all his work, was a hunger for the truth that transcends mere facts: the infinite and eternal Reality which was beyond the finite and temporal perceptions of humanity.

The deep theology behind the Creation Myth at the start of *The Silmarillion* was discussed by Brian Rosebury in *Tolkien: A Critical Assessment*:

Ainulindalë, the Elves' version of *Genesis*, seems to me a success: its central image, the world as a Great Music made visible, its history a fulfilment of creative purposes which proceed both directly from God and mediately from him, through the sub-creativity of created beings, is elaborately worked out and represents a profound meditation on the

Augustinian theology, its address to the problem of evil and its account of the contingency of temporal existence. And its prose is at once appropriately 'scriptural' and distinctive of Tolkien.[6]

Not surprisingly, Tolkien's 'profound meditation on Augustinian theology' has found many admirers among the Christian clergy. The Jesuit, Father Robert Murray, a friend of Tolkien's, alluded to the 'biblical' nature of Tolkien's Creation myth:

> The Bible contains traces of various poetic creation myths besides the accounts in Genesis, especially in Job and the Psalms. But in all literatures since the formation of the sacred books of humankind surely there is hardly a creation myth to equal, in beauty and imaginative power, the one with which *The Silmarillion* begins. Here Tolkien projected his idea of sub-creation back to the beginning of all things, and conceived it in terms of music. Ilúvatar, the One, first created the Ainur, 'the Holy Ones ... the offspring of his thought', and proposed themes for them to make music on. At last he called a halt, and then revealed that this music, both in its beauty and in the discords which had arisen within it, formed the archetypes and 'script' for a whole world and its history.[7]

Father Murray's view was echoed by another Jesuit, Father James V. Schall, who told a friend, 'I have never read anything quite so beautiful as the first page of *The Silmarillion*, the chapter entitled, "Ainulindalë: The Music of the Ainur."'[8] Father Schall not only liked to read the opening lines of *The Silmarillion* but to have them read aloud, echoing Rosebury's view that the prose was 'appropriately scriptural':

There was Eru, the One, who in Arda is called Ilúvatar; and he made first the Ainur, the Holy Ones, that were the offspring of his thought, and they were with him before aught else was made. And he spoke to them themes of music; and they sang before him, and he was glad.[9]

A more whimsical view of Tolkien's Creation myth is provided by Richard Jeffery, a leading member of the C.S. Lewis Society who has made a life-long study of Tolkien. Jeffery had met Tolkien in 1956, soon after the third volume of *The Lord of the Rings* had been published, and they discussed *The Silmarillion*. At the time, Tolkien had recently resumed work on it. More than forty years later, Jeffery remains convinced of the book's merits:

I am rather fond of *The Silmarillion* … the idea that God allows the archangels to take part in the Creation … It strikes me that his picture of the archangels is surprisingly like small children with their father, rather trying to get the advantage over each other. Also, the one who rebels is rather like a child who refuses to co-operate in the making of grand sand castles … so is told not to join in … He responds by trying to smash them up. Of course because the Valar are immortal they can't really do anything to each other so they can only smash up each other's creation. All of this is the background to *The Lord of the Rings* as having been created by the archangels, the Valar, under the direction of the One.[10]

Jeffery's one crucial sin of omission in this amusing rendition of Tolkien's Creation myth was his failure to stress that Elves and Men, known together as the Children of Ilúvatar, were *not* created by the Valar, or the Ainur, but by the One directly.

Describing the Ainur at the beginning of *The Silmarillion*, Tolkien wrote:

> The Ainur know much of what was, and is, and is to come, and few things are unseen by them. Yet some things there are that they cannot see, neither alone nor taking counsel together; for to none but to himself has Ilúvatar revealed all that he has in store, and in every age there come forth things that are new and have no foretelling, for they do not proceed from the past. And so it was that as this vision of the world was played before them, the Ainur saw that it contained things which they had not thought. And they saw with amazement the coming of the Children of Ilúvatar, and the habitation that was prepared for them; and they perceived that they themselves in the labour of their music had been busy with the preparation of this dwelling, and yet knew not that it had any purpose beyond its own beauty. For the Children of Ilúvatar were conceived by him alone; and they came with the third theme, and were not in the theme which Ilúvatar propounded at the beginning, and none of the Ainur had part in their making. Therefore when they beheld them, the more did they love them, being things other than themselves, strange and free, wherein they saw the mind of Ilúvatar reflected anew, and learned yet a little more of his wisdom, which otherwise had been hidden even from the Ainur.[11]

Tolkien then states that 'amid all the splendours of the World, its vast halls and wheeling fires', Ilúvatar chose a place for the habitation of his Children 'in the Deeps of Time and in the midst of the innumerable stars'.[12] Thus, in a feat of ingenious invention, or sub-creation, Tolkien not only distinguishes

Men and Elves as being made directly 'in the image of God', essentially different from the rest of Creation, but at the same time accommodates the theory of evolution. The evolution of the cosmos was simply the unfolding of the Music of the Ainur within which the One places his Children in a habitation prepared for them. The enormity of the concept, and its apparent paradox, was addressed by Tolkien in words of poignant mysticism: 'this habitation might seem a little thing to those who consider only the majesty of the Ainur, and not their terrible sharpness'.[13]

In a similar feat of ingenuity, Tolkien explains that the Valar, the angelic powers given the responsibility of shaping the cosmos, have often been called 'gods' by Men.[14] In this way he manages to accommodate paganism as well as evolution within his mythology, making both subsist within Christian orthodoxy.

Following his whimsical exposition of Tolkien's Creation myth, Richard Jeffery added, more seriously, 'I think Tolkien and Lewis would have both said that God's relationship with the world is very complex, good and evil are very complex.'[15] Doubtless they would have, but they would not have allowed the complexity to become an excuse for sophistry. For both Tolkien and Lewis the explanation of good and evil was to be found in orthodox Christian teaching. In fact, for all Tolkien's much publicized disdain for allegory, there is no mistaking his allegorical treatment of the Christian doctrine of the Fall in *The Silmarillion*. Melkor, later known as Morgoth, is Middle Earth's equivalent of Lucifer, also known as Satan. Melkor is described by Tolkien as 'the greatest of the Ainur' as Lucifer was the greatest of the archangels. Like Lucifer, Melkor is the embodiment and the ultimate source of the sin of pride, intent on corrupting mankind for his own purposes.

Melkor desired 'to subdue to his will both Elves and Men, envying the gifts with which Ilúvatar promised to endow them; and he wished himself to have subjects and servants, and to be called Lord, and to be master over other wills'.[16]

The allegory becomes even less mistakable when Tolkien describes the war between Melkor and Manwë, who is clearly cast in the role of the archangel Michael:

When therefore Earth was yet young and full of flame Melkor coveted it, and he said to the other Valar: 'This shall be my own kingdom; and I name it unto myself!'

But Manwë was the brother of Melkor in the mind of Ilúvatar, and he was the chief instrument of the second theme that Ilúvatar had raised up against the discord of Melkor; and he called unto himself many spirits both greater and less, and they came down into the fields of Arda and aided Manwë, lest Melkor should hinder the fulfilment of their labour for ever, and Earth should wither ere it flowered. And Manwë said unto Melkor: 'This kingdom thou shalt not take for thine own, wrongfully, for many others have laboured here no less than thou.' And there was strife between Melkor and the other Valar; and for that time Melkor withdrew and departed to other regions and did there what he would; but he did not put the desire of the Kingdom of Arda from his heart.[17]

The parallels between Melkor and Lucifer are made even more apparent when Tolkien explains that the name, Melkor, means 'He who arises in Might' – 'But that name he has forfeited; and the Noldor, who among the Elves suffered most from his malice, will not utter it, and they name him Morgoth, the Dark Enemy of the World.'[18] Similarly, Lucifer, brightest of all the angels, means 'Light Bringer', whereas Satan, like 'Morgoth', means 'Enemy'. Tolkien's intention, both as a Christian and as a philologist, in identifying Melkor with Lucifer is plain enough.

Taking his inspiration, no doubt, from the Book of Isaiah ('Thy pomp is brought down to the grave, and the noise of thy viols: the worm is spread under thee, and the worms cover thee. How art thou fallen from heaven, O Lucifer, son of the morning' (Isaiah 14:11–12)), Tolkien says of Melkor:

> From splendour he fell through arrogance to contempt for all things save himself, a spirit wasteful and pitiless. Understanding he turned to subtlety in perverting to his own will all that he would use, until he became a liar without shame. He began with the desire of Light, but when he could not possess it for himself alone, he descended through fire and wrath into a great burning, down into Darkness. And darkness he used most in his evil works upon Arda, and filled it with fear for all living things.[19]

As well as the scriptural influence, the other over-riding influence, as discussed already, is clearly Augustinian theology. Evil, as symbolized by darkness, has no value of its own but is only a negation of that which is good, as symbolized by light.

Shortly after this description of Melkor, Tolkien introduces Sauron, the Dark Enemy in *The Lord of the Rings*. Sauron is described as a 'spirit' and as the 'greatest' of Melkor's, alias Morgoth's, servants: 'But in after years he rose like a shadow of Morgoth and a ghost of his malice, and walked behind him on the same ruinous path down into the Void.'[20]

Thus, the evil powers in *The Lord of the Rings* are specified as direct descendants of Tolkien's Satan, rendering impossible,

or at any rate implausible, anything but a theistic interpretation of the book. Furthermore, as has been seen, the theology
of *The Silmarillion* is orthodox in nature, paralleling the
teachings of traditional Christianity to a remarkable degree.
This throws into question Lewis's view that Tolkien created
his own theology, along with his own 'myths, geography,
history, palaeography, languages, and orders of beings'. In fact,
far from creating a new theology Tolkien merely adopted and
adapted an old one to his own use. This Catholic theology,
explicitly present in *The Silmarillion* and implicitly present in
The Lord of the Rings, is omnipresent in both, breathing life
into the tales as invisibly but as surely as oxygen. Whether
Tolkien was consciously aware of this is another matter, but
subconsciously he was so saturated with the Christian
concept of reality that it permeates his myth profoundly.

He admitted as much in a letter he wrote on 14 October
1958. Referring to *The Lord of the Rings* as 'a tale, which is
built on or out of certain "religious" ideas, but is *not* an allegory of them', he discussed its theology: 'Theologically (if the
term is not too grandiose) I imagine the picture to be less
dissonant from what some (including myself) believe to be the
truth.'[21] This letter, which implies that Tolkien was surprised
to find how orthodox his work actually was, suggests that the
theology was introduced subconsciously. However, Tolkien's
efforts to explain, or explain away, the awkward (or orcward?)
position of the orcs from a theological point of view, indicate
his over-riding desire that his myth should be seen as essentially orthodox in nature.

The awkwardness of orcs had been pointed out to Tolkien
by Peter Hastings, manager of a Catholic bookshop in Oxford,
who suggested that 'Treebeard's statement that the Dark Lord
created the Trolls and the Orcs' contradicted Christian

teaching that evil was incapable of creating anything. In reply, Tolkien was at pains to point out that 'Creation, the act of Will of Eru the One that gives Reality to conceptions, is distinguished from Making, which is permissive':

> I think I agree about the 'creation by evil'. But you are more free with the word 'creation' than I am. Treebeard does not say that the Dark Lord 'created' Trolls and Orcs. He says he 'made' them in *counterfeit* of certain creatures pre-existing. There is, to me, a wide gulf between the two statements, so wide that Treebeard's statement could (in my world) have possibly been true. It is *not* true actually of the Orcs – who are fundamentally a race of 'rationally incarnate' creatures, though horribly corrupted, if no more so than many Men to be met today. Treebeard is a *character* in my story, not me: and though he has a great memory and some earthy wisdom, he is not one of the Wise, and there is quite a lot he does not know or understand ... Suffering and experience (and possibly the Ring itself) gave Frodo more insight; and you will read in Ch. I of Book VI the words to Sam. 'The Shadow that bred them can only mock, it cannot make real new things of its own. I don't think it gave life to the Orcs, it only ruined them and twisted them.' In the legends of the Elder Days it is suggested that the Diabolus subjugated and corrupted some of the earliest Elves, before they had ever heard of the 'gods', let alone of God.[22]

The orcs, therefore, are seen by Tolkien as victims of the Fall, as is Man, with the difference that their corruption by Tolkien's Satan was much worse than that of Man.

The ramifications of the Fall are evident throughout *The Silmarillion*, as indeed they are throughout *The Lord of the Rings*, in the recurring theme of conflict between the creative force of Good and the destructive force of Evil. The effects of this perennial conflict on the history of mankind was summed up succinctly towards the end of *The Silmarillion*:

> It is said by the Eldar that Men came into the world in the time of the Shadow of Morgoth, and they fell swiftly under his dominion; for he sent his emissaries among them, and they listened to his evil and his cunning words, and they worshipped the Darkness and yet feared it. But there were some that turned from evil and left the lands of their kindred, and wandered ever westward; for they had heard a rumour that in the West there was a light which the Shadow could not dim.[23]

Since Tolkien saw his own myth as a reflection of the True Myth, which was the fullness of Reality flowing from God, it is not surprising to see these views reflected in his life as well as his work. Tolkien believed that the perennial conflict between good and evil was as much a part of Earth as of Middle Earth. In a letter to his son Christopher on 14 May 1944, he wrote:

> A small knowledge of history depresses one with the sense of the everlasting mass and weight of human iniquity: old, old, dreary, endless repetitive unchanging incurable wicked-ness. All towns, all villages, all habitations of men – sinks! And at the same time one knows that there is always good: much more hidden, much less clearly discerned, seldom breaking out into recognizable, visible, beauties of word or deed or face – not even when in fact sanctity, far greater than

the visible advertised wickedness, is really there. But I fear that in the individual lives of all but a few, the balance is debit – we do so little that is positively good, even if we negatively avoid what is actively evil. It must be terrible to be a priest![24]

If the recurring theme of conflict between good and evil runs through *The Silmarillion* as a defining pattern, it remains only a part of the wealth of theology and mysticism with which Tolkien embroiders the fabric of his myth. In the moving story of Beren and Lúthien there is love, prayer, angelic intercession, sacrifice, the wisdom of accepted sorrow, and even a dim prefiguring of the Incarnation and Redemption. Elsewhere in *The Silmarillion*, there are even, on occasions, moments of sublime poetic beauty as, for example, this description of water and the sea:

> And they observed the winds and the air, and the matters of which Arda was made, of iron and stone and silver and gold and many substances: but of all these water they most greatly praised. And it is said by the Eldar that in water there lives yet the echo of the Music of the Ainur more than in any substance else that is in the Earth; and many of the Children of Ilúvatar hearken still unsated to the voices of the Sea, and yet know not for what they listen.[25]

In this passage, as in so many others throughout *The Silmarillion*, Tolkien succeeds in synthesizing the physical with the metaphysical in a way which marks him as a mystic. This mysticism was evident in a letter he wrote to one of his sons in November 1944, significantly at a time when he was in the midst of writing *The Lord of the Rings*:

Your reference to the care of your guardian angel makes me fear that 'he' is being specially needed. I dare say it is so ... It also reminded me of a sudden vision ... I had not long ago when spending half an hour in St Gregory's before the Blessed Sacrament ... I perceived or thought of the Light of God and in it suspended one small mote (or millions of motes to only one of which was my small mind directed), glittering white because of the individual ray from the Light which both held and lit it ... And the ray was the Guardian Angel of the mote: not a thing interposed between God and the creature, but God's very attention itself, personalized. And I do not mean 'personified', by a mere figure of speech according to the tendencies of human language, but a real (finite) person. Thinking of it since – for the whole thing was very immediate, and not recapturable in clumsy language, certainly not the great sense of joy that accompanied it and the realization that the shining poised mote was myself (or any other human person that I might think of with love) – it has occurred to me that ... this is a finite parallel to the Infinite. As the love of the Father and Son ... is a Person, so the love and attention of the Light to the Mote is a person (that is both with us and in Heaven): finite but divine: i.e. angelic. Anyway, dearest, I received comfort ... which I have (I fear) failed to convey: except that I have with me now a definite awareness of you poised and shining in the Light – though your face (as all our faces) is turned from it. But we might see the glimmer in the faces (and persons as apprehended in love) of others.[26]

If this is both heavy and heady, it is nonetheless important to any understanding of Tolkien's life, his personality and his work. Those who fail to share Tolkien's faith or philosophy may find his line of reasoning utterly incomprehensible; yet it was, for Tolkien, a logically reasoned exposition of an aspect of truth which he had perceived and experienced. In Tolkien's view, truth, and therefore reality, was ultimately metaphysical in nature, the physical universe being merely a reflection of some greater metaphysical purpose. This is reflected in *The Silmarillion*, in which the whole of physical creation is envisaged as a Great Music, played by angelic sub-creators in accordance with the will of God. The interposing of Tolkien's letter to his son with the myth propounded in *The Silmarillion* illustrates that Tolkien did not consider his sub-created myth as 'fiction', as popularly understood, but as a figment of truth.

Christopher Tolkien, the son to whom the above letter was addressed, has said that his father became 'more and more interested in the metaphysical aspect of *The Silmarillion*'[27] and it is a pity that he never wrote more about this facet of his work. It is clear, however, that *The Silmarillion*, the myth which formed the background to Tolkien's creative life for more than half a century, from his youth until his death, was probably the most important of all his works as regards the personal effect it had on him as the author, or sub-creator. It accompanied him throughout his life and created the frame-work, the context, into which *The Lord of the Rings* was slotted. If Tolkien was the man behind the myth, its sub-creator, *The Silmarillion* was also the myth behind the man, moulding his creative vision.

CHAPTER 7

ORTHODOXY IN MIDDLE EARTH:
THE TRUTH BEHIND THE MYTH

You cannot afford to *ignore* Dante's philosophical and theological beliefs, or to skip the passages which express them
most clearly; but ... on the other hand you are not called
upon to believe them yourself.[1]

In spite of Tolkien's statement that 'I do not seriously dream
of being measured against Dante, a supreme poet',[2] these
words of T.S. Eliot concerning the reading of Dante are just as
applicable to anyone reading *The Lord of the Rings*.

One cannot afford to ignore Tolkien's philosophical and
theological beliefs, central as they are to his whole conception
of Middle Earth and the struggles within it, but on the other
hand one can enjoy Tolkien's epic without sharing the beliefs
which gave it birth. This, of course, is evident from the many
millions who have read and enjoyed Tolkien's books without
sharing his Christianity. However, as his friend George Sayer
has remarked, '*The Lord of the Rings* would have been very
different, and the writing of it very difficult, if Tolkien hadn't
been a Christian. He thought it a profoundly Christian book.'[3]

In a letter to another friend, Tolkien had written, '*The Lord
of the Rings* is of course a fundamentally religious and
Catholic work; unconsciously so at first, but consciously in
the revision.'[4] These words were written to Father Robert
Murray on 2 December 1953, more than four years after

Tolkien had completed *The Lord of the Rings* and eight months before the first volume of it was finally published. Father Murray was the grandson of Sir James Murray, the founder of the *Oxford English Dictionary*, and was a close friend of the Tolkien family. At Tolkien's request, Murray had read part of *The Lord of the Rings* in typescript and galley-proofs, and had responded with both comments and criticism. He wrote that the book left him with a strong sense of 'a positive compatibility with the order of Grace', and compared the image of Galadriel to that of the Virgin Mary.[5]

Murray's comments elicited a candid response from Tolkien:

I have been cheered specially by what you have said ... because you are more perceptive, especially in some directions, than any one else, and have even revealed to me more clearly some things about my work. I think I know exactly what you mean by the order of Grace; and of course by your references to Our Lady, upon which all my own small perception of beauty both in majesty and simplicity is founded.[6]

Following his assertion that *The Lord of the Rings* was 'fundamentally religious and Catholic', Tolkien added that he was 'grateful for having been brought up (since I was eight) in a Faith that has nourished me and taught me all the little that I know; and that I owe to my mother, who clung to her conversion and died young, largely through the hardships of poverty resulting from it'.

The reference to his mother's conversion may have been prompted by the fact that Father Murray was a convert himself, having been received into the Church several years earlier largely under Tolkien's influence. Murray had arrived in Oxford in 1944 and soon discovered 'the joy of friendship with the Tolkiens'. 'Less than eighteen months later, when they realised that I was being drawn to share their faith, they introduced me to Father Carter, which led to a lasting friendship with that wonderful man and preacher.'[7]

Father Douglas Carter was Tolkien's parish priest, and Murray recalled that Tolkien had a high opinion of the priest, 'one of whose sermons inspired a long and theologically rich letter to his son Christopher'.[8] This letter needs quoting at length because it throws important light on Tolkien's faith and philosophy at the time he was writing *The Lord of the Rings*. He wrote that he and his daughter Priscilla had cycled to St Gregory's where they had heard one of Father Carter's 'best sermons (and longest)'. It had been a 'wonderful commentary on the Gospel of the Sunday (healing of the woman and of Jairus' daughter)' which had been 'made intensely vivid by his comparison of the three evangelists ... and also by his vivid illustrations from modern miracles':

The similar case of a woman similarly afflicted (owing to a vast uterine tumour) who was cured instantly at Lourdes, so that the tumour could not be found, and her belt was twice too large. And the most moving story of the little boy with tubercular peritonitis who was *not* healed, and was taken sadly away in the train by his parents, practically dying with two nurses attending him. As the train moved away it passed within sight of the Grotto. The little boy sat up. 'I want to go and talk to the little girl' – in the same train there was a little girl who had been healed. And he got up and walked there and played with the little girl; and then he came back, and he said 'I'm hungry now'. And they gave him cake and two bowls of chocolate and enormous potted meat sandwiches, and he ate them! (This was in 1927). So Our Lord told them to give the little daughter of Jairus something to eat. So plain and matter of fact: for so miracles are. They are intrusions (as we say, erring) into real or ordinary life, but they do intrude into real life, and so need ordinary meals and other results ... But at the story of the little boy (which is a fully attested *fact* of course) with its apparent sad ending and then its sudden unhoped-for happy ending, I was deeply moved and had that peculiar emotion we all have – though not often. It is quite unlike any other sensation. And all of a sudden I realized what it was: the very thing that I have been trying to write about and explain – in that fairy-story essay that I so much wish you had read that I think I shall send it to you. For it I coined the word 'eucatastrophe': the sudden happy turn in a story which pierces you with a joy that brings tears (which I argued it is the highest function of fairy-stories to produce).[9]

The essay, 'On Fairy Stories', to which Tolkien referred, was originally an Andrew Lang lecture given at the University of St Andrews on 8 March 1939. At the time of this letter to his son it still had not been published, not appearing in print until publication of the memorial volume *Essays Presented to Charles Williams* in 1947. In this essay Tolkien elaborated his view of the function of fairy stories, expressing the theory which *The Lord of the Rings* attempted to put into practice. Fairy stories offered 'consolation' through the 'imaginative satisfaction of ancient desires' but, more importantly, the fairy story offered 'the Consolation of the Happy Ending'. Whereas Tragedy was 'the true form of Drama, its highest function', the opposite was true of fairy story: 'Since we do not appear to possess a word that expresses this opposite – I will call it *Eucatastrophe*. The *eucatastrophic* tale is the true form of fairy-tale, and its highest function.' This good catastrophe, this 'sudden joyous "turn"' representing a 'miraculous grace, never to be counted on to recur', did not deny the existence of '*dyscatastrophe*, of sorrow and failure'. On the contrary, 'the possibility of these is necessary to the joy of deliverance'. Rather, it denied the 'universal final defeat and in so far is *evangelium*, giving a fleeting glimpse of Joy, Joy beyond the walls of the world, poignant as grief':

It is the mark of a good fairy-story, of the higher or more complete kind, that however wild its events, however fantastic or terrible the adventures, it can give to a child or man that hears it, when the 'turn' comes, a catch of the breath, a beat and lifting of the heart, near to (or indeed accompanied by) tears, as keen as that given by any form of literary art, and having a peculiar quality.[10]

Tolkien wrote an epilogue to this essay because this 'joy' which he had specified 'as the mark of the true fairy-story (or romance), or as the seal upon it, merits more consideration':

The peculiar quality of the 'joy' in successful Fantasy can thus be explained as a sudden glimpse of the underlying reality or truth. It is not only a 'consolation' for the sorrow of this world, but a satisfaction, and an answer to that question, 'Is it true?' ... in the 'eucatastrophe' we see a brief vision ... a far-off gleam or echo of *evangelium* in the real world...

I would venture to say that approaching the Christian Story from this direction, it has long been my feeling (a joyous feeling) that God redeemed the corrupt making-creatures, men, in a way fitting to this aspect, as to others, of their strange nature. The Gospels contain a fairy-story, or a story of a larger kind which embraces all the essence of fairy-stories. They contain many marvels – peculiarly artistic, beautiful, and moving: 'mythical' in their perfect, self-contained significance; and among the marvels is the greatest and most complete conceivable eucatastrophe. But this story has entered History and the primary world; the desire and aspiration of sub-creation has been raised to the fulfilment of Creation. The Birth of Christ is the eucatastrophe of Man's history. The Resurrection is the eucatastrophe of the story of the Incarnation. This story begins and ends in joy. It has pre-eminently the 'inner consistency of reality'. There is no tale ever told that men would rather find was true, and none which so many sceptical men have accepted as true on its own merits. For the Art of it has the supremely convincing tone of Primary Art, that is, of Creation. To reject it leads either to sadness or to wrath.[11]

In conclusion, Tolkien stressed that Christianity, the True Myth, had reconciled all lesser myths to itself. The lesser myths, in the form of fairy story or romance, were 'derived from Reality, or are flowing into it'. However inadequate in themselves, they still offered a glimpse of the greater truth from which they spring or into which they flow. Since the 'Christian joy, the *Gloria*' has redeemed Man it has also redeemed the sub-creativity of Man:

This story is supreme; and it is true. Art has been verified. God is the Lord, of angels, and of men – and of elves. Legend and History have met and fused.

But in God's kingdom the presence of the greatest does not depress the small. Redeemed Man is still man. Story, fantasy, still go on, and should go on. The Evangelium has not abrogated legends; it has hallowed them, especially the 'happy ending'. The Christian has still to work, with mind as well as body, to suffer, hope, and die; but he may now perceive that all his bents and faculties have a purpose, which can be redeemed. So great is the bounty with which he has been treated that he may now, perhaps, fairly dare to guess that in Fantasy he may actually assist in the effoliation and multiple enrichment of creation. All tales may come true: and yet, at the last, redeemed, they may be as like and as unlike the forms that we give them as Man, finally redeemed, will be like and unlike the fallen that we know.[12]

The views expressed in this final paragraph came to imaginative fruition in Tolkien's short story, *Leaf by Niggle*, which he wrote during the war at a time when he was finding it difficult to make progress on *The Lord of the Rings*. It was therefore appropriate that 'On Fairy Stories', *Leaf by Niggle* and his poem 'Mythopoeia', the three of his works which expressed most evocatively his view of the relationship of myth to truth, should be published together under the title *Tree and Leaf* many years later.

Colin Gunton, a theologian at King's College London, believed that Tolkien's view of fairy stories in general was especially true of *The Lord of the Rings* in particular: 'May not, then, one reason for taking Tolkien's splendid tale seriously theologically be that it is in so many respects "a far-off gleam or echo of *evangelium*"; perhaps, indeed, not so very far-off a gleam?'[13]

Meanwhile, Stratford Caldecott, in his essay on 'Tolkien,

Lewis, and Christian Myth', discussed Tolkien's view of fairy stories with both depth and poignancy:

> The Gospels contain a fairy story – even the sum total of all fairy stories rolled together, the one story we would most wish to be true in all literature. But although we cannot make the story true by wishing, and must not deceive ourselves into thinking that it is true *because we wish it*, we still cannot rule out the possibility that it did all actually happen. It may be that the very *reason* we wish it were true is because we were *made* to wish it, by the One who made it true. God created us incomplete, because the kind of creature that can only be perfected by its own choices (and so through Quest and trial) is more glorious than the kind that has only *to be* whatever it was made to be by another.[14]

This was discussed explicitly by Tolkien in a letter to his son:

> Of course I do not mean that the Gospels tell what is *only* a fairy-story; but I do mean very strongly that they do tell a fairy-story: the greatest. Man the story-teller would have to be redeemed in a manner consonant with his nature: by a moving story. *But* since the author of it is the supreme Artist and the Author of Reality, this one was also made to Be, to be true on the Primary Plane. So that in the Primary Miracle (the Resurrection) and the lesser Christian miracles too though less, you have not only that sudden glimpse of the truth behind the apparent Ananke of our world, but a glimpse that is actually a ray of light through the very chinks of the universe about us.[15]

These, then, were the theories which Tolkien was endeavouring to put into practice in the writing of *The Lord of the Rings*. Indeed, it is no coincidence that his lecture on fairy stories, his long letter to his son on the same subject, and *Leaf by Niggle*, his short story on the same theme, were all written in the years in which he was writing *The Lord of the Rings*. It was scarcely surprising therefore that *The Lord of the Rings* should resonate with the same sense of Christian orthodoxy that permeated *The Silmarillion*, the latter being both its parent and the source of the myth-pool from which it drew so richly.

Charles Moseley wrote in his study of Tolkien that 'Tolkien's Christian understanding of the nature of the world was fundamental to his thinking and to his major fiction.' He then proceeded to describe the Christian metaphysics which underpin Tolkien's sub-creation:

> Neither propaganda nor allegory, at its root lies the Christian model of a world loved into being by a Creator, whose creatures have the free will to turn away from the harmony of that love to seek their own will and desires, rather than seeking to give themselves in love to others. This world is one of cause and consequence, where everything matters, however seemingly insignificant: action plucks on other actions, and the end of this self-love is the reduction of freedom, the imprisonment in the self, and the inability to give or receive the love that is the only thing desired ... Christianity sees the universe as a place of struggle between good and evil where individuals are crucial.[16]

A similar view was expressed by Paul Pfotenhauer in his article on 'Christian Themes in Tolkien'.[17] The fact that Sauron's evil presence is always felt though always in the background, Pfotenhauer argued, may help us to recognize the demonic in our own midst. Meanwhile the more significant, yet more hidden, presence of the One, ultimately determining the outcome of events, may help us to recognize Divine Providence. Like several other writers, Pfotenhauer stressed the importance of Augustinian theology to *The Lord of the Rings* as well as singling out the recurring theme of the Suffering Servant who gives himself willingly, even unto death, that others might live.

Throughout the years since its publication, many other writers have written of the Christian orthodoxy which breathes life into *The Lord of the Rings*, notable examples being Willis B. Glover's essay, 'The Christian Character of Tolkien's Invented World'[18] and C.S. Kilby's talk on 'The Christian Interpretation of Tolkien'.[19]

However, the fact that Tolkien consciously spurned allegory and preferred instead to leave the Christianity in his work implicit rather than explicit has led to much misunderstanding. Patrick Curry, author of *Defending Middle Earth*, has declared that Tolkien's Christianity 'cannot be allowed to limit interpretations of his work to Christian ones. My own, as you will find, is an explicitly non-theistic reading, and I believe that that is more typical among his many readers than otherwise.'[20] Regardless of whether Curry's view is shared by many of Tolkien's readers, it was certainly not shared by Tolkien himself. In the same letter in which he had described *The Lord of the Rings* as 'fundamentally religious and Catholic', Tolkien explained that, paradoxically, his decision to remove all references to institutional religion was the result of his desire that the work should remain theologically orthodox: 'That is why I have not put in, or have cut out, practically all references to anything like "religion", to cults or practices, in the imaginary world. For the religious element is absorbed into the story and the symbolism.'[21] In another letter, written shortly after *The Lord of the Rings* was published, Tolkien gave the ultimate practical reason for omitting overt references to religion: 'The Incarnation of God is an *infinitely* greater thing than anything I would dare to write.'[22] He overcame the problem and at the same time enhanced the mystery of the myth by placing the history of Middle Earth long before the Incarnation.

Tolkien still described the historical setting of *The Lord of the Rings* in specifically theistic terms, however: 'The Fall of Man is in the past and off stage; the Redemption of Man is in the far future. We are in a time when the One God, Eru, is known to exist by the wise, but is not approachable save by or through the *Valar*, though He is still remembered in (unspoken) prayer by those of Númenórean descent.'[23] Although the world of Middle Earth is nominally 'pagan', in the sense that God is only approachable through what are perceived as 'the gods', it is 'pre-Christian' only in a temporal and peripheral sense. In the eternal sense with which Tolkien is principally concerned it is a Christian world created by the Christian God who has not, as yet, revealed Himself in the fullness of the truth made explicit in the Incarnation and Resurrection. Consequently, although the characters in Middle Earth have a knowledge of God that is less complete than that which has been revealed to the Christian world, the God who is dimly discerned in Middle Earth is nonetheless the same God as the One worshipped by Tolkien himself. The God of Earth and the God of Middle Earth are One. This follows both logically and theologically from Tolkien's belief that his sub-created secondary world was a reflection, or a glimpse, of the truth inherent in the Created Primary World.

Having ascertained that the only 'true' reading of *The Lord of the Rings* is a specifically theistic one, there is a wealth of spiritual meaning to be found in its pages. To reiterate Tolkien's words, it is a question of discerning 'the religious element ... absorbed into the story and the symbolism'.

In general terms the religious element falls into three distinct but inter-related areas: the sacrifice which accompanies the selfless exercise of free will; the intrinsic conflict between good and evil; and the perennial question of time and eternity, particularly in relation to life and death.

The spirit of sacrifice is omnipresent throughout the three volumes of *The Lord of the Rings*, particularly in the actions of the principal heroes. It reaches the level of the sublime as Sam and Frodo approach the gates of Mordor:

> Frodo seemed to be weary, weary to the point of exhaustion. He said nothing, indeed he hardly spoke at all; and he did not complain, but he walked like one who carries a load, the weight of which is ever increasing; and he dragged along, slower and slower, so that Sam had often to beg Gollum to wait and not to leave their master behind.
>
> In fact with every step towards the gates of Mordor Frodo felt the Ring on its chain about his neck grow more burdensome. He was now beginning to feel it as an actual weight dragging him earthwards. But far more he was troubled by the Eye: so he called it to himself. It was that more than the drag of the Ring that made him cower and stoop as he walked. The Eye: that horrible growing sense of a hostile will that strove with great power to pierce all shadows of cloud, and earth, and flesh, and to see you: to pin you under its deadly gaze, naked, immovable. So thin, so frail and thin, the veils were become that still warded it off. Frodo knew

just where the present habitation and heart of that will now was: as certainly as a man can tell the direction of the sun with his eyes shut. He was facing it, and its potency beat upon his brow.[24]

The parallels with Christ's carrying of the Cross are obvious. Furthermore, such is the potency of the prose and the nature of Tolkien's mysticism that the parable of Frodo's burden may even lead the reader to a greater understanding of Christ's burden. All of a sudden one sees that it was not so much the weight of the Cross that caused Christ to stumble but the weight of evil, symbolized by Tolkien as the Eye of Sauron.

Frodo's response to the burden was not to cast it off but to carry it willingly, though fearfully, into the very heart of Mordor. He had not sought the burden, but once it had been laid upon his reluctant shoulders he accepted it, and the sacrifice it involved, becoming a suffering servant to a greater good. In many ways, however, Frodo's companion, Sam Gamgee, is an even greater hero, the more so because he is cast in the role of Frodo's servant, serving his master with a selfless love: 'Sam's mind was occupied mostly with his master, hardly noticing the dark cloud that had fallen on his own heart. He put Frodo in front of him now, and kept a watchful eye on every movement of his, supporting him if he stumbled, and trying to encourage him with clumsy words.'[25]

The character of Sam Gamgee is representative of another powerful sub-theme running through *The Lord of the Rings*: the exaltation of the humble. 'My "Sam Gamgee",' Tolkien wrote, 'is indeed a reflexion of the English soldier, of the privates and batmen I knew in the 1914 war, and recognised as so far superior to myself.'[26] This was reflected in *The Lord of the Rings* where Sam emerges, in some respects, as 'far superior' to Frodo. As they approach Mount Doom, Frodo begins to despair of ever achieving the quest and it is only Sam's strength and encouragement that keep him going. When Sam himself is faced with the temptation to despair, arguing with himself about the futility of continuing, he overcomes and resolves to carry his master to the Cracks of Doom himself if necessary: 'I'll get there, if I leave everything but my bones behind ... And I'll carry Mr Frodo up myself, if it breaks my back and heart.'[27]

When, due to Frodo's physical exhaustion, Sam is forced to put his resolution into practice, the strangest thing happens:

> As Frodo clung upon his back, arms loosely about his neck, legs clasped firmly under his arms, Sam staggered to his feet; and then to his amazement he felt the burden light. He had feared that he would have barely the strength to lift his master alone, and beyond that he had expected to share in the dreadful dragging weight of the accursed Ring. But it was not so. Whether because Frodo was so worn by his long pains, wound of knife, and venomous sting, and sorrow, fear, and homeless wandering, or because some gift of final strength was given to him, Sam lifted Frodo with no more difficulty than if he were carrying a hobbit-child pig-a-back in some romp on the lawns or hayfields of the Shire.[28]

Earlier, Sam had experienced a similar sensation when, believing Frodo had been killed by Shelob, he had taken the burden of the Ring upon himself: 'And then he bent his own neck and put the chain upon it, and at once his head was bowed to the ground with the weight of the Ring, as if a great stone had been strung on him. But slowly, as if the weight became less, or new strength grew in him, he raised his head, and then with a great effort got to his feet and found that he could walk and bear his burden.'[29]

Again, images of the Cross are unmistakable, and particularly Christ's promise that those who take up their Cross to follow Him will find their burden light.

Another Christian image of sacrifice which recurs throughout *The Lord of the Rings* is the reflection of Christ's teaching that there is no greater love than to lay down one's life for a friend. Notable examples include Boromir's heroic death in order to save his companions, a death which followed shortly after his repentance for his earlier effort to seize the Ring by force from Frodo. There is also Gandalf's apparent death on the Bridge of Khazad-Dûm as he fought to save the rest of the company from the Balrog – followed, of course, by his 'resurrection'.

This recurring theme of selfless sacrifice was discussed by Sean McGrath in an essay which was appropriately titled 'The Passion According to Tolkien':

The Lord of the Rings myth depicts the dynamics of this fundamental option to give up our lives for the sake of a higher good, that lies at the heart of human ethics. The pretty poison that lures us away from God's design toward a kind of temporary personal omnipotence is subtler than the evil at work in Middle Earth. In my daily life in middle class North America, no winged Nazgûl block out the sun with their huge black wings; no emaciated Smeagols remind us of the price of unchecked selfishness; or do they? This 'escapist' literature presents in vivid dramatic pictures what is otherwise intangible and inexpressible: our battle for salvation, for overcoming the all-pervasive, crippling legacy of sin. It gives form and substance to our very real quest and projects it into an imaginary universe where the ultimate questions are blazingly clear...

...in Frodo's agonizing pilgrimage to Mordor and the cracks of Doom the depth of our sacrifice is at last adequately portrayed. For when God asks us to transcend our present state of being he is asking us to break and spend ourselves as relentlessly as Frodo gives his entire being to the quest.[30]

Perhaps, however, the depth of sacrifice is again portrayed most adequately by the humble figure of Sam Gamgee. Stratford Caldecott suggests that 'in some ways, Sam is more central to the story than Frodo, and certainly more so than Aragorn':

As soon as we start to read the book as Sam's Quest, we notice that the maturing of Sam and the healing of the Shire go hand in hand. This makes perfect sense if, as Tolkien once wrote (*Letters*, no. 181), the plot is concerned with 'the ennoblement (or sanctification) of the humble'. It is, at bottom, a *Christian* myth, in which 'the first will be last and the last will be first'. Sam is a 'humble man', close to the earth, without pretension. For him to leave the Shire, out of love for his Master, involves a great sacrifice. It is fidelity to that sacrifice, and to his relationship with Frodo, that remains the guiding star throughout. The plans of the Wise and the fate of Middle Earth are never his concern. He only knows he has to do his bit to help Frodo, however hopeless the task may seem. At a crucial moment in Mordor he must carry the Ringbearer, and even the Ring itself. He moves from *immature* innocence to mature innocence: and finally, in his own world (that is, in Tolkien's inner world of the Shire), this 'gardener' becomes a 'king' – or at least a Mayor.[31]

In other respects Caldecott's interpretation of the Christian aspects of *The Lord of the Rings* echoes that of McGrath. Like McGrath, Caldecott also believes that Tolkien's epic holds up a magic mirror to our world which 'penetrates below the skin to expose the archetypes within'. 'It undermines our normal habits of perception, and lays bare the nature and scale of the universal Quest in which we are every one of us engaged: what we stand to lose, and what we stand to gain.'[32] Caldecott calls *The Lord of the Rings* a 'Christian myth' because it is 'a story that embodies Christian wisdom'. Specifically, Christianity and *The Lord of the Rings* both concern themselves with 'choice, free will, and sacrifice'.[33] Caldecott also concurs with McGrath in perceiving a parallel between the Passion of Tolkien and the Passion of Christ: 'Each of the four main heroes undergoes a kind of death and rebirth as part of their quest, a descent into the underworld. In this way each participates to a greater and lesser degree in the archetypal journey of Christ.'[34]

Besides the themes of 'choice, free will, and sacrifice', another of the central precepts upon which *The Lord of the Rings* is built is the intrinsic conflict between good and evil. The spiritual warfare between the forces of dark and light in Tolkien's world forms the landscape within which the characters exercise their free will and make their sacrifices. Indeed, it is the knowledge of this conflict, and the responses to it, which give meaning to the sacrifices that the heroes make. 'Good and ill have not changed since yesteryear,' says Aragorn to Éomer, 'nor are they one thing among Elves and Dwarves and another among Men. It is a man's part to discern them.'[35]

'*The Lord of the Rings*,' writes the theologian Colin Gunton, 'may not be an overtly theological book, but it is certainly in a broad sense about salvation. It is about the winning back of Middle Earth from the powers of evil.'[36] Gunton considered Frodo's role in the quest to destroy the power of the Dark Lord to be 'strongly marked by Christian notions':

> If we recall Jesus' temptation by the devil to worship him and gain power over all the cities of the world, we shall see the point of Frodo's behaviour. Again and again, actors in the drama are tempted to use the ring to overcome the Dark Lord. But Frodo, taught by Gandalf who, like him, has some of the marks of a Christ figure, realises that to use evil, even in the battle against evil, is to become enslaved by it. The Dark Lord might be overcome, but those who overcome him will in their turn be corrupted into playing the same role.[37]

Gunton also emphasized Tolkien's adherence to orthodox Christian teaching on the nature of evil:

> ...evil is parasitic upon the good: it has an awful power, it corrupts and destroys, and yet has no true reality of its own. So it is with Tolkien's depiction of evil. The ring-wraiths represent some of the most horrifyingly evil agencies in literature. They are wraiths, only half real, but of a deadly and dreadful power. Their cries evoke despair – the incapacity to act – and terror in the forces of light. Their touch brings a dreadful coldness, like the coldness of Dante's hell. And yet they are finally insubstantial. When the ring is melted in the furnaces of Mount Doom, they 'crackled, withered, and went out' (p. 982). Similarly, just as the devils of Christian mythology are fallen angels, so all the creatures of the dark Lord are hideous parodies of creatures from the true creation: goblins of elves, trolls of those splendid creatures, the ents, and so on (p. 507). Evil is the corruption of good, monstrous in power yet essentially parasitic.[38]

The parasitic nature of evil is the key to its inherent weakness. Since, of its nature, it is counter-creative and can only destroy, it often destroys itself in the blindness of its malice. 'Often does hatred hurt itself,' says Gandalf, a view which is reiterated by Théoden: 'Strange powers have our enemies, and strange weaknesses! But it has long been said: *oft evil will shall evil mar.*'[39]

Gunton also saw 'interesting parallels to and borrowings from Christian theology' in the Christ-like way in which Frodo triumphed against the odds: 'Like Jesus, Frodo goes into the heart of the enemy's realm in order to defeat him. And like him he is essentially weak and defenceless in worldly terms, but finally strong and invincible because he refuses to use the enemy's methods.'[40]

The other central precept at the heart of *The Lord of the Rings* is the relationship between time and eternity, particularly in relation to the question of life and death. The importance of this aspect was stressed by Tolkien himself on more than one occasion. In April 1956 he compared the relative effect on Men and Elves of mortality and immortality respectively. 'I do not think that even Power or Domination is the real centre of my story,' he wrote. 'The real theme for me is about something much more permanent and difficult: Death and Immortality: the mystery of the love of the world in the hearts of a race "doomed" to leave and seemingly lose it; the anguish in the hearts of a race "doomed" not to leave it, until its whole evil-aroused story is complete.'[41]

This sense of the 'doom' of death at the heart of Tolkien's tale was discussed by Kevin Aldrich in his essay on 'The Sense of Time in J.R.R. Tolkien's *The Lord of the Rings*'. 'A good place to begin an examination of the theme of death and immortality,' Aldrich wrote, 'is the Ring Rhyme that begins each of the volumes of *The Lord of the Rings*.' In particular, Aldrich stressed the importance of the line, 'Nine for Mortal Men doomed to die...': 'The heavily stressed alliterative syllables "Mortal Men" and "doomed to die" sound ominous. And in the space of six syllables we are told three times of man's mortality. We are "mortal", we are "doomed", and we will "die". The main note of man's existence, then, in this apparently simple little poem seems to be his mortality.'[42]

The Elves, on the other hand, are immortal and, in Tolkien's words, are 'doomed not to leave' the world. This difference between Elves and Men plays an important part in the unfolding of events in *The Lord of the Rings* and, as with the rest of the tale, has its roots in *The Silmarillion*:

It is one with this gift of freedom that the children of Men dwell only a short space in the world alive, and are not bound to it, and depart soon whither the Elves know not. Whereas the Elves remain until the end of days, and their love of the Earth and all the world is more single and more poignant therefore, and as the years lengthen ever more sorrowful. For the Elves die not till the world dies, unless they are slain or waste in grief (and to both these seeming deaths they are subject); neither does age subdue their strength, unless one grow weary of ten thousand centuries; and dying they are gathered to the halls of Mandos in Valinor, whence they may in time return. But the sons of Men die indeed, and leave the world; wherefore they are called the Guests, or the Strangers. Death is their fate, the gift of Ilúvatar, which as Time wears even the Powers shall envy. But Melkor has cast his shadow upon it, and confounded it with darkness, and brought forth evil out of good, and fear out of hope. Yet of old the Valar declared to the

Elves in Valinor that Men shall join in the Second Music of the Ainur; whereas Ilúvatar has not revealed what he purposes for the Elves after the World's end, and Melkor has not discovered it.[43]

In this solitary paragraph from *The Silmarillion* there is much of importance to a deeper understanding of *The Lord of the Rings*.

The fact that the One has not revealed what he purposes for the Elves after the world's end, whereas he has stated specifically that Man has a destiny beyond the grave which he shares with the angelic Ainur, illustrates Tolkien's concern that his myth should remain true to Christian orthodoxy. Indeed, the fact that he resolutely refuses to bestow an eternal, as opposed to a temporal, destiny on Elves, Dwarves, or Orcs, illustrates that, contrary to the claims of C.S. Lewis, he is unprepared to sub-create a new theology. He is prepared to sub-create mythical creatures and legendary histories, but he is not prepared to tamper with the Primary Art of the Creator Himself which Tolkien believed had been revealed through the Incarnation, the scriptures and the traditional teaching of the Church down the ages.

The other 'truth' which finds expression in this key passage from *The Silmarillion* is the fact that death, far from being a curse to mankind, is a gift of God. It is only considered cursed because it has been cursed by Melkor, or Morgoth, who curses all the gifts of the One. Therefore, 'Melkor has cast his shadow upon it, and confounded it with darkness, and brought forth evil out of good, and fear out of hope.' This was reiterated in Tolkien's account of the Downfall of Númenor, when the men of Númenor began to curse their mortality and to envy the immortality of the Elves and the angelic Valar. 'Why should we not envy the Valar, or even the least of the

Deathless?' the Númenóreans ask the angelic Messengers who had been sent to them by the Valar. 'For of us is required a blind trust, and a hope without assurance, knowing not what lies before us in a little while.' To this, the Messengers replied:

> Indeed the mind of Ilúvatar concerning you is not known to the Valar, and he has not revealed all things that are to come. But this we hold to be true, that your home is not here, neither in the Land of Aman nor anywhere within the Circles of the World. And the Doom of Men, that they should depart, was at first a gift of Ilúvatar. It became a grief to them only because coming under the shadow of Morgoth it seemed to them that they were surrounded by a great darkness, of which they were afraid ... if that grief has returned to trouble you, as you say, then we fear that the Shadow arises once more and grows again in your hearts.[44]

The angelic Messengers then warned the men of Númenor that their death was the will of the One and that they should not 'withhold the trust' to which they were called.

The Númenóreans failed to heed the warning and Tolkien uses their rebellion to illustrate the sociological impact of their theological ignorance:

> But the fear of death grew ever darker upon them, and they delayed it by all means that they could; and they began to build great houses for their dead, while their wise men laboured unceasingly to discover if they might the secret of recalling life, or at the least of the prolonging of Men's days. Yet they achieved only the art of preserving incorrupt the dead flesh of Men, and they filled all the land with silent tombs in which the thought of death was enshrined in the

darkness. But those that lived turned the more eagerly to pleasure and revelry, desiring ever more goods and more riches; and after the days of Tar-Ancalimon the offering of the first fruits to Eru was neglected, and men went seldom any more to the Hallow upon the heights of Meneltarma in the midst of the land.[45]

Significantly, it was in this age of decadence that 'Sauron arose again in Middle-earth'.[46]

Yet, in spite of Melkor's efforts to cloud the issue with confusion and despair, Man's mortality remains a gift which goes to the very heart of his being and points his will in the right direction. It was the will of the One 'that the hearts of Men should seek beyond the world and should find no rest therein; but they should have a virtue to shape their life, amid the powers and chances of the world, beyond the Music of the Ainur, which is as fate to all things else; and of their operation everything should be, in form and deed, completed, and the world fulfilled unto the last and the smallest.'[47] In this way, the three central themes in *The Lord of the Rings* are bound together, connecting the essential nature of man's mortality with the importance of free will and the intrinsic conflict between good and evil.

As usual, Tolkien was at pains to ensure that the theology of his sub-created world conformed with the theology of the Church. In October 1958, he wrote:

In this mythical 'prehistory' *immortality* ... was part of the given nature of the Elves; beyond the End nothing was revealed. *Mortality* ... is spoken of as the given nature of Men: the Elves called it the *Gift of Ilúvatar* (God) ... This is therefore an 'Elvish' view, and does not necessarily have anything to say for or against such beliefs as the Christian that 'death' is not part of human nature, but a punishment for sin (rebellion), a result of the 'Fall'. It should be regarded as an Elvish perception of what *death* – not being tied to the 'circles of the world' – should now become for Men, however it arose. A divine 'punishment' is also a divine 'gift', if accepted, since its object is ultimate blessing, and the supreme inventiveness of the Creator will make 'punishments' (that is changes of design) produce a good not otherwise to be attained.[48]

Of course, from a Christian perspective the 'ultimate blessing' of the gift of death was not the extinction of life but, paradoxically, the *fullness* of life. As Kevin Aldrich explained, '*The Lord of the Rings* is about immortality and escape from death. But there is no escape *from* death except *through* death, if at all ... What *The Lord of the Rings* has to say ultimately is that if true happiness is to be found by mortals, it will be found not in time but in eternity.'[49] This was the source and the essence of the 'shadowlands' imagery which permeates so much of Tolkien's work, and so much of the work of his friend C.S. Lewis. To both writers this world was but a land of shadows, a *veil* of tears as well as a vale of tears, which shielded mortal men from the fullness of the light of God. In Tolkien's work this can be seen most clearly in his story *Leaf by Niggle* where everything becomes more real after death than it has been before.

Yet this 'shadowlands' imagery dominates the concluding pages of *The Lord of the Rings* also. The book ends with Frodo and Gandalf leaving Middle Earth forever, bound for the Blessed Realm beyond the world of Men:

Then Frodo kissed Merry and Pippin, and last of all Sam, and went aboard; and the sails were drawn up, and the wind blew, and slowly the ship slipped away down the long grey firth ... And the ship went out into the High Sea and passed on into the West, until at last on a night of rain Frodo smelled a sweet fragrance on the air and heard the sound of singing that came over the water. And then it seemed to him that as in his dream in the house of Bombadil, the grey rain-curtain turned all to silver glass and was rolled back, and he beheld white shores and beyond them a far green country under a swift sunrise.[50]

This scene was also recounted in *The Silmarillion*, though more metaphysically: 'And latest of all the Keepers of the Three Rings rode to the Sea ... In the twilight of autumn it sailed out of Mithlond, until the seas of the Bent World fell away beneath it, and the winds of the round sky troubled it no more, and borne upon the high airs above the mists of the world it passed to the Ancient West, and an end was come for the Eldar of story and of song.'[51]

Meanwhile, the other three hobbits who had accompanied Frodo on the quest to destroy the Ring were left behind, watching the ship disappear over the horizon. Their sense of exile is intense:

But to Sam the evening deepened to darkness as he stood at the Haven; and as he looked at the grey sea he saw only a shadow on the waters that was soon lost in the West. There still he stood far into the night, hearing only the sigh and murmur of the waves on the shores of Middle-earth, and the sound of them sank deep into his heart. Beside him stood Merry and Pippin, and they were silent.[52]

The sense of exile is heightened when put into the metaphysical context of the Creation, as described in *The Silmarillion*: 'And it is said by the Eldar that in water there lives yet the echo of the Music of the Ainur more than in any substance else that is in the Earth; and many of the Children of Ilúvatar hearken still unsated to the voices of the Sea, and yet know not for what they listen.'[53]

Although *The Lord of the Rings* ends with the echo of the music of the angels accentuating Man's exile from the fullness of truth beyond the grave, Tolkien adds an appendix which concludes with the sense of homecoming awaiting those who accept the gift of death. Aragorn's final words before his death encapsulate the sense of hope at the heart of Tolkien's sub-creation: 'In sorrow we must go, but not in despair. Behold! we are not bound forever to the circles of the world, and beyond them is more than memory. Farewell!'[54]

CHAPTER 8

THE WELL AND THE SHALLOWS:
TOLKIEN AND THE CRITICS

We have come out of the shallows and the dry places to the one deep well; and the Truth is at the bottom of it.[1]

Eight months before *The Lord of the Rings* was published, Father Robert Murray had written to Tolkien expressing his doubts concerning its likely reception. Murray feared that many critics would not know what to make of it, believing that 'they will not have a pigeon-hole neatly labelled for it'.[2]

'I am afraid it is only too likely to be true,' Tolkien replied. '... I am dreading publication, for it will be impossible not to mind what is said. I have exposed my heart to be shot at. I think the publishers are very anxious too; and they are very keen that as many people as possible should read advance copies, and form a sort of opinion before the hack critics get busy ...'[3]

The critics, hack and otherwise, gave *The Fellowship of the Ring*, the first volume of *The Lord of the Rings*, a decidedly mixed response following its publication in August 1954. Peter Green, the biographer of Kenneth Grahame, wrote in the *Daily Telegraph* on 27 August that it was a 'shapeless work' and that it 'veers from Pre-Raphaelite to Boy's Own Paper'. He also set the patronizing tone adopted by many other critics both at the time and in the years that followed: 'I presume it is meant to be taken seriously, and am apprehensive that I can find no adequate reasons for doing so...' Green was not alone in this inability to discern the depths beneath the surface of Tolkien's myth. J.W. Lambert, writing in the *Sunday Times* on 8 August, declared that the story had 'no religious spirit of any kind', asking whether it was anything other than 'a book for bright children'.

The charge that the book was juvenile in character, belonging to the 'Boy's Own Paper', was caused in part by Tolkien's connection with C.S. Lewis whose 'Narnia' stories were being published at the time to a discordant chorus of popular acclaim and critical hostility. Lewis's 'smuggling of theology' into his children's fiction had made him unpopular in secular circles, and his works of popular Christian apologetics provoked a great deal of hostility. In fact, when Tolkien's publisher had asked Lewis to contribute a short piece for the dust jacket of the first edition of *The Fellowship of the Ring*, Lewis wrote the following cautionary words to Tolkien: 'Even if he and you approve my words, think twice before using them: I am certainly a much, and perhaps an increasingly, hated man whose name might do you more harm than good.'[4] Lewis's warning was prophetic. More than one critic reviewing the book in August 1954 displayed 'an extraordinary personal animosity to Lewis, and used (or wasted) a good deal of space in mocking Lewis's comparison of Tolkien to Ariosto'.[5] Edwin Muir, writing in the *Observer* on 22 August, was typical of those who scoffed at Lewis's praise: 'This remarkable book makes its appearance at a disadvantage. Nothing but a great masterpiece could survive the bombardment of praise directed at it from the blurb.'

On 9 September, Tolkien wrote to his publisher about the hostility that Lewis had provoked:

As for the reviews they were a great deal better than I feared, and I think might have been better still, if we had not quoted the Ariosto remark, or indeed got involved at all with the extraordinary animosity that C.S.L. seems to excite in certain quarters. He warned me long ago that his support might do me as much harm as good. I did not take it seriously, though in any case I should not have wished other than to be associated with him – since only by his support and friendship did I ever struggle to the end of the labour. All the same many commentators seem to have preferred lampooning his remarks or his review to reading the book.[6]

The reason that Tolkien believed the reception of *The Fellowship of the Ring* to be 'a great deal better' than he had feared was the presence among the sneers of a few genuinely positive reviews. 'It is an amazing piece of work,' wrote A.E. Cherryman in *Truth* on 6 August. 'He has added something, not only to the world's literature, but to its history.' Howard Spring, in *Country Life* on 26 August, concurred with this view: 'This is a work of art ... It has invention, fancy and imagination ... It is a profound parable of man's everlasting struggle against evil.' A reviewer in the *Manchester Guardian* on 20 August had described Tolkien as 'one of those born storytellers who makes his readers as wide-eyed as children for more'. The *Oxford Times* review on 13 August was perceptive in its belief that Tolkien's book would divide opinion into opposing camps: 'The severely practical will have no time for it. Those who have imagination to kindle will find themselves completely carried along, becoming part of the eventful quest and regretting that there are only two more books to come.'

Those in the pro-Tolkien camp did not have long to wait for the next book. The second volume, *The Two Towers*, was published in mid-November, accompanied by a similar selection of mixed reviews. In America, where *The Fellowship of the Ring* had been published in October and *The Two Towers* shortly after, the reviews were even more negative than in England. Tolkien's champion in the United States was the poet W.H. Auden, who wrote enthusiastic articles in the *New York Times*. Auden's view that 'no fiction I have read in the last five years has given me more joy' helped to boost sales, and a large number of copies were bought by American readers in the ensuing year.

The second volume ended abruptly with Frodo imprisoned in the Tower of Cirith Ungol, prompting a reviewer in the *Illustrated London News* to declare that 'the suspense is cruel', but it would be nearly a year before the third and final volume, *The Return of the King*, was published on 20 October 1955. Following its publication, the critics were able to judge *The Lord of the Rings* in its entirety and C.S. Lewis, its greatest champion, was as affirmative as ever in his praise. 'When I reviewed the first volume of this work,' he wrote in a review for *Time and Tide* on 22 October, 'I hardly dared to hope it would have the success which I was sure it deserved. Happily I am proved wrong.' In his conclusion to the same review Lewis made a prediction which subsequently has been proved right in the eyes of millions of readers throughout the world: 'The book is too original and too opulent for any final judgment on a first reading. But we know at once that it has done things to us. We are not quite the same men. And though we must ration ourselves in our re-readings, I have little doubt that the book will soon take its place among the indispensables.'

Meanwhile, W.H. Auden continued his vociferous support for Tolkien, declaring in the course of a radio talk on *The Lord of the Rings* on 16 November, 'If someone dislikes it I shall never trust their literary judgement about anything again.'[7] Bernard Levin added his own formidable voice to the chorus of praise, writing in *Truth* that he believed Tolkien's book to be 'one of the most remarkable works of literature in our, or any, time. It is comforting, in this troubled day, to be once more assured that the meek shall inherit the earth.'[8]

Others begged to differ and were as damning in their indictments as Lewis, Levin and Auden had been fulsome in their praise. Edmund Wilson dismissed *The Lord of the Rings* as 'juvenile trash' in *The Nation* on 14 April 1956 and a similar line of attack was employed by Edwin Muir in a review in the *Observer*, headed 'A Boy's World', on 27 November 1955: 'The astonishing thing is that all the characters are boys masquerading as adult heroes. The hobbits, or halflings, are ordinary boys; the fully human heroes have reached the fifth form; but hardly one of them knows anything about women, except by hearsay. Even the elves and the dwarfs and the ents are boys, irretrievably, and will never come to puberty.'

'Blast Edwin Muir and his delayed adolescence,' Tolkien wrote in a letter to his publisher on 8 December. 'He is old enough to know better. It might do him good to hear what women think of his "knowing about women", especially as a test of being mentally adult.'[9]

It was ironic that Edwin Muir should become one of Tolkien's most outspoken critics, especially as the two men had much in common. Muir's *Autobiography*, published at the same time as *The Lord of the Rings*, expressed the author's belief that there was a transcendent mystery at the heart of life which meant that truth was best expressed in the language of Story and Fable. This, of course, was remarkably similar to the beliefs behind Tolkien's work. Neither did the similarities end there. Like Tolkien, Muir had been wrenched from the halcyon days of a rural childhood into an alienating existence in an industrialized city (Muir's parents had

migrated from his native Orkney to Glasgow in 1901, at about
the same time that Tolkien and his brother had been uprooted
to Birmingham from their rural idyll in Sarehole). Like
Tolkien, this uprooting experience had left an indelible mark
on his psyche, shaping his creative outlook to a profound
extent. Like Tolkien, the experience led him to traditional
Christian conclusions.

Yet if Tolkien had found in Muir an unlikely enemy, Muir's
criticism that *The Lord of the Rings* was 'childish' was also
levelled against the book by several other critics. Tolkien had
previously made his own defence to such criticism in his
essay 'On Fairy Stories', and C.S. Lewis clearly had this essay
in mind when he wrote an article entitled 'Sometimes Fairy
Stories May Say Best What's To Be Said' for the *New York
Times Book Review* on 18 November 1956:

> You will notice that I have throughout spoken of Fairy Tales,
> not 'children's stories'. Professor J.R.R. Tolkien in *The Lord
> of the Rings* has shown that the connection between fairy
> tales and children is not nearly so close as publishers and
> educationalists think. Many children don't like them and
> many adults do. The truth is, as he says, that they are now
> associated with children because they are out of fashion
> with adults; have in fact retired to the nursery as old furni-
> ture used to retire there, not because the children had begun
> to like it but because their elders had ceased to like it...
>
> The Fantastic or Mythical is a Mode available at all ages for
> some readers; for others, at none. At all ages, if it is well used
> by the author and meets the right reader, it has the same
> power: to generalise while remaining concrete, to present in
> palpable form not concepts or even experiences but whole
> classes of experience, and to throw off irrelevancies. But at its

best it can do more; it can give us experiences we have never had and thus, instead of 'commenting on life', can add to it...

'Juveniles', indeed! Am I to patronise sleep because children sleep sound? Or honey because children like it?[10]

In spite of the best endeavours of Tolkien and Lewis to counter the charge of immaturity, it has remained one of the most common criticisms of their work. This inability on the part of many modern critics to recognize the universal value of myth was put into a psychological context by Ursula Le Guin, who wrote of the 'deep puritanical distrust of fantasy' by those who 'confuse fantasy, which in the psychological sense is a universal and essential faculty of the human mind, with infantilism and pathological regression'.[11] This distrust of Tolkien's medium has resulted in 'serious' reference works downplaying his importance as a writer of influence. Patrick Curry, in his unpublished study of 'Tolkien and His Critics', highlighted the anomaly inherent in the space given to Tolkien in leading reference works compared with his undoubted position as one of the most popular and influential writers of the twentieth century. Curry points out that Margaret Drabble's *The Oxford Companion to English Literature* gives Tolkien 'exactly thirteen lines out of 1154 pages'; the *Oxford Concise Companion to English Literature* devotes twelve lines to Tolkien; while Andrew Saunders's *The Short Oxford History of English Literature* fails to mention Tolkien at all in any of its 678 pages. Curry calls this 'an unconscionable dereliction of duty on the part of people whose profession is supposedly to comprehend literature'.[12]

Those who have not simply wished Tolkien away by refusing to acknowledge his importance have gone to the other extreme, resorting to either ridicule or vitriolic abuse.

Curry has listed the following epithets amongst those which have been employed in describing *The Lord of the Rings*: 'paternalistic, reactionary, anti-intellectual, racist, fascistic and, perhaps worst of all in contemporary terms, irrelevant.'[13] Coupled with this abuse is ridicule. John Goldthwaite, in his recent book, *The Natural History of Make-Believe*, which claimed to be 'a guide to the principal works', dismissed *The Lord of the Rings* as 'Faerie-land's answer to *Conan the Barbarian*'.[14] In similar, though more amusing, vein the poet John Heath-Stubbs remarked that Tolkien's epic was 'a combination of Wagner and Winnie-the-Pooh'.[15] Finally, besides ridicule and abuse, there is, to cap it all, the juvenile combination of both: ridiculous abuse. In this category, Patrick Curry quotes the example of Humphrey Carpenter: 'Even Tolkien's own biographer (*Et tu, Brute?*) has fatuously opined that "he doesn't really belong to literature or to the arts, but more to the category of people who do things with model railways in their garden sheds".'[16]

A more serious allegation, because more damning if true, is the claim that Tolkien and his sub-creation are in some way 'racist' or 'fascist'. The claim can be easily disposed of in Tolkien's own words. He discussed his political opinions rarely, but when he did it is clear that he was very much a libertarian, distrusting the encroachments of central government: 'My political opinions lean more and more to Anarchy (philosophically understood, meaning abolition of control not whiskered men with bombs) – or to "unconstitutional" Monarchy.'[17] These words were written in November 1943 when Tolkien was in the middle of writing *The Lord of the Rings*. It is, therefore, scarcely surprising that Mordor is depicted as a fascist- or communist-style slave-state under the tyrannical control of Sauron the

Dictator, whereas the lands beyond his dominion are happily rustic and free from 'state planning' or 'direct government control'. This aversion to state interference found expression in a letter he wrote in 1956: 'I am not a "socialist" in any sense – being averse to "planning" (as must be plain) most of all because the "planners", when they acquire power, become so bad ... The present design of destroying Oxford in order to accommodate motor-cars is a case. But our chief adversary is a member of a "Tory" Government.'[18] Clearly Tolkien was unprepared to take part in what the Catholic writer Christopher Derrick has called the 'damn-fool dichotomy of left and right'.[19]

Neither was Tolkien an imperialist. He despised both British imperialism and the cultural imperialism of the United States, as is clear from a letter he wrote to his son shortly after the war-time leaders of Britain, America and Russia had met at the Teheran Conference in November 1943:

I must admit that I smiled a kind of sickly smile ... when I heard of that bloodthirsty old murderer Josef Stalin inviting all nations to join a happy family of folks devoted to the abolition of tyranny and intolerance! ... The bigger things get the smaller and duller or flatter the globe gets. It is getting to be all one blasted little provincial suburb. When they have introduced American sanitation, morale-pep, feminism, and mass production throughout the Near East, Middle East, Far East, U.S.S.R., Hither Further and Inner Mumbo-land, Gondhwanaland, Lhasa, and the villages of darkest Berkshire, how happy we shall be. At any rate it ought to cut down travel. There will be nowhere to go. So people will (I opine) go all the faster.

Referring to a newspaper report that one-eighth of the world's population now spoke English, Tolkien continued in plaintive terms:

> If true, damn shame – say I. May the curse of Babel strike all their tongues till they can only say "baa baa". It would mean much the same. I think I shall have to refuse to speak anything but Old Mercian. But seriously: I do find this Americo-cosmopolitanism very terrifying … I am not really sure that its victory is going to be so much the better for the world as a whole in the long run … I love England (not Great Britain and certainly not the British Commonwealth (grr!)), and if I was of military age, I should, I fancy, be grousing away in a fighting service, and willing to go on to the bitter end – always hoping that things may turn out better for England than they look like doing.[20]

These are strong words but scarcely the words of a 'fascist'. In fact, Tolkien reserved some of his strongest words for an attack on fascism. 'I suppose I know better than most what is the truth about this "Nordic" nonsense,' Tolkien wrote in a letter to his son Michael on 9 June 1941, shortly after the latter had become an Officer Cadet at the Royal Military College, Sandhurst:

> Any way, I have in this War a burning private grudge – which would probably make me a better soldier at 49 than I was at 22: against that ruddy little ignoramus Adolf Hitler … Ruining, perverting, misapplying, and making for ever accursed, that noble northern spirit, a supreme contribution to Europe, which I have ever loved, and tried to present in its true light. Nowhere, incidentally, was it nobler than in England, nor more early sanctified and Christianized …[21]

Years later, when two writers suggested that Tolkien's Middle Earth 'corresponds spiritually to Nordic Europe', Tolkien was at pains to put the record straight:

> Not *Nordic*, please! A word I personally dislike; it is associated, though of French origin, with racialist theories...
>
> Auden has asserted that for me 'the North is a sacred direction'. That is not true. The North-west of Europe, where I (and most of my ancestors) have lived, has my affection, as a man's home should. I love its atmosphere, and know more of its histories and languages than I do of other parts; but it is not 'sacred', nor does it exhaust my affections. I have, for instance, a particular love for the Latin language, and among its descendants for Spanish. That it is untrue for my story, a mere reading of the synopses should show. The North was the seat of the fortresses of the Devil. The progress of the tale ends in what is far more like the re-establishment of an effective Holy Roman Empire with its seat in Rome than anything that would be devised by a 'Nordic'.[22]

Tolkien's most convincing defence against the charge of 'fascism' or 'racism' dates back to 1938. In the summer of that year the German publishers, Rutten & Loening of Potsdam, were showing an interest in publishing a German translation of *The Hobbit* and had written to Tolkien, via his British publishers, asking if he was of 'arisch', i.e. aryan, origin. Tolkien's publishers, Allen & Unwin, forwarded the letter and Tolkien replied to Rutten & Loening on 25 July:

> I regret that I am not clear as to what you intend by *arisch*. I am not of *Aryan* extraction: that is Indo-iranian; as far as

I am aware none of my ancestors spoke Hindustani, Persian, Gypsy, or any related dialects. But if I am to understand that you are enquiring whether I am of *Jewish* origin, I can only reply that I regret that I appear to have *no* ancestors of that gifted people. My great-great-grandfather came to England in the eighteenth century from Germany: and the main part of my descent is therefore purely English, and I am an English subject – which should be sufficient.[23]

Referring to the letter from the German publishers in a letter to Allen & Unwin, Tolkien asked: 'Do I suffer this impertinence because of the possession of a German name, or do their lunatic laws require a certificate of "arisch" origin from all persons of all countries?' Clearly incensed, Tolkien told his publishers to 'let a German translation go hang'. 'In any case I should object strongly to any such declaration appearing in print. I do not regard the (probable) absence of all Jewish blood as necessarily honourable; and I have many Jewish friends, and should regret giving any colour to the notion that I subscribed to the wholly pernicious and unscientific race-doctrine.'[24]

The lack of evidence, and indeed the overwhelming weight of evidence to the contrary, has not deterred some critics from labelling Tolkien as a fascist or, where the label will not stick, as a fellow traveller. Fred Inglis, in his essay 'Gentility and Powerlessness: Tolkien and the New Class', was at pains to prove that *The Lord of the Rings* was a proto-fascist myth:

The other side of contemporary individualism is the longing for a lost Eden of membership, community, ceremony ... even at the expense of rationality. All political leaders need myths which rouse this longing, but Fascism is founded on it. Tolkien is no Fascist, but his great myth may be said, as

Wagner's was, to prefigure the genuine ideals and nobilities of which Fascism is the dark negation. Instead of the raucous bawling of *Il Duce*, the pentameter; instead of tanks and the goose step, horses and cloaks and lances; instead of Nuremberg, Frodo's farewell. But I noted Tolkien's Englishness, and if Fascism were to come to England it would, in E.P. Thompson's phrase, come by 'steady vegetable pressure' rather than by murder and burning down the House of Commons.[25]

Inglis has clearly failed to find the pulse at the heart of *The Lord of the Rings*. The 'longing for a lost Eden', the sense of exile, at the core of Tolkien's myth is a mystical expression of the desire for Heaven, a closer union with God *beyond this world*, which is the very opposite of those creeds of both left and right which offer quick-fix solutions to the world's needs. To Tolkien, and to Frodo, Galadriel and Gandalf, there is no heaven on earth; nor would they have listened to any demagogue of left or right, be they Hitler, Mussolini, Marx, Mao, Lenin, Sauron or Saruman, who suggested otherwise.

Perhaps the issue should be laid to rest by quoting the words of Evelyn Waugh, another writer who has been falsely accused of fascism. Waugh had written plaintively to the *New Statesman* on 5 March 1938, four months before Tolkien's letter to the German publishers:

There was a time in the early twenties when the word 'Bolshie' was current. It was used indiscriminately of refractory schoolchildren, employees who asked for a rise in wages, impertinent domestic servants, those who advocated an extension of the rights of property to the poor, and anything or anyone of whom the speaker disapproved. The only result was to impede reasonable discussion and clear thought.

I believe we are in danger of a similar, stultifying use of the word 'Fascist'. There was recently a petition sent to English writers ... asking them to subscribe themselves, categorically, as supporters of the Republican Party in Spain, or as 'Fascists'. When rioters are imprisoned it is described as a 'Fascist sentence'; the Means Test is Fascist; colonisation is Fascist; military discipline is Fascist; patriotism is Fascist; Catholicism is Fascist; Buchmanism is Fascist; the ancient Japanese cult of their Emperor is Fascist; the Galla tribes' ancient detestation of theirs is Fascist; fox-hunting is Fascist ... Is it too late to call for order?

The sub-editors at the *New Statesman* headed Waugh's letter 'Fascist', presumably as a juvenile jibe intended to annoy their hostile correspondent. In doing so they were only reinforcing his point. In fact, the *reductio ad absurdum* of labelling everyone and everything as either 'Bolshie' or 'Fascist' was finding tragi-comic expression in Spain even as Waugh was writing. The communists and the anarchists, erstwhile allies against Franco's fascists, had begun turning their guns on each other, each accusing the other of being 'Fascist'. In such circumstances it had certainly become 'too late to call for order' because order itself was deemed 'Fascist'.

The madness caused by this reductionism was at its height in the mid-'50s when *The Lord of the Rings* was published. As the Cold War threatened nuclear devastation, and with the East calling the West 'Fascist' and the West calling the East 'Bolshie', it was not surprising that many perceived the importance of the political dimension in Tolkien's myth. Although Tolkien was at pains to stress that the parable of Power within *The Lord of the Rings* was a sub-theme, subsisting within the greater religious themes at the heart of the work, many saw in Middle Earth the same sense of sanity in an increasingly mad world which had made Orwell's *Nineteen Eighty-four* and *Animal Farm* so poignant and popular.

Fascism was not the only f-word thrown at *The Lord of the Rings* by critics. For Nigel Walmsley, the key to understanding Middle Earth was not to see Tolkien as Fascist but to see him as Fashion:

> The popularity of *The Lord of the Rings* has to be understood in the context of that group which most surely guaranteed its reputation, the young, disaffected section of the Western industrial middle class of the mid-1960s. The book was a seminal influence on the popular sub-culture of that period, an artifact as commercially enticing as a Bob Dylan record. As an apparent literary success it has perplexed some academics, and in 1967 a protracted correspondence on the merits of the book took place in the letters column of *The Times* between British University teachers anxious at what they saw as a sign of the collapse of their students' critical judgement in embracing Middle-earth. The key years in establishing Tolkien's popularity as a writer were from 1965 to 1968, during which period *The Lord of the Rings* sold 3,000,000 copies in paperback.[26]

Like many good pop stars, Tolkien's success would be short lived and Walmsley states that by 1968 'the style of Middle-earth had become passé':

> Those who had a year before aspired to look like Bilbo Baggins now sought political credibility and sub-cultural acceptance by cloning themselves on Che Guevara; knee-length leather bikers' boots replaced bare feet, paramilitary

berets replaced ethnic woolly hats, beards were shaped to imitate two months hard-won growth in the Bolivian jungle instead of the gnome-like outcrops of pubic-type facial hair … Harsh aggressive leather, dark and sombre hues, ousted soft, agrarian wools and the bright, kaleidoscope Hobbit colours of '67; action displaced contemplation, electric blues displaced acoustic folk. The fashionable gaze was no longer open and beatific but forbidding and pugnacious. And the reading: Marx, Engels, Regis Debray and Herbert Marcuse's 1966 work, *The Ethics of Revolution*. Tolkien was back on the shelf.

These were the signs, the surface indicators, of a sharp change in cultural attitude which was effectively to end Tolkien's brief period of coruscating contemporary relevance.[27]

One wonders if 'Nigel Walmsley' is really a pseudonym of John Cleese, and his essay 'Tolkien and the Sixties' a Pythonesque pastiche, but if, as one suspects, the author is in deadly earnest, he has not only missed the point but, to employ the modern fashionable idiom, he has 'lost the plot completely'. Walmsley concludes his essay with the assertion that the success of *The Lord of the Rings* was due to 'its radically imaginative appeal to a transient sub-cultural atavism and a related hallucinogenic hedonism which forced it into mainstream international popularity and academic acceptability'. Perhaps no reply is necessary, or possible, but one wonders how this theory squares with Tolkien's continuing popularity in the 'glam' '70s, the cynical '80s and the 'techno' '90s, culminating in his emergence as the most popular writer of the century in several nationwide polls.

Other critics, having failed to fathom the philosophical depths, have floundered in the sexual shallows of Freudian 'analysis'. Perhaps the most comic, and tragic, of these 'sexual' readings of Tolkien's myth is Brenda Partridge's 'No Sex Please – We're Hobbits: The Construction of Female Sexuality in *The Lord of the Rings*'. Partridge's sex-obsession, omnipresent throughout the essay, is most noticeable in her interpretation of Frodo's and Sam's battle with the giant spider, Shelob:

> Shelob's lair, reached by entering a hole and journeying along tunnels, may also be seen to represent the female sexual orifice. At the entrance Frodo and Sam have to force themselves through the bushy, clutching growths (the pubic hair) ... These growths turn out to be cobwebs which enmesh the victim but Frodo, with the obvious phallic symbolism of the sword, pierces the web ... The diction used to describe the tearing of the web, 'rent' and 'veil', is traditionally associated with the tearing of the hymen.
>
> Galadriel's phial ... also represents a phallus more potent than their swords...
>
> Despite the phial's powers, Frodo as a man is ultimately overpowered by the female Shelob; paralysed by her venom he lies helpless waiting to be sacrificed at her will. He is rescued only through the valiant struggle of his male companion, Sam.
>
> The description of Sam's battle with Shelob is not only a life and death struggle of man and monster, good against evil but also represents a violent sexual struggle between man and woman. Shelob's 'soft squelching body' is a metaphor for the female genitals swollen and moist in sexual arousal ... Her impenetrable skin hangs in folds like the layers of the labia...
>
> So Sam valiantly stabs at the monster, pitifully helpless as she rears over him ... The male organ puny compared with

the vast, evil smelling mass of the female is described in euphemistic sexual terms as his 'little impudence'...

And so Sam and Shelob interlocked climax in an orgasm with the male phallus thrusting hard inflicting great pain and a deadly blow deep into the female sexual organ ... In the aftermath of the climax as the erection subsides the male, though victor, is again seen as frail and overwhelmed by the female's bulk.

Shelob then crawls away in agony as Sam in a final gesture holds up the phial, once more asserting male supremacy, brandishing the phallus, male symbol of power...

The imagery portraying this gesture appears at first sight to be more overtly religious, representing the Christian victory over paganism. However, as we have seen before, in *The Lord of the Rings* sexual implications are shrouded in religious symbolism ... Once again Tolkien interprets myth in such a way as to reveal his inner fear or abhorrence of female sexuality, but his attitude is reinforced by the prejudices inherent in religious symbolism itself.[28]

It is ironic that a similar sex-obsession has afflicted many later writers in the fantasy genre with results that Brenda Partridge would doubtless find horrific. These writers have forsaken the 'religious symbolism' altogether so that the 'struggle' between good and evil in much modern 'fantasy' is reduced to the level of 'voyeuristic sadism, where good is "beautiful", over-muscled (if male) and scantily clad (if female), and evil revoltingly and not very plausibly ugly, in a world where, in the end, right is right because it wins'.[29] Such 'fantasy', so prevalent today in comics, computer games and films, as well as in fiction, are imitations of Tolkien which are as much a travesty of the original as are orcs to elves.

Ultimately what both the sexist and the anti-sexist inter-pretations have in common, apart from the overemphasis on sex itself, is a spiritual blindness. They have left out the most important part of the picture because they cannot see it. The 'soul' that breathes life and meaning into Tolkien's myth is the religious dimension and it is a failure to recognize this which is at the root of much of the misunderstanding about *The Lord of the Rings*. Many critics have failed to see this dimension and have looked for meaning in the wrong places, while others have assumed that there is no meaning at all. 'The trouble is,' wrote the critic Derek Robinson, 'Tolkien's message is that there is no message.'[30] In both cases the failure to understand the deeper meaning results in an assumption that Tolkien's myth is 'unrealistic' and 'escapist'. 'It is perhaps the escapism which its mythology offers,' wrote the literary editor of *The Times* in the wake of the triumph of *The Lord of the Rings* in the Waterstone's poll, 'that has provided its enduring appeal, the same escapism that has kept Gene Roddenberry's *Star Trek* going for decades.'[31]

As 'escapism' is probably the most persistently recurring label to be attached to *The Lord of the Rings* by critics desperate to find a 'pigeon-hole' for it, it is fortunate that Tolkien discussed the subject in his essay 'On Fairy Stories':

I will now conclude by considering Escape and Consolation, which are naturally closely connected. Though fairy-stories are of course by no means the only medium of Escape, they are today one of the most obvious and (to some) outrageous forms of 'escapist' literature; and it is thus reasonable to attach to a consideration of them some considerations of this term 'escape' in criticism generally.

I have claimed that Escape is one of the main functions of fairy-stories, and since I do not disapprove of them, it is plain that I do not accept the tone of scorn or pity with which 'Escape' is now so often used: a tone for which the uses of the word outside literary criticism give no warrant at all ... Evidently we are faced by a misuse of words, and also by a confusion of thought. Why should a man be scorned, if, finding himself in prison, he tries to get out and go home? Or if, when he cannot do so, he thinks and talks about other topics than jailers and prison-walls? The world outside has not become less real because the prisoner cannot see it. In using Escape in this way the critics have chosen the wrong word, and, what is more, they are confusing ... the Escape of the Prisoner with the Flight of the Deserter.[32]

There is much in this incisive riposte to the critics that helps to illumine both *The Lord of the Rings* and the failure of many critics to come to terms with it. Tolkien perceives that 'realist' critics use the word escapism in a negative, patronizing or derisive sense because they object to what they see as the wilful *desertion* by 'escapist' writers from the 'realities' of life. To these 'realists' all views of life which are not constrained by the straitjacket of their own scepticism and their implicit philosophical humanism is 'escapist', a desertion from modernist dogma. Yet Tolkien did not accept this dogma, believing it fundamentally flawed and therefore not 'realist' at all. For Tolkien, true reality, the fullness of reality, was to be found beyond the physical in the metaphysical, beyond the natural in the supernatural. 'Nature is no doubt a life-study,' Tolkien wrote, 'or a study for eternity (for those so gifted); but there is a part of man which is not "Nature", and which therefore is not obliged to study it, and is, in fact, wholly unsatisfied by it.'[33]

There are parallels here with the work of the Jesuit poet Gerard Manley Hopkins, whose concept of 'inscape' is as relevant to an understanding of Tolkien as any concept of 'escape'. Hopkins was one of 'those so gifted' who made the loving observation of Nature 'a study for eternity'. For Hopkins, as for Tolkien, the true reality of a thing, be it a tree, a kestrel, a cloud, a sunset or a man, was to be found in its beauty not in the physical properties defined by its molecular composition. This concept of *inscape*, the metaphysical design which gives a thing its beauty, was developed by Hopkins from his reading of philosophy, and particularly the metaphysical writings of Duns Scotus, who stressed that each thing had an essence, something intrinsically essential, beyond its outward appearance. This was its *haecceitas*, its 'thisness'. An entry Hopkins made in his Journal in July 1872 is remarkably applicable to Tolkien's critics: 'I thought how sadly beauty of inscape was unknown and buried away from simple people and yet how near at hand it was if they had eyes to see it.'[34]

The metaphysical insight which can be gleaned from *The Lord of the Rings* was stressed by Stephen R. Lawhead in his essay on Tolkien:

> ...the best of fantasy offers not an escape away from reality, but an escape to a heightened reality – a world at once more vivid and intense and real, where happiness and sorrow exist in double measure, where good and evil war in epic conflict, where joy is made more potent by the possibility of universal tragedy and defeat.
>
> In the very best fantasy literature, like *Lord of the Rings*, we escape into an ideal world where ideal heroes and heroines (who are really only parts of our true selves) behave

ideally. The work describes human life as it might be lived, perhaps ought to be lived, against a backdrop, not of all happiness and light, but of crushing difficulty and over-whelming distress.[35]

In Lawhead's view, Tolkien's achievement in *The Lord of the Rings* was the transporting of the reader to a 'heightened reality' which was only dimly discernible in the partial reality in which we live. This heightened reality led the reader closer to ultimate truth which Tolkien believed was God Himself. Therefore, since Truth, properly understood, was Perfect, it was to perfection that our quest for reality, or realism, should be directed. The imperfections of life, the ambiguities and ambivalences of everyday existence, though real in a limited sense, only detract from the greater reality, blurring the vision. This was the view of the Jesuit, Father James V. Schall, expressed in his essay 'On the Reality of Fantasy': 'The unsus-pecting reader who thinks he is only reading "fantasy" in reading Tolkien will suddenly find himself pondering the state of his own soul because he recognizes his own soul in each fairy-tale.'[36]

Father Schall's view also illustrates the chasm of difference between the 'escapism' of *The Lord of the Rings* and that of science fiction creations such as *Star Trek*. The latter, however much its language is couched in scientific 'reality', offers an escape *from* ourselves and a distancing of ourselves from the 'real world'. This is the 'escape' which Tolkien likens to the Flight of the Deserter. *The Lord of the Rings*, on the other hand, is an escape *into* ourselves, the quest to rediscover the essence of the self amidst life's distractions, the 'escape' which Tolkien likened to the prisoner who tries to escape in order to 'go home'. Whereas *Star Trek* expresses the desire to leave home and explore the universe, *The Lord of the Rings* expresses the desire to find home and discover the universals.

Concomitant with this desire to escape *into* spiritual truth is the realization that complete 'escape' is impossible in this life. Hence the sense of longing and the feeling of exile which is integral to the spiritual quest.

This sorrow at the heart of life was expressed by Tolkien soon after the publication of *The Lord of the Rings*, in a letter dated 15 December 1956: 'Actually I am a Christian, and indeed a Roman Catholic, so that I do not expect "history" to be anything but a "long defeat" – though it contains (and in a legend may contain more clearly and movingly) some samples or glimpses of final victory.'[37] Such glimpses were certainly present in *The Lord of the Rings*, but they were always tempered by the sorrow of the 'long defeat', particularly in Sam's sense of exile following Frodo's departure from the Grey Havens.

Tolkien sought to give theological voice to the sorrow and suffering which are interwoven into the fabric of life in *The Silmarillion*, embodying its perennial nature in the myth surrounding Nienna, one of the Queens of the angelic Valar:

> Mightier than Estë is Nienna, sister of the Fëanturi; she dwells alone. She is acquainted with grief, and mourns for every wound that Arda has suffered in the marring of Melkor. So great was her sorrow, as the Music unfolded, that her song turned to lamentation long before its end, and the sound of mourning was woven into the themes of the World before it began. But she does not weep for herself; and those who hearken to her learn pity, and endurance in hope ... for she brings strength to the spirit and turns sorrow to wisdom. The windows of her house look outward from the walls of the world.[38]

In this passage Tolkien again emerges as a mystic, seeing suffering as the result of an evil beyond the power of man, the work of Satan, 'the marring of Melkor'. Yet, because God can always bring good out of the evil designs of the Enemy, this suffering, properly understood and accepted, teaches both 'pity, and endurance in hope', as well as bringing 'strength to the spirit' and turning 'sorrow to wisdom'. Most profound, and most poetic, is the image of sorrow and suffering as the teachers of selflessness, prompting those who bear the pains of life to seek for the joys beyond the world: 'The windows of her house look outward from the walls of the world.'

Tolkien's wisdom was echoed by another Catholic writer, Maurice Baring, in the words of one of the characters in his last novel, *Darby and Joan*:

> 'One has to *accept* sorrow for it to be of any healing power, and that is the most difficult thing in the world ... A Priest once said to me, "When you understand what *accepted* sorrow means, you will understand everything. It is the secret of life".'

There are several other interesting parallels between Baring and Tolkien which help to shed light on the critical reception of Tolkien's work. Like Tolkien, Baring was also much maligned and misunderstood by the critics, most notably by Virginia Woolf, who attacked what she perceived as his 'superficiality'. Baring found such criticism frustrating, especially as he felt that failure to understand his work was due itself to superficiality. Both the frustration he felt and the superficiality which caused it were expressed plaintively in his book, *Have You Anything to Declare?*

It is utterly futile to write about the Christian faith from the outside. A good example of this is the extremely conscientious novel by Mrs Humphry Ward called *Helbeck of Bannisdale*. It is a study of Catholicism from the outside, and the author has taken scrupulous pains to make it accurate, detailed and exhaustive. The only drawback is that, not being able to see the matter from the inside, she misses the whole point.[39]

This, of course, was the fate suffered by Baring and Tolkien alike at the hands of critics who had failed to comprehend the philosophical foundations upon which their work was based. G.K. Chesterton, writing to Baring in 1929, shortly after Baring's novel *The Coat Without Seam* was published, put the problem succinctly: 'It is, as you say, extraordinary how the outer world can see everything about it except the point. It is curiously so with much of the good Catholic work now being done in literature, especially in France ... I am only a vulgar controversial journalist, and never pretended to be a novelist; my writing cannot in any case be so subtle or delicate as yours. But even I find that if I make the point of a story stick out like a spike, they carefully go and impale themselves on something else.'[40]

In contrast, the Catholic writer François Mauriac told the actor and writer Robert Speaight, 'What I admire most about Baring's work is the sense he gives you of the penetration of grace.'[41] The same could be said of Tolkien's work, particularly of the theological thread running through the length of *The Lord of the Rings*. One is reminded of Tolkien's wholehearted approval of Father Robert Murray's statement that *The Lord of the Rings* left him with a strong sense of 'a positive compatibility with the order of Grace'.[42]

The stark contrast between the critical assessment of Christians and non-Christians, between those who can see the matter from the 'inside' and those who cannot, is exemplified by the views of Father Ricardo Irigaray, an Argentinian priest who has written a full-length study of Tolkien, sadly not thus far translated into English. Father Irigaray's study is a comprehensive exposition of Tolkien's world, covering the relationship between myth and truth; the monotheistic principle at the centre of the creation of Middle Earth; the origin and nature of evil; the ways in which moral evil, the result of Original Sin, finds expression in possessiveness and the rejection of hope; the relationship of fate, freedom and providence; the role of humility and the exaltation of the humble; the way to sanctity through the shaping of the personality in the process of maturity, especially in relation to interior tribulation and purification in sacrifice; and concluding with the mystery of faith and the 'faith atmosphere' of the Tolkienian world.[43]

Similar views were expressed by Father Charles Dilke, a priest at the London Oratory, who re-reads *The Lord of the Rings* regularly, 'trying to avoid learning it by heart':

I first read it when I was at Cambridge, about the end of the fifties ... I was in the process of becoming a Catholic at that time and it seemed to me that the world of Tolkien was a basically Catholic world, so it supported though indirectly what I was doing ... When I first read it I was impressed by the way that Frodo cannot throw the Ring away without the help of the luckless Gollum. This seemed to me an expression of the doctrine of grace ... Another highly theological bit is Galadriel and the Land of Lórien, almost transparently a vision of the Immaculate. 'There is no stain over Lórien.'[44]

Meanwhile the writer and poet Charles A. Coulombe concluded his essay, 'The Lord of the Rings: A Catholic View', with the following overall assessment of the book's importance:

> It has been said that the dominant note of the traditional Catholic liturgy was intense longing. This is also true of her art, her literature, her whole life. It is a longing for things that cannot be in this world: unearthly truth, unearthly purity, unearthly justice, unearthly beauty. By all these earmarks, Lord of the Rings is indeed a Catholic work, as its author believed; but it is more. It is this age's great Catholic epic, fit to stand beside the Grail legends, Le Morte d'Arthur, and The Canterbury Tales. It is at once a great comfort to the individual Catholic, and a tribute to the enduring power and greatness of the Catholic tradition, that JRRT created this work. In an age which has seen an almost total rejection of the Faith on the part of the Civilisation she created, the loss of the Faith on the part of many lay Catholics, and apparent uncertainty among her hierarchy, Lord of the Rings assures us, both by its existence and its message, that the darkness cannot triumph forever.[45]

Compared with the posturings and postulations of many of Tolkien's critics, these deeply Christian perceptions represent a journey from the shallows to the depths, from superficiality to profundity. Yet The Lord of the Rings is still enjoyed by many thousands of readers who are not Christians but who discern in its pages, perhaps unconsciously, a 'far-off gleam or echo of evangelium in the real world'.[46] To many of Tolkien's millions of readers, Christian and otherwise, the myth he sub-created is not a flight from reality but an escape to reality.

CHAPTER 9

TOLKIEN AS HOBBIT:
THE ENGLISHMAN BEHIND THE MYTH

I am in fact a Hobbit (in all but size). I like gardens, trees and unmechanized farmlands; I smoke a pipe, and like good plain food (unrefrigerated), but detest French cooking; I like, and even dare to wear in these dull days, ornamental waistcoats. I am fond of mushrooms (out of a field); have a very simple sense of humour (which even my appreciative critics find tiresome); I go to bed late and get up late (when possible). I do not travel much.[1]

This confession of 'hobbitness' by Tolkien is of more than merely amusing significance. The hobbits in his sub-creation are an imaginative incarnation and personification of an 'Englishness' which was rooted deep in his own psyche. 'The hobbits are just rustic English people,' Tolkien told an interviewer, 'made small in size because it reflects the generally small reach of their imagination – not the small reach of their courage or latent power.'[2] The character of Sam Gamgee was, Tolkien wrote, 'a reflexion of the English soldier, of the privates and batmen I knew in the 1914 war, and recognised as so far superior to myself,'[3] and he reported in a letter to his son on 28 July 1944 that his intention in characterizing Sam was 'precisely to bring out the comicness, peasantry, and if you will Englishry of this jewel among the hobbits. Had I thought it out at the beginning, I should have given all the hobbits very English names to match the Shire.'[4]

On 3 July 1956 Tolkien wrote to Rayner Unwin, his publisher, 'The Shire is based on rural England and not any other country in the world ... The toponymy of The Shire ... is a "parody" of that of rural England, in much the same sense as are its inhabitants: they go together and are meant to. After all the book is English, and by an Englishman ...'[5]

The 'Englishry' of the hobbits and the Englishness of their creator were explained in a letter to W.H. Auden: 'If you want to write a tale of this sort you must consult your roots, and a man of the North-west of the Old World will set his heart and the action of his tale in an imaginary world of that air, and that situation.'[6]

Although his un-English surname derived from an eighteenth-century German ancestor, Tolkien wrote that he was not German, 'whatever some remote ancestors may have been. They migrated to England more than 200 years ago, and became quickly intensely English (not British).'[7] Like his forebears, Tolkien was also 'intensely English (not British)', declaring to his son that 'I love England (not Great Britain and certainly not the British Commonwealth (grr!))'.[8]

This anti-imperialism found expression in Middle Earth in the incarnation of hobbits as idealized Little Englanders. The localized patriotism of the Shire represents a contented, idyllic and inward-looking Little England, as distinct from the imperialism of Great Britain or the glorification of the British Empire. Indeed, Tolkien's local patriotism even prefigures the current revival of regionalism in so far as the Shire is not modelled on an abstract, generalized 'England' but very specifically on the area of the rural West Midlands which was closest to his heart: 'I am indeed in English terms a West-midlander at home only in the counties upon the Welsh Marches; and it is, I believe, as much due to descent as to opportunity that Anglo-Saxon and Western Middle English and alliterative verse have been both a childhood attraction and my main professional sphere.'[9] To W.H. Auden he stressed that he was 'a West-midlander by blood (and took to early west-midland Middle English as a known tongue as soon as I set eyes on it)'.[10] To his son Christopher he wrote of 'the origins of our peculiar people. And indeed of us in particular. For barring the Tolkien (which must long ago have become a pretty thin strand) you are a Mercian or Hwiccian (of Wychwood) on both sides.'[11] To another of his sons, Michael, he wrote of his maternal ancestors, the Suffields, who were particularly associated with the county of Worcestershire: 'Though a Tolkien by name, I am a Suffield by tastes, talents, and upbringing, and any corner of that county (however fair or squalid) is in an indefinable way "home" to me, as no other part of the world is.'[12]

Even more specifically, Tolkien drew heavily on the childhood experiences in the Warwickshire village of Sarehole, where he had spent four years that were forever enshrined as a rural and romantic idyll in his memory. Alluding to these years, he wrote that it was 'really significant' that he had 'lived for my early years in "the Shire" in a pre-mechanical age'.[13]

Tolkien's memories of 'a pre-mechanical age' stayed with him throughout his life, shaping both his view of modern society and his creativity as a writer. 'He disliked the modern world,' his son Christopher recalled, '... the modern world meant for him, essentially, the machine. One of the underlying things in *The Lord of the Rings* is the machine.'[14] This implicit anti-industrialism pervades both *The Hobbit* and *The Lord of the Rings* so that the 'evil' parts of Middle Earth are depicted as polluted industrial waste lands, while the 'good' parts which have not been corrupted are modelled on pre-industrial societies. Just as Tolkien's anti-imperialism had borne fruit in parallels between the Shire and Little England, so his anti-industrialism found fruition in the depiction of the Shire as the Merrie England of mediaeval legend. Thus the Shire is a land in which machine-based mass-production has not been introduced and where individual craftsmanship still prevails.

In *The Hobbit* the intrinsic worth of traditional craftsmanship is contrasted with the materialism of those who hoard possessions that they do not have the skills to make themselves. This disdain by the craftsman for the possessiveness of the hoarder is voiced by the dwarf Thorin: 'Dragons steal gold and jewels, you know, from men and elves and dwarves, wherever they can find them; and they guard their plunder as long as they live (which is practically for ever, unless they are killed), and never enjoy a brass ring of it. Indeed they hardly know a good bit of work from a bad, though they usually have a good notion of the current market value; and they can't make a thing for themselves, not even mend a little loose scale of their armour.'[15] A depiction of this possessiveness is given later in *The Hobbit* after the dragon Smaug notices that a two-handled cup is missing from his hoard: 'His rage passes description – the sort of rage that is only seen when rich folk that have more than they can enjoy suddenly lose something that they have long had but have never before used or wanted.'[16]

The possessive nature of the dragon finds its human equivalent in the Master of Lake Town who is criticized for preferring trade to tradition: 'Nor did he think much of old songs, giving his mind to trade and tolls, to cargoes and gold, to which habit he owed his position.'[17] When Smaug attacks Lake Town in his rage, the Master deserts the townsfolk who are bravely trying to defend their homes and makes straight for 'his great gilded boat, hoping to row away in the confusion and save himself'.[18] His betrayal is noticed after the dragon is slain, and some of the Lake-people murmur their contempt: 'He may have a good head for business – especially his own business ... but he is no good when anything serious happens!'[19] The Master returns and talks himself out of trouble, winning back the trust of the people in a manner which resembles the skilful polemic of Wormtongue in *The Lord of the Rings* but, as with Wormtongue, he eventually receives his just deserts: 'The old Master had come to a bad end. Bard had given him much gold for the help of the Lake-people, but being of the kind that easily catches such disease he fell under the dragon-sickness, and took most of the gold and fled with it, and died of starvation in the Waste, deserted by his companions.'[20]

These interlocked themes of morality and economics, sketched in outline in *The Hobbit*, were further developed in *The Lord of the Rings*, where the principle of craftsmanship was enshrined in the phrase of the leader of the Elves in Lórien: 'We put the thought of all that we love into all that we make.'[21]

On the very first page of the Prologue to *The Lord of the Rings* Tolkien paints a picture of hobbits and their life in the Shire which is evocative of a Merrie England peopled by rustic craftsmen, peasant farmers and small-holders: 'Hobbits are an unobtrusive but very ancient people, more numerous formerly than they are today; for they love peace and quiet and good tilled earth: a well-ordered and well-farmed countryside was their favourite haunt. They do not and did not understand or like machines more complicated than a forge-bellows, a water-mill, or a hand-loom, though they were skilful with tools.' Furthermore, hobbits enjoy 'a close friendship with the earth'.[22] The idyllic, unspoilt and unpolluted lifestyle of the Shire is contrasted with the industrial wastelands of Mordor:

> The air, as it seemed to them, grew harsh, and filled with a bitter reek that caught their breath and parched their mouths.
>
> ...Frodo looked round in horror. Dreadful as the Dead marshes had been, and the arid moors of the Noman-lands, more loathsome far was the country that the crawling day now slowly unveiled to his shrinking eyes ... here neither spring nor summer would ever come again. Here nothing lived, not even the leprous growths that feed on rottenness. The gasping pools were choked with ash and crawling muds, sickly white and grey, as if the mountains had vomited the filth of their entrails upon the lands about. High mounds of crushed and powdered rock, great cones of earth fire-blasted and poison-stained, stood like an obscene graveyard in endless rows, slowly revealed in the reluctant light.
>
> They had come to the desolation that lay before Mordor: the lasting monument to the dark labour of its slaves that should endure when all their purposes were made void; a land defiled, diseased beyond all healing – unless the Great Sea should enter it and wash it with oblivion. 'I feel sick,' said Sam. Frodo did not speak.[23]

As the hobbits pass further into the Dark Lord's polluted realm, the industrial desolation engulfs them in its stench and ugliness: 'North amid their noisome pits lay the first of the great heaps and hills of slag and broken rock and blasted earth, the vomit of the maggot-folk of Mordor ...'[24]

Tolkien's rage against the machine surfaces again and again throughout *The Lord of the Rings*. Sam sees a vision in

Galadriel's Mirror of trees being felled in the Shire and of 'a large red-brick building' being put up on the site where the Old Mill had stood: 'Lots of folk were busily at work. There was a tall red chimney nearby. Black smoke seemed to cloud the surface of the Mirror.'[25] Elsewhere, Treebeard complains that Saruman 'has a mind of metal and wheels; and he does not care for growing things, except as far as they serve him for the moment'.[26] Treebeard is further angered that Saruman's orcs have been destroying trees:

> He and his foul folk are making havoc now. Down on the borders they are felling trees – good trees. Some of the trees they just cut down and leave to rot – orc-mischief that; but most are hewn up and carried off to feed the fires of Orthanc. There is always a smoke rising from Isengard these days. Curse him, root and branch! Many of those trees were my friends, creatures I had known from nut and acorn; many had voices of their own that are lost for ever now. And there are wastes of stump and bramble where once were singing groves.[27]

The recurrence of anti-industrialism in *The Lord of the Rings* has been singled out for attention by several critics. Roger Sale observed that 'Tolkien has always spoken ... as though only fools and madmen would contemplate the twentieth century without horror.'[28] On a more positive note, Paul Kocher wrote that 'Tolkien was ecologist, champion of the extraordinary, hater of "progress", lover of handicrafts, detester of war long before such attitudes became fashionable.'[29] Although such attitudes were certainly 'fashionable' in 1972 when Kocher wrote these lines, and were about to become even more so following the publication during the following year of E.F. Schumacher's *Small is Beautiful*, it would be inaccurate to suggest that Tolkien was ahead of his time. He was in fact merely following a long tradition of opposition to the evils of the industrial age, stretching back to William Blake and William Cobbett almost two centuries earlier, to the very dawn of industrialism itself.

The context in which Tolkien's own opposition should be seen was discussed by Charles A. Coulombe in his essay on *The Lord of the Rings*:

> The concept of society as an organic whole, without class conflict, with a communal structure, is one that has characterized Catholic social thought since the Roman Empire. In many ways the Shire expresses perfectly the economic and political ideals of the Church, as expressed by Leo XIII in *Rerum novarum*, and Pius XI in *Quadragesimo anno*. Traditional authority (the Thain), limited except in times of crisis; popular representation (the Mayor of Michel Delving), likewise limited; subsidiarity; and above all, minimal organization and conflict. It is the sort of society envisioned by Distributists Belloc and Chesterton in Britain, by Salazar in Portugal, by the framers of the Irish Constitution, by Dollfuss in Austria, and by Smetona in Lithuania. How ever far short or close these dwellers in the real world came to their goal, the fact remains that it is something very close to the Shire they had in mind.[30]

The linking of the Shire with the Distributism of G.K. Chesterton and Hilaire Belloc is particularly important. Tolkien's vision of the Shire was strikingly similar to that espoused during the '20s and '30s by the Distributist League, of which Chesterton was President. The Distributist credo that private property should be enjoyed by as many of the population as possible, so that people could be freed from the 'wage slavery' of Big Business or State Monopoly, was put succinctly into the thoughts of Sam Gamgee in *The Lord of the Rings*: 'Deep down in him lived still unconquered his plain hobbit-sense ... The one small garden of a free gardener was all his need and due, not a garden swollen to a realm; his own hands to use, not the hands of others to command.'[31]

The consequences for the Shire when this 'plain hobbit-sense' gave way to greed and the desire for power was illustrated when the hobbits returned home to find the land they loved in desolation. Their beloved Shire was becoming a Mordor in microcosm:

> 'It all began with Pimple, as we call him,' said Farmer Cotton; 'and it began as soon as you'd gone off, Mr Frodo. He'd funny ideas had Pimple. Seems he wanted to own everything himself, and then order other folk about. It soon came out that he already did own a sight more than was good for him; and he was always grabbing more, though where he got the money was a mystery: mills and malt-houses and inns, and farms, and leaf-plantations ...'[32]

If Tolkien's vision of the Shire, threatened by the evils of industrial 'development', was similar in many respects to the vision of England held by the Distributists, it is also indicative of other remarkable parallels between the writings of Tolkien and those of Chesterton.

The full extent of G.K. Chesterton's influence in the first third of this century was considerable, especially among 'orthodox' Christians, both Anglican and Catholic, who considered him their champion. As Tolkien was growing up at the very time that Chesterton's flame was brightest and his

powers waxing, it would be inconceivable that the tradition-
ally minded young Catholic would not have read many, if not
most, of his books. Certainly, there is much to suggest that
Tolkien and Chesterton were kindred spirits.

Like Tolkien, Chesterton saw Merrie England as an idealized view of what England had been and what she could be. It
was an England free from post-Reformation Puritanism and
post-industrial proletarianism, an England where individuals
owned the land on which they lived and worked. It was
Blake's green and pleasant land liberated from the dominion
of dark, satanic mills.

Chesterton wrote a study of Blake and also a full-length biography of William Cobbett, the other great early opponent of
industrialism. 'In Mr Chesterton's view,' wrote a reviewer of the
latter book, 'Cobbett stood for England: England unindustri-
alised, self-sufficient, relying on a basis of agriculture and sound
commerce for her prosperity, with no desire for inflation.'[33]
Chesterton considered Cobbett the champion of England's
dispossessed rural population, the last rustic radical: 'After him
Radicalism is urban – and Toryism suburban.'[34] He also
compared Cobbett to Shelley: 'Going through green Warwickshire, Cobbett might have thought of the crops and Shelley of
the clouds. But Shelley would have called Birmingham what
Cobbett called it – a hell-hole.'[35] This was certainly a view
with which Tolkien would have concurred wholeheartedly,
especially as he had seen his beloved Sarehole swallowed up
during his own life-time by the 'hell-hole' of the West Midlands
conurbation. It is also interesting that Chesterton's description
of Cobbett is equally applicable to Tolkien:

What he saw was not an Eden that cannot exist, but rather
an Inferno that can exist, and even that does exist. What he

saw was the perishing of the whole English power of self-support, the growth of cities that drain and dry up the countryside ... the toppling triumphs of machines over men ... the wealth that may mean famine and the culture that may mean despair; the bread of Midas and the sword of Damocles.[36]

The evident convergence of opinions raises the question of Chesterton's role in shaping Tolkien's perceptions. While it is clear from Tolkien's own writings that he knew and admired Chesterton's work, it is less clear to what extent this had affected his own philosophical, ideological or creative outlook.

In his essay 'On Fairy Stories', Tolkien quotes Chesterton on several occasions, always in favourable terms, to reinforce a point he is making. He also quotes Chesterton favourably in one or two of his letters, but on another occasion is critical of Chesterton's *The Ballad of the White Horse*. On 3 September 1944 he wrote, in a letter to his son, that his daughter Priscilla, then fifteen, 'had been wading through' Chesterton's *Ballad*: 'My efforts to explain the obscurer parts to her convince me that it is not as good as I thought. The ending is absurd. The brilliant smash and glitter of the words and phrases (when they come off, and are not mere loud colours) cannot disguise the fact that G.K.C. knew nothing whatever about the "North", heathen or Christian.'[37] Ironically, these words of criticism serve as evidence of Chesterton's influence on Tolkien. Since Tolkien had probably read *The Ballad of the White Horse* shortly after its publication in 1911, it would appear that for more than thirty years he had been under the impression, albeit a largely false impression according to his later revised judgement, that Chesterton's romantic ballad was 'good'. This impression may have been reinforced by discussions with C.S. Lewis at the weekly meetings of the Inklings. Lewis knew much of the *Ballad* by heart, declaring to George Sayer, one of his pupils who later became his biographer, that it was 'marvellous' and that 'here and there it achieves the heroic, the rarest quality in modern literature'.[38]

There is little to suggest that Tolkien's view was as laudatory as Lewis's and one wonders whether the critic Christopher Clausen, in his essay on 'The Lord of the Rings and The Ballad of the White Horse',[39] had overstated the case for Chesterton's influence. Clausen claims that *The Lord of the Rings* is 'heavily indebted' to Chesterton's ballad, particularly in the similarity of Galadriel's role to that of the Virgin Mary in *The Ballad of the White Horse*. Clausen also sees Tolkien's Dwarves, Elves and Men as parallels of Saxons, Celts and Romans. The basic structure and conception of the two works are similar, in Clausen's view, because both tell the story of a war between good and evil forces in which an alliance of the forces of good, despite all the odds, gains the victory against the vastly more powerful forces of evil. In both works the culmination of events is the return of the king to his rightful state. Clausen also alludes to the symbolism implicit in the fact that Gandalf's horse, Shadowfax, is the archetypal white horse of English legend.

However convincing the parallels, Tolkien's knowledge and scholarship were so extensive that *The Ballad of the White Horse* can only be seen, at most, as one of many influences at work in the shaping of *The Lord of the Rings*.

None the less, and regardless of the alleged nature of Chesterton's *direct* influence upon Tolkien, there is considerable evidence of his *indirect* influence. Tolkien certainly sympathized with Chesterton's work and, for all their differences of approach, there are clearly discernible links of affinity between the two men.

One of the most notable of these is the over-riding sense of wonder that permeates both men's work, and indeed both men's outlook and philosophy. In *The Lord of the Rings* the enigmatic figure of Tom Bombadil seems to embody this sense of wonder, in which wisdom and innocence are unified, to a sublime degree: 'Tom sang most of the time, but it was chiefly nonsense, or else perhaps a strange language unknown to the hobbits, an ancient language whose words were mainly those of wonder and delight.'[40]

Bombadil is paradox personified. Older than the world, he is perennially young. He has the wisdom to wonder, the wisdom *of* wonder, which sees through worldly cynicism. He has childlike innocence without childish naivety. These qualities are also present in the character of Quickbeam, an ent who is introduced to the hobbits by Treebeard:

All that day they walked about in the woods with him, singing, and laughing; for Quickbeam often laughed. He laughed if the sun came out from behind a cloud, he laughed if they came upon a stream or spring: then he stooped and splashed his feet and head with water; he laughed sometimes at some sound or whisper in the trees. Whenever he saw a rowan-tree he halted a while with his arms stretched out, and sang, and swayed as he sang.[41]

T.A Shippey, author of *The Road to Middle Earth*, referred to the infectious nature of this sense of wonder in Tolkien's work when he said that Tolkien had 'turned me into an observer. Tolkien turns people into birdwatchers, tree spotters, hedgerow-grubbers.'[42] This was certainly one of Tolkien's intentions, springing from his belief that one of the highest functions of fairy stories was the recovery of a clear view of reality:

>...we need recovery. We should look at green again, and be startled anew (but not blinded) by blue and yellow and red ... This recovery fairy-stories help us to make...
>
>Recovery (which includes return and renewal of health) is a re-gaining – regaining of a clear view. I do not say 'seeing things as they are' and involve myself with the philosophers, though I might venture to say 'seeing things as we are (or were) meant to see them' – as things apart from ourselves. We need, in any case, to clean our windows; so that the things seen clearly may be freed from the drab blur of triteness or familiarity – from possessiveness ... This triteness is really the penalty of 'appropriation': the things that are trite, or (in a bad sense) familiar, are the things that we have appropriated, legally or mentally. We say we know them. They have become like the things which once attracted us by their glitter, or their colour, or their shape, and we laid hands on them, and then locked them in our hoard, acquired them, and acquiring ceased to look at them.
>
>Of course, fairy-stories are not the only means of recovery, or prophylactic against loss. Humility is enough. And there is (especially for the humble) *Mooreeffoc*, or Chestertonian Fantasy. *Mooreeffoc* is a fantastic word, but it could be seen written up in every town in this land. It is Coffee-room, viewed from the inside through a glass door, as it was seen by Dickens on a dark London day; and it was used by Chesterton to denote the queerness of things that have become trite, when they are seen suddenly from a new angle. [43]

This Chestertonian principle was used by Tolkien when Gandalf was trying to work out the password to the doors of Moria. The wording in Elvish above the doors read: 'The Doors of Durin, Lord of Moria. Speak, friend, and enter.' Gandalf spent a long time trying different Elvish incantations but to no avail. The doors to the Mines of Moria remained firmly shut. Suddenly the wizard sprang to his feet laughing. The password had been staring him in the face all the time, too obvious to be seen. The words should have been translated literally as 'say "friend" and enter': 'I had only to speak the Elvish word for *friend* and the doors opened. Quite simple. Too simple for a learned lore-master in these suspicious days. Those were happier times.'[44]

Tolkien and Chesterton also shared a love for tradition and traditionalism. In 1909 Chesterton had defended Tradition-alism by labelling it the philosophy of the Tree:

> I mean that a tree goes on growing, and therefore goes on changing; but always in the fringes surrounding something unchangeable. The innermost rings of the tree are still the same as when it was a sapling; they have ceased to be seen, but they have not ceased to be central. When the tree grows a branch at the top, it does not break away from the roots at the bottom; on the contrary, it needs to hold more strongly by its roots the higher it rises with its branches. That is the true image of the vigorous and healthy progress of a man, a city, or a whole species.[45]

A sense of tradition was as important to Tolkien as it was to Chesterton and the whole of *The Lord of the Rings* resonates with its presence. Yet it is interesting that the mythological figure that Tolkien uses to embody Tradition is Treebeard, a tree-like creature who was the oldest living being in the whole of Middle Earth. Treebeard is Tolkien's personification of Chesterton's philosophy of the Tree.

When Pippin and Merry had first seen Treebeard they felt that the wisdom of the ages could be glimpsed in the depths of his eyes:

> These deep eyes were now surveying them, slow and solemn, but very penetrating. They were brown, shot with a green light. Often afterwards Pippin tried to describe his first impression of them.
>
> 'One felt as if there was an enormous well behind them, filled up with ages of memory and long, slow, steady thinking; but their surface was sparkling with the present: like sun shimmering on the outer leaves of a vast tree, or on the ripples of a very deep lake. I don't know, but it felt as if something that grew in the ground – asleep, you might say, or just feeling itself as something between roof-tip and leaf-tip, between deep earth and sky had suddenly waked up, and was considering you with the same slow care that it had given to its own inside affairs for endless years.'[46]

The strong links of affinity between Tolkien and Chesterton, glimpsed implicitly in Middle Earth, are more easily discerned in Tolkien's lighter and lesser known works. In *The Father Christmas Letters*, *Leaf by Niggle*, *Smith of Wootton Major* and, most notably of all, in *Farmer Giles of Ham*, one sees more clearly the parallels between his work and the 'Chestertonian Fantasy' referred to by Tolkien in his essay 'On Fairy Stories'.

The Father Christmas Letters, though not published until three years after Tolkien's death, are amongst the earliest of all his writings. Written each Christmas from 1920 until the start of the Second World War, they were not intended for publication but were written solely for the amusement and enchantment of his own children. Above all, as we saw earlier, they display a childlike charm and cheerfulness which helps to dispel the image, portrayed by those who misunderstand *The Lord of the Rings*, that Tolkien is too serious and gloomy.

The parallels with Chesterton in this instance, both in the meticulous writing and illustrating of books intended not for publication but purely for the amusement of individual children, and also in the love for the mythology surrounding the person of Father Christmas, seem to go beyond the celebrated Chestertonian *joie de vivre*. Although Chesterton had no children of his own, his life is peppered with incidents of him writing verses, plays, stories, imaginative letters and even entire mini-books as gifts to various children. He was a talented artist and he often added drawings to his handwritten children's stories, similar to the elaborate illustrations with which Tolkien accompanied his letters from Father Christmas. Chesterton shared Tolkien's love for Christmas and wrote several poems and essays on the subject. 'Personally, of course, I believe in Santa Claus,' Chesterton wrote in one of his essays for the *Daily News*, 'but it is the season of forgiveness, and I will forgive others for not doing so.'[47] In another of his essays he described an imaginary meeting with Santa Claus in which Santa bemoans the fact that the modern world misunderstands him:

'How can one be too good, or too jolly? I don't understand. But I understand one thing well enough. These modern people are living and I am dead.'

'You may be dead,' I replied. 'You ought to know. But as for what they are doing – do not call it living.'[48]

The same melancholy in the face of loss of faith, symbolized in the myth of Father Christmas, was present in the final paragraph of the last of Tolkien's *Father Christmas Letters*, written when his youngest child, Priscilla, was ten years old:

I suppose after this year you will not be hanging your stocking any more. I shall have to say 'goodbye', more or less: I mean, I shall not forget you. We always keep the names of our old friends, and their letters; and later on we hope to come back when they are grown up and have houses of their own and children ...[49]

This melancholy is the dominant characteristic of *Smith of Wootton Major*, written in 1965 and published in 1967. Yet it is not, as Richard Jeffery claimed in his talk to the Oxford C.S. Lewis Society, 'unhappy and pessimistic'.[50] Although the atmosphere throughout is heavy with a sense of wistful resignation, the same degrees of faith and hope are present in *Smith of Wootton Major* as are present in Tolkien's other books. The whole story can be seen as a parable on, and as a reiteration of, Chesterton's contrasting image of the Well of faith compared with the Shallows of scepticism. When Smith enters the realm of Fairy he sees everything far more clearly than is possible in the shadowlands of the 'real' world: 'There the air is so lucid that eyes can see the red tongues of birds as they sing on the trees upon the far side of the valley, though that is very wide and the birds are no greater than wrens.'[51] The theme of selflessness, so crucial to *The Lord of the Rings*, is present in Smith's relinquishing of his possession of the fay-star, the gift which allows him to visit the realm of Fairy where these lucid visions are possible.

In stark contrast to the figure of Smith is the character of Nokes, the Master Cook. Nokes is an arch-sceptic whose motto should be 'seeing is believing', to which Tolkien's riposte in the telling of the tale is that 'there are none so blind as those who will not see'. Alf the Prentice says to Nokes: 'Well, if you won't believe it was Smith, I can't help you.'[52] This simple statement is more potent and poignant than it may at first appear. Alf, cast in a role which parallels that of Gandalf in certain respects, has many powers but he is not able to over-ride Nokes's free will. If Nokes remains obstinate in his refusal of the gift of faith there is nothing that can be done. Nokes does remain obstinate and it is this obstinacy, even in the face of magical or miraculous evidence, that gives potency to the final parts of the story. When Nokes's wish to become slim is granted by Alf he explains it away; and when Alf finally leaves, Nokes is more pleased than anyone to see him go. If Tolkien's tale is 'unhappy and pessimistic' in any sense at all, it is not about truth or ultimate reality but about the inability of people to see it. This is paralleled in 'Chestertonian Fantasy' in both *The Ball and the Cross* and *Manalive*, and is the crux of many of Chesterton's 'Father Brown' stories.

There are similarities between *Smith of Wootton Major* and Tolkien's short story, *Leaf by Niggle*, written more than twenty years earlier. Whereas in *Smith of Wootton Major* things can be seen more clearly in the realm of Fairy, in *Leaf by Niggle* things become more real in the 'purgatorial' realm after death. Tolkien himself used the word 'purgatorial' with reference to *Leaf by Niggle*[53], and it is perhaps the closest he came to writing an overtly Christian allegory. Perhaps *Leaf by Niggle* was discussed most perceptively by Paul H. Kocher in *Master of Middle Earth*, his literary study of Tolkien published in 1972. In Kocher's view, *Leaf by Niggle* was an effort on Tolkien's part 'to find some underlying meaning for all his labours, if not in this life then in the next':

Along this line of interpretation we notice that Niggle's world, like Tolkien's, is unmistakably Christian. It is governed by very strict laws (moral and religious in nature) requiring each man to help his needy neighbour, even at painful cost to himself and even in the absence of both gratitude and desert. These laws are enforced externally by an inspector. Internally their sanction lies in Niggle's own conscience and his imperfectly generous heart. He was 'kind-hearted in a way. You know the sort of kind heart: it made him uncomfortable more often than it made him do anything; and even when he did anything it did not prevent him from grumbling, losing his temper, and swearing ... All the same it did land him in a good many odd jobs for his neighbour, Mr Parish, a man with a lame leg.' Other interruptions to Niggle's painting, however, come from his own idleness, failure of concentration, and lack of firmness. Meantime he neglects to prepare for the long journey he has been told is imminent, and he is taken unawares by the coming of the Black Driver to take him through the dark tunnel. The situation inevitably recalls that in the medieval drama Everyman, to which Tolkien is giving a modern adaptation.

In the workhouse on the other side (an updated version of Dante's *Purgatorio*) Niggle is assigned hard labours aimed at correcting his sins and weaknesses. He learns to work at set intervals, to be prompt, to finish every task, to plan, to think in orderly fashion, to serve without grumbling. He is then ready to hear a dialogue between two voices, discussing what is to be done with him, one voice insisting on justice, the other pleading for mercy. Here the resemblance is to the debate between the four daughters of God – Righteousness and Truth against Mercy and Peace – at the judging of souls, a favourite theme in medieval drama and poetry ... That Tolkien should employ techniques and ideas drawn from the literature of a period he knew so well is not surprising. But his success in acclimatizing them to our times is remarkable. Again we are justified in stressing that they were, and still are, Catholic.[54]

There would seem little to add to this lucid exposition of Niggle's journey from earthly life to purgatorial life, but there is another theme within the story which was equally important to Tolkien's conception of his life's purpose. Above all, *Leaf by Niggle* was Tolkien's effort to put the conclusion of his essay 'On Fairy Stories' into a fairy story. It was an effort to practise what he preached.

In the conclusion to his essay Tolkien had suggested that the sub-creativity of man was capable of being a true reflection of the Primary Creation of God:

...in God's kingdom the presence of the greatest does not depress the small. Redeemed Man is still man. Story, fantasy, still goes on, and should go on. The Evangelium has not abrogated legends; it has hallowed them, especially the 'happy ending'. The Christian has still to work, with mind as well as body, to suffer, hope, and die; but he may now perceive that all his bents and faculties have a purpose, which can be redeemed. So great is the bounty with which he has been treated that he may now, perhaps, fairly dare

to guess that in Fantasy he may actually assist in the effoliation and multiple enrichment of creation. All tales may
come true; and yet, at the last, redeemed, they may be as like
and as unlike the forms that we give them as Man, finally
redeemed, will be like and unlike the fallen that we know.[55]

This paragraph was the inspiration for *Leaf by Niggle* and the
reason why Priscilla Tolkien believed this story to be the
'most autobiographical' of all her father's work.[56]

Niggle was a painter, not a writer, but the parallels with
Tolkien are obvious. Niggle's 'Tree' is clearly a euphemism for
Tolkien's own sub-creation, principally *The Lord of the Rings*
but also *The Silmarillion* on which he laboured all his life and
which, like Niggle's Tree, would ultimately remain uncom-
pleted at his death. Priscilla Tolkien quotes the following
passage from *Leaf by Niggle* as an illustration of the autobiographical element in the story:

Niggle pushed open the gate, jumped on the bicycle, and
went bowling downhill in the spring sunshine. Before long
he found that the path on which he had started had disap-
peared, and the bicycle was rolling along over a marvellous
turf. It was green and close; and yet he could see every blade
distinctly. He seemed to remember having seen or dreamed
of that sweep of grass somewhere or other. The curves of the
land were familiar somehow. Yes: the ground was becoming
level, as it should, and now, of course, it was beginning to
rise again. A great green shadow came between him and the
sun. Niggle looked up, and fell off his bicycle.

Before him stood the Tree, his Tree, finished. If you could
say that of a Tree that was alive, its leaves opening, its
branches growing and bending in the wind that Niggle had

so often felt or guessed, and had so often failed to catch. He gazed at the Tree, and slowly he lifted his arms and opened them wide.

'It's a gift!' he said. He was referring to his art, and also to the result; but he was using the word quite literally.[57]

This episode occurs after Niggle had heard the two Voices discussing his purgatorial destiny and the bicycle ride was part of the 'gentle treatment' which the Voices had prescribed for the continued recovery of his soul. The fact that Niggle is able to see every blade of grass distinctly is reminiscent of the enhanced vision in Fairy depicted in *Smith of Wootton Major*, and the open-armed joy at the gift of Creation reflects the joy of Quickbeam in *The Lord of the Rings*. A further parallel between *Smith of Wootton Major* and *Leaf by Niggle* is the similarity between the sceptic, Nokes, and Niggle's neighbour, Parish, who is cast in the role of a 'realist' critic who fails to see the underlying truth in myth. Now, after his own death, Parish is able to see reality as it truly is. Accompanied by Niggle in the incarnated world of Niggle's painting, though not knowing it, he asks a shepherd to tell him the name of the country in which he finds himself:

'Don't you know?' said the man. 'It is Niggle's Country. It is Niggle's Picture, or most of it; a little of it is now Parish's Garden.'

'Niggle's Picture!' said Parish in astonishment. 'Did *you* think of all this, Niggle? I never knew you were so clever. Why didn't you tell me?'

'He tried to tell you long ago,' said the man; 'but you would not look. He had only got canvas and paint in those days, and you wanted to mend your roof with them. This is

what you and your wife used to call Niggle's Nonsense, or
That Daubing.'

'But it did not look like this then, not *real*,' said Parish.

'No, it was only a glimpse then,' said the man; 'but you
might have caught the glimpse, if you had ever thought it
worth while to try.'[58]

It was indeed apt that Tolkien's publishers should publish
Leaf by Niggle in a combined volume with the essay 'On Fairy
Stories' under the collective title *Tree and Leaf*, especially as
the one had given birth to the other. Both, however, were
developments from the philosophy of myth which Tolkien
had expressed most eloquently in his poem 'Mythopoeia'.
It was also apt, therefore, that this was added to later editions
of *Tree and Leaf*. The final lines of 'Mythopoeia', as well as
being Tolkien's highest achievement in verse, offer a glimpse
of the vision of Paradise which Tolkien saw beyond the purgatorial vision in *Leaf by Niggle*:

In Paradise perchance the eye may stray
from gazing upon everlasting Day
to see the day-illumined, and renew
from mirrored truth the likeness of the True.
Then looking on the Blessed Land 'twill see
that all is as it is, and yet made free:
Salvation changes not, nor yet destroys,
garden nor gardener, children nor their toys.
Evil it will not see, for evil lies
not in God's picture but in crooked eyes,
not in the source but in malicious choice,
and not in sound but in the tuneless voice.
In Paradise they look no more awry;

and though they make anew, they make no lie.
Be sure they still will make, not being dead,
and poets shall have flames upon their head,
and harps whereon their faultless fingers fall:
there each shall choose for ever from the All.[59]

If, as Paul Kocher maintains, there are parts of *Leaf by Niggle*
which resemble 'an updated version of Dante's *Purgatorio*',
this part of 'Mythopoeia' certainly resembles Dante's
Paradiso. Like Dante, Tolkien was concerned with what the
critic Lin Carter described in her study of *The Lord of the
Rings* as 'the eternal verities of human nature'.[60] What was
important to both Tolkien and Dante was not the accidental
trappings of everyday life but the essential nature of everlasting life, not what human society was becoming but what
humanity was being, not the peripheral but the perennial.
The same concerns were central to Chesterton. Robert J.
Reilly, in his essay on 'Tolkien and the Fairy Story', links
Chesterton and Tolkien as modern inheritors of a long history
of related ideas:

> Why such a position as Tolkien's should exist now is a ques-
> tion for the historian of ideas to answer. That Tolkien's
> Christian romanticism is not unique is, of course, obvious
> by reference to such people as C.S. Lewis and Charles
> Williams. The historian will in turn find back of all three the
> face of Chesterton, and behind him one of Lewis and
> Chesterton's longtime favourites, George Macdonald.[61]

These, in turn, were only relatively recent beneficiaries of
a Christian tradition stretching back almost two thousand
years to the Gospels themselves. 'Chesterton's romances of

Being, such as *Manalive*, follow on and are part of his Thomistic-mystical religious view,' Reilly wrote.[62] This shared religious vision may in itself explain the links of affinity between Chesterton and Tolkien, but a letter Tolkien wrote to his son on 14 May 1944 suggests that Chesterton's influence may on occasions have been more direct:

> I suddenly got an idea for a new story (of about length of Niggle) – in church yesterday, I fear. A man sitting at a high window and seeing not the fortunes of a man or of people, but of one small piece of *land* (about the size of a garden) all down the ages. He just sees it illumined, in borders of mist, and things, animals and men just walk on and off, and the plants and trees grow and die and change. One of the points would be that plants and animals change from one fantastic shape to another but men (in spite of different dress) don't change at all. At intervals all down the ages from Palaeolithic to Today a couple of women (or men) would stroll across scene saying exactly the same thing (e.g. It oughtn't to be allowed. They ought to stop it. Or, I said to her, I'm not one to make a fuss, I said, but ...)[63]

Sadly this story never appears to have come to fruition but the idea bears a remarkable similarity to the central premise of Chesterton's *The Everlasting Man*, the non-fictional work which had been so instrumental in C.S. Lewis's conversion to Christianity.

Five years after this letter to his son was written, Tolkien's *Farmer Giles of Ham* was published. This children's book serves as a living refutation of the charge of gloom or pessimism which is all too often, and wrongly, levelled against Tolkien. Like so much of his other lighter work,

Farmer Giles of Ham shares an affinity with 'Chestertonian Fantasy', perhaps more so than any of his other books. Whereas Tolkien's other works exhibit the Chestertonian sense of wonder, the 'Manalive', and include images of Everyman and the 'Everlasting Man', *Farmer Giles of Ham* exhibits the Chestertonian sense of fun. It is a lighthearted and riotous romp in the tradition of Chesterton's *The Flying Inn* and *The Napoleon of Notting Hill*. Links with the latter work are all too obvious on the very first page when Tolkien sets his story in an idyllic Merrie England, reminiscent of the Mediaeval vision which inspires Adam Wayne, Chesterton's 'Napoleon':

Aegidius de Hammo was a man who lived in the midmost parts of the Island of Britain. In full his name was Aegidius Ahenobarbus Julius Agricola de Hammo; for people were richly endowed with names in those days, now long ago, when this island was still happily divided into many kingdoms. There was more time then, and folk were fewer, so that most men were distinguished. However, those days are now over, so I will in what follows give the man his name shortly, and in the vulgar form: he was Farmer Giles of Ham, and he had a red beard. Ham was only a village, but villages were proud and independent still in those days.[64]

The plot unfolds as Farmer Giles, a reluctant hero, tames the dragon and gains fame as a result. The villagers gain their freedom from a covetous King and his decadent court who are more interested in the latest fashion in hats or in 'discussing points of precedence and etiquette'[65] than with acts of heroism. There are many amusing characters, such as the village blacksmith who is cast in the role of a comic

Wormtongue, and the story's chronology is given in Saints' Days, placing it solidly in a Christian context. Farmer Giles's dog reminds one of Quoodle, the lovably excitable dog in *The Flying Inn*, but the most notable similarity between *Farmer Giles of Ham* and *The Flying Inn* is the eulogizing of good English ale. There are no rumbustious drinking songs in Tolkien's tale, as there are in Chesterton's novel, but the praise and celebration of ale is the same in both works:

> They sat round in the kitchen drinking his health and loudly praising him. He made no effort to hide his yawns, but as long as the drink lasted they took no notice. By the time they had all had one or two (and the farmer two or three), he began to feel quite bold; when they had all had two or three (and he himself five or six), he felt as bold as his dog thought him. They parted good friends; and he slapped their backs heartily.[66]

There are similar allusions to the qualities of ale, and of village inns, in *The Lord of the Rings*. Pippin regrets that the route they are taking out of the Shire does not go via the Golden Perch at Stock: 'The best beer in the Eastfarthing, or used to be: it is a long time since I tasted it.'[67] Most memorably there is the sojourn of the hobbits at the Prancing Pony at Bree where Sam is 'much relieved by the excellence of the beer'.[68] In fact, the beer is so excellent that Frodo ends up singing a drinking song with near disastrous consequences. Such frivolities are soon lost in the seriousness of the Quest, but upon their return to the Shire they are horrified to discover that the evil of Mordor has even invaded their own homeland with dire results, not least of which is the closing of all the inns: 'They're all closed,' said Robin. 'The Chief doesn't hold with beer. Leastways that is how it started. But now I reckon it's his Men that has it all.'[69]

This conjures up yet another parallel between Chesterton and Tolkien. Chesterton had written *The Flying Inn* partly as a risible riposte to the Temperance movement and to the spectre of Prohibition, and Tolkien would have sympathized fully with Chesterton's jocular jousting with these puritanical 'killjoys'. Tolkien's regular meetings with Lewis and the other Inklings in the Eagle and Child were as important to him as the meetings with Belloc and Baring in the inns of Fleet Street had been to Chesterton. The consumption of traditional ale in traditional inns was as central to each man's image of Englishness as it was to Frodo's and Sam's image of hobbitness.

Tolkien had stated that his conceptions of 'Englishry' and 'hobbitry' were synonymous and, according to these criteria, Chesterton certainly qualifies as an honorary hobbit. The two writers seem to epitomize Englishness, quintessentially so, and one can almost picture them being perfectly at home in the Shire. Indeed, they would be more appreciated in the Shire than they are in modern England. Hobbits, Tolkien wrote, are very fond of stories and it is easy to imagine *Farmer Giles of Ham* and *The Flying Inn* at the very top of the hobbits' reading list!

'Tolkienian Fantasy' aside, the two writers were certainly kindred spirits. As Tolkien would no doubt have said, if Chesterton had not already done so, 'The more truly we can see life as a fairy-tale, the more clearly the tale resolves itself into war with the dragon who is wasting fairyland.'[70]

Chapter 10

Approaching Mount Doom:
Tolkien's Final Years

In late July 1955, three months before the third and final volume of *The Lord of the Rings* was published, Tolkien and his daughter Priscilla visited Italy. Throughout the visit he kept a diary, and recorded that he felt as though he had 'come to the heart of Christendom: an exile from the borders and the far provinces returning home, or at least to the home of his fathers'. Among the canals of Venice he found himself 'almost free of the cursed disease of the internal combustion engine of which all the world is dying'. Later he wrote that 'Venice seemed incredibly, elvishly lovely – to me like a dream of Old Gondor, or Pelargir of the Númenórean Ships, before the return of the Shadow.'[1] In a letter to his son and daughter-in-law Tolkien wrote that 'for pure fun and pleasure, I enjoyed the first days at Venice most',[2] and on their last day they attended a performance of Verdi's *Rigoletto* which he described as 'perfectly astounding'.[3] On the following day he and Priscilla travelled to Assisi 'for the great feast of Santa Chiara', where they attended 'High Mass sung by Cardinal Micara with silver trumpets at the elevation!' In the letter to his son and daughter-in-law, he reported being 'staggered by the frescos of Assisi' and wrote that 'I remain in love with Italian, and feel quite lorn without a chance of trying to speak it!'[4]

Tolkien returned to England to find himself besieged by anxious publishers, pressing him to deal with the last few remaining queries from the printers concerning the overdue third volume of *The Lord of the Rings*. This finally reached the bookshops on 20 October, a year after the publication of the first two volumes.

The Lord of the Rings was soon established as an international bestseller and its success attracted the attention of the film world. On 4 September 1957 Tolkien was approached by three American businessmen, Forrest J. Ackerman, Morton Grady Zimmerman and Al Brodax, who showed him drawings for a proposed animated motion picture of *The Lord of the Rings*. Tolkien was impressed by the 'really astonishingly good pictures' which were 'Rackham rather than Disney', but he was not impressed by the proposed 'Story Line': 'The Story Line or Scenario was, however, on a lower level. In fact bad.'[5] 'People gallop about on Eagles at the least provocation,' Tolkien complained in a letter to his publisher, 'Lórien becomes a fairy-castle with "delicate minarets", and all that sort of thing.'[6] A number of names were consistently misspelt in the synopsis – Boromir being rendered as 'Borimor' – and *lembas*, the elvish waybread which several critics had compared to the Blessed Sacrament, was described as a 'food concentrate'.

Negotiations with the film moguls were discontinued, but the celebrity status Tolkien was to enjoy and endure in the wake of the international success of *The Lord of the Rings* was only just beginning.

At around the time he was being courted by rich American film makers, he became the winner of the International Fantasy Award, which was presented to him at the Fifteenth World Science Fiction Convention on 10 September. 'What it boiled down to,' Tolkien wrote, 'was a lunch at the Criterion ... with speeches, and the handing over of an absurd "trophy".

A massive metal "model"' of an upended Space-rocket (combined with a Ronson lighter).'[7]

Tolkien's new-found fame was far removed from his academic career as Merton Professor of English Language and Literature, and the incongruity of his dual role as popular fantasy writer and internationally acclaimed philologist caused both bemusement and a certain wry amusement among his fellow dons at Oxford. He was now in his sixties and his academic career was coming to an end even as his international fame as a writer was beginning. He retired in 1959, at the age of sixty-seven, and gave his Valedictory Address to the University of Oxford on 5 June of that year. It was full of the self-effacing humility befitting the occasion and he displayed an attitude to the subject of philology which was both modest and moderate: 'Philology was part of my job, and I enjoyed it. I have always found it amusing. But I have never had strong views about it. I do not think it necessary to salvation. I do not think it should be thrust down the throats of the young, as a pill, the more efficacious the nastier it tastes.'[8] Yet his self-effacement should not detract from his key role in reconciling the formerly estranged schools of language and literature at Oxford. During the years 1925–35 he had been, in the words of his obituarist in *The Times*, 'more than any other single man, responsible for closing the old rift between "literature" and "philology" in English studies at Oxford and thus giving the existing school its characteristic temper. His unique insight at once into the language of poetry and into the poetry of language qualified him for this task.'[9] In his Valedictory Address Tolkien referred to this aspect of his life's work in terms which alluded to his birth in South Africa: 'I have the hatred of *apartheid* in my bones; and most of all I detest the segregation or separation of Language and Literature. I do not care which of them you think White.'[10]

One of the best descriptions of Tolkien as an Oxford professor, viewed from the perspective of one of the many undergraduates he taught over the years, was given by Desmond Albrow, writing in the *Catholic Herald*. Albrow's first meeting with Tolkien had taken place in Tolkien's study at his home in Northmoor Road, north Oxford, in 1943:

Tolkien was not then widely known outside the narrow confines of Oxbridge and academe ... I, with my provincial ignorance of the ways of the literary and intellectual world, had never even heard of Tolkien. But he was the first Oxford professor that I had ever met face to face and the delightful fact was that he behaved to me like a true scholar-gentleman.

I was then a fairly clever, but fairly callow, 18-year-old, fresh and unbruised by life from the North of England for whom Oxford at first taste was almost a foreign hinterland with bizarre rules and traps to snare both the arrogant and the innocent. In about a quarter of an hour Tolkien gave me a confidence and an optimism that he so easily could have destroyed with a cutting phrase or a supercilious quip. Just imagine if I had encountered one of those modern-day, smart-alec, television-preening dons who have now despoiled what is left of the high tables of Oxford.

Here was a professor who looked like a professor ... Tolkien wore cords and a sports jacket, smoked a reassuring pipe, laughed a lot, sometimes mumbled when his thoughts outstripped words, looked in those days to my idealistic eyes like the young Leslie Howard, the film actor. There was a sense of civilisation, winsome sanity and sophistication about him...

After the conclusion of the interview, Albrow left Tolkien's house, 'with its books, pipesmoke and obvious testaments to children and family life', with a 'jaunty step' and a new confidence about his future as an Oxford undergraduate.

Years later, when Albrow became engaged to be married, he discovered that his future wife's family had been friends in north Oxford with the Tolkiens for many years. His future father-in-law had bought Tolkien's last car after Tolkien's dislike for the internal combustion engine had finally led to his forsaking car ownership. 'I liked this,' Albrow recalled. 'Somehow Hobbits and motor-cars did not seem to make sense.'

As a good friend of the family into which Albrow was marrying, Tolkien had re-entered his life:

> He was still the kind man who had befriended me when there was no need, still laughed and gently mocked the world, still mumbled and puffed his pipe. Later he made a gracious and witty speech at our wedding ...[11]

In his memoir, Albrow compared Tolkien, 'a professor who looked like a professor', with C.S. Lewis, who 'looked more like an intellectual butcher'. Yet during the 1950s differences had emerged between Tolkien and Lewis which went deeper than the sartorial. There was never a breach in their friendship, just a gradual, almost imperceptible cooling of relations which was exacerbated by Lewis's controversial marriage to Joy Davidman in March 1957. None of Lewis's friends were told of the marriage, learning of the event only through the notice in *The Times*, and Tolkien was only one of several of Lewis's closest friends who were astonished and offended by the news. Since Lewis's love affair with Joy Davidman has now been immortalized, and partially fictionalized, in the

BBC and Hollywood productions of *Shadowlands*, it is difficult to sympathize with, or understand, the opposition which
the marriage provoked at the time. Yet to Lewis's friends,
Tolkien included, only the bare facts were visible. Lewis, a
confirmed bachelor who was not far short of his sixtieth
birthday, had married an American divorcée, in itself
shocking in the eyes of those who saw Lewis as a bastion of
traditional Christian teaching on marriage. Furthermore, this
divorcee was seen as an *arriviste*, exerting an unhealthy influence on Lewis. However unjust such a viewpoint may seem in
hindsight, it was not so easy for those closest to Lewis to see
things dispassionately at the time.

The depth of Tolkien's feelings for Lewis and his regrets at
their estrangement were expressed in a letter to Priscilla four
days after Lewis's death on 22 November 1963:

> So far I have felt the normal feelings of a man of my age – like
> an old tree that is losing its leaves one by one: this feels like
> an axe-blow near the roots. Very sad that we should have
> become so separated in the last years; but our time of close
> communion endured in our memory for both of us. I had a
> mass said this morning, and was there, and served.[12]

R.E. Havard and James Dundas-Grant, two other members of
the Inklings, were also present at the Mass.

At Lewis's funeral at Holy Trinity, the Headington Quarry
church which Lewis attended throughout the last years of his
life, Tolkien met up with several other old friends, including
Owen Barfield, George Sayer and John Lawlor. They had their
own memories of Lewis, unique to each of them, but the deep
sense of loss was shared by all. Tolkien expressed his own feelings in several letters to members of his family. To his son

Michael he wrote that 'many people still regard me as one of his intimates. Alas! that ceased to be so some ten years ago. We were separated first by the sudden apparition of Charles Williams, and then by his marriage. Of which he never even told me ... But we owed each a great debt to the other, and that tie with the deep affection that it begot, remains. He was a great man of whom the cold-blooded official obituaries only scraped the surface, in places with injustice.'[13] The grief which Tolkien felt at the loss of Lewis was expressed in a letter to his publisher on 23 December in which he bemoaned 'a troublous year, of endless distraction and much weariness, ending with the blow of C.S.L.'s death'.[14] In a letter to Christopher Bretherton in July of the following year Tolkien wrote that Lewis 'was my closest friend from about 1927 to 1940, and remained very dear to me. His death was a grievous blow.'[15]

In the following month Tolkien was moved to defend Lewis from comments which George Bailey, one of Lewis's former pupils, had made in an article in *The Reporter*:

C.S.L. of course had some oddities and could sometimes be irritating. He was after all and remained an Irishman of Ulster. But he did nothing for effect; he was not a professional clown, but a natural one, when a clown at all. He was generous-minded, on guard against all prejudices, though a few were too deep-rooted in his native background to be observed by him. That his literary opinions were ever dictated by envy (as in the case of T.S. Eliot) is a grotesque calumny. After all it is possible to dislike Eliot with some intensity even if one has no aspirations to poetic laurels oneself.[16]

Lewis's and Tolkien's negative attitude towards Eliot is certainly curious and perhaps a little anomalous. In both cases their disdain for Eliot's verse dated back to the early '20s when *The Waste Land* had shocked the sensibilities of the poetic establishment while striking a pessimistic chord with the post-war generation. Tolkien's and Lewis's intense tradition-alism prevented them from coming to terms with the freeness of form employed by Eliot, even though the sentiments expressed in his verse echoed their own view of life to a remarkable extent. In his later verse, *Choruses from 'The Rock'* and *Four Quartets*, Eliot expressed an opposition to materialism and scientism with a profundity which few, if any, have matched this century. If anything, he was probably even more traditionalist than either Tolkien or Lewis, as dismayed as they about the cultural decline throughout the century, and in the specifically religious context he slots somewhere between the two of them. As an Anglo-Catholic he was 'higher' than Lewis in Anglican terms while never actually 'poping' and becoming a convert to Roman Catholicism.

In spite of Tolkien's inability to appreciate Eliot's verse, many critics have been quick to see parallels between their respective visions. Charles Moseley, in his study of Tolkien, stressed the similarities between the image of the Waste Land and the image of Mordor:

Already the motif to which Tolkien often returned, the Quest journey through a Waste Land, the challenge to a dark Tower – a challenge that in turn tests the maturity and integrity of the challenger – is dominant. The echoes of medieval Arthurian romance are patent, just as they are in T.S. Eliot's *The Waste Land*; and both writers share an interest in the way the mythic stirs half-understood reso-nances in a reader's mind.[17]

Another parallel was drawn by Colin Wilson: 'The Lord of the Rings is a criticism of the modern world and of the values of technological civilization. It asserts its own values, and tries to persuade the reader that they are preferable to current values ... In fact, like The Waste Land, it is at once an attack on the modern world and a credo, a manifesto.'[18]

More recently, in the aftermath of Tolkien's triumph in the Waterstone's poll, John Clute, editor of the Encyclopedia of Fantasy, sought to explain the cultural criteria which underpin The Lord of the Rings in terms which culminated naturally in Eliot's 'waste land' motif. Clute described The Lord of the Rings, with its hard-won triumph of good over evil and its 'earned happy ending', as 'a comprehensive counter-myth to the story of the twentieth century', stressing that it enshrined Tolkien's sense 'that what had happened to life in the twentieth century was profoundly inhuman'. Tolkien's counter-myth, Clute concluded, was 'a description of a universe that feels right – another reality that the soul requires in this waste-land century'.[19]

Meanwhile, Charles W. Moorman endeavoured to place the connections in a wider context. Moorman argued that the image of the City formulated by St Augustine largely shaped and regulated the tone and form of the work of Tolkien, Lewis, Eliot, Charles Williams and Dorothy L. Sayers.[20] When Eliot died in January 1965 Tolkien became the only survivor of this group of Christian writers, intensifying his feeling that he had outstayed his welcome in the 'waste land' century he had grown to despise. The previous decade had seen the death of most of the generation of literary figures whose tradition-alist response to twentieth-century materialism had consti-tuted a significant Christian cultural revival. Ronald Knox, Dorothy L. Sayers and Roy Campbell had all died in 1957,

Alfred Noyes the following year, and Edith Sitwell in 1964. Evelyn Waugh would die in 1966 and Siegfried Sassoon in 1967. As he watched his literary peers, and his world, quite literally pass away before his eyes, the sense of exile surfaced as never before. This was evident in a letter to his friend Amy Ronald, dated 16 November 1969:

> What a dreadful, fear-darkened, sorrow-laden world we live in – especially for those who have also the burden of age, whose friends and all they especially care for are afflicted in the same way. Chesterton once said that it is our duty to keep the Flag of This World flying: but it takes now a sturdier and more sublime patriotism than it did then. Gandalf added that it is not for us to choose the times into which we are born, but to do what we could to repair them; but the spirit of wickedness in high places is now so powerful and so many-headed in its incarnations that there seems nothing more to do than personally to refuse to worship any of the hydras' heads ...²¹

In such circumstances Tolkien gained much consolation from his faith, writing in the same letter to Amy Ronald of his belief in the power of prayer: 'I pray for you – because I have a feeling (more near a certainty) that God, for some ineffable reason which to us may seem almost like humour, is so curiously ready to answer the prayers of the *least* worthy of his suppliants – if they pray for others. I do not of course mean to say that he only answers the prayers of the unworthy (who ought not to expect to be heard at all), or I should not now be benefitting by the prayers of others.'

Tolkien's faith in old age was expressed with eloquence in a letter to his son Michael on 1 November 1963. Written three weeks before Lewis's death and only two months before his own seventy-second birthday, this letter needs quoting at length because it provides a comprehensive exposition of Tolkien's philosophical and religious outlook as he approached the end of his life:

> You speak of 'sagging faith'... In the last resort faith is an act of the will, inspired by love. Our love may be chilled and our will eroded by the spectacle of the shortcomings, folly, and even sins of the Church and its ministers, but I do not think that one who has once had faith goes back over the line for these reasons (least of all anyone with any historical know-ledge). 'Scandal' at most is an occasion of temptation – as indecency is to lust, which it does not make but arouses. It is convenient because it turns our eyes away from ourselves and our own faults to find a scape-goat ... The temptation to 'unbelief' (which really means rejection of Our Lord and His claims) is always there within us. Part of us longs to find an excuse for it outside us. The stronger the inner temptation the more readily shall we be 'scandalized' by others. I think I am as sensitive as you (or any other Christian) to the 'scan-dals', both of clergy and laity. I have suffered grievously in my life from stupid, tired, dimmed, and even bad priests; but I now know enough about myself to be aware that I should not leave the Church (which for me would mean leaving the allegiance of Our Lord) for any such reasons: I should leave because I did not believe ... I should deny the Blessed Sacrament, that is: call Our Lord a fraud to His face.
>
> If He is a fraud and the Gospels fraudulent – that is: garbled accounts of a demented megalomaniac (which is the only alternative), then of course the spectacle exhibited by the Church ... in history and today is simply evidence of a

gigantic fraud. If not, however, then this spectacle is alas! only what was to be expected: it began before the first Easter, and it does not affect *faith* at all – except that we may and should be deeply grieved. *But* we should grieve on our Lord's behalf and for Him, associating ourselves with the scandal-izers not with the saints, not crying out that we cannot 'take' Judas Iscariot, or even the absurd and cowardly Simon Peter, or the silly women like James' mother, trying to push her sons.

It takes a fantastic will to unbelief to suppose that Jesus never really 'happened', and more to suppose that he did not say the things recorded of him – so incapable of being 'invented' by anyone in the world at that time: such as 'before Abraham came to be *I am*' (John viii). 'He that hath seen me hath seen the Father' (John ix); or the promulgation of the Blessed Sacrament in John v: 'He that eateth my flesh and drinketh my blood hath eternal life'. We must therefore either believe in Him and in what he said and take the conse-quences; or reject him and take the consequences. I find it for myself difficult to believe that anyone who has ever been to Communion, even once, with at least right intention, can ever again reject Him without grave blame. (However, He alone knows each unique soul and its circumstances.)

The only cure for sagging or fainting faith is Communion. Though always Itself, perfect and complete and inviolate, the Blessed Sacrament does not operate completely and once for all in any of us. Like the act of Faith it must be contin-uous and grow by exercise. Frequency is of the highest effect. Seven times a week is more nourishing than seven times at intervals...

I myself am convinced by the Petrine claims, nor looking around the world does there seem much doubt which (if Christianity is true) is the True Church, the temple of the Spirit dying but living, corrupt but holy, self-reforming and rearising. But for me that Church of which the Pope is the acknowledged head on earth has as chief claim that it is the one that has (and still does) ever defended the Blessed Sacrament, and given it most honour, and put it (as Christ plainly intended) in the prime place. 'Feed my sheep' was His last charge to St Peter; and since His words are always first to be understood literally, I suppose them to refer primarily to the Bread of Life. It was against this that the W. European revolt (or Reformation) was really launched – 'the blasphemous fable of the Mass' – and faith/works a mere red herring. I suppose the greatest reform of our time was that carried out by St Pius X: surpassing anything, however needed, that the Council will achieve.[22]

The 'Council' to which Tolkien was referring was the Second Vatican Council which had convened in 1962 and would last for four years. Like Evelyn Waugh, who died under its shadow, Tolkien was apprehensive about many of the reforms instituted by the Council. 'We discussed religion often,' remembers George Sayer, who met Tolkien regularly during the 1960s. 'Tolkien was a very strict Roman Catholic. He was very orthodox and old fashioned and he opposed most of the new developments in the Church at the time of the Second Vatican Council.'[23] This was confirmed by Father John Tolkien, the eldest of Tolkien's sons, who had been ordained in the 1940s. Father Tolkien emphasized that his father's Catholicism 'pervaded all his thinking, beliefs and everything else', that 'he was very much, always a Christian', but added that he was 'against the changes' brought about by the Council, 'especially the loss of Latin'.[24] Tolkien expressed his love for Latin in a letter to his old parish priest Father Douglas Carter in June 1972.[25] Several years earlier he discussed the changes wrought by the Council in a letter to his son, Michael:

> 'Trends' in the Church are ... serious, especially to those accustomed to find in it a solace and a 'pax' in times of temporal trouble, and not just another arena of strife and change. But imagine the experience of those born (as I) between the Golden and Diamond Jubilee of Victoria. Both senses or imaginations of security have been progressively stripped away from us. Now we find ourselves nakedly confronting the will of God, as concerns ourselves and our position in Time ... I know quite well that, to you as to me, the Church which once felt like a refuge, now often feels like a trap. There is nowhere else to go! (I wonder if this desperate feeling, the last state of loyalty hanging on, was not, even more often than is actually recorded in the Gospels, felt by Our Lord's followers in His earthly life-time?) I think there is nothing to do but to pray, for the Church, the Vicar of Christ, and for ourselves; and meanwhile to exercise the virtue of loyalty, which indeed only becomes a virtue when one is under pressure to desert it.[26]

In the same letter Tolkien questioned some of the erroneous thinking which he believed had undermined the proceedings of the Council. In his arguments against the demands for greater 'simplicity' in the Church's liturgy, Tolkien fell back on the arboreal imagery of Chesterton's Philosophy of the Tree and his own vision of the perennial wisdom of Treebeard:

> The 'protestant' search backwards for 'simplicity' and direct-ness – which, of course, though it contains some good or at

least intelligible motives, is mistaken and indeed vain. Because 'primitive Christianity' is now and in spite of all 'research' will ever remain largely unknown; because 'primitiveness' is no guarantee of value, and is and was in great part a reflection of ignorance. Grave abuses were as much an element in Christian 'liturgical' behaviour from the beginning as now. (St Paul's strictures on eucharistic behaviour are sufficient to show this!) Still more because 'my church' was not intended by Our Lord to be static or remain in perpetual childhood; but to be a living organism (likened to a plant), which develops and changes in externals by the interaction of its bequeathed divine life and history – the particular circumstances of the world into which it is set. There is no resemblance between the 'mustard-seed' and the full-grown tree. For those living in the days of its branching growth the Tree is the thing, for the history of a living thing is part of its life, and the history of a divine thing is sacred. The wise may know that it began with a seed, but it is vain to try and dig it up, for it no longer exists, and the virtue and powers that it had now reside in the Tree. Very good: but in husbandry the authorities, the keepers of the Tree, must look after it, according to such wisdom as they possess, prune it, remove cankers, rid it of parasites, and so forth. (With trepidation, knowing how little their knowledge of growth is!) But they will certainly do harm, if they are obsessed with the desire of going back to the seed or even to the first youth of the plant when it was (as they imagine) pretty and unafflicted by evils.[27]

The 'other motive' behind the calls for reform of the liturgy which caused Tolkien consternation was 'aggiornamento: bringing up to date' which, Tolkien believed, 'has its own grave dangers, as has been apparent throughout history'.[28]

There are distinct similarities between Tolkien's view and that of Evelyn Waugh, who also singled out the alliance of 'primitivists' and 'aggiornamentists' for scorn. In an article in the *Spectator* at the very start of the Council's proceedings, Waugh had written of the threat posed by the new liturgists:

> It is not, I think, by a mere etymological confusion that the majority of English-speaking people believe that 'venerable' means 'old'. There is a deep-lying connection in the human heart between worship and age. But the new fashion is for something bright and loud and practical. It has been set by a strange alliance between archaeologists absorbed in their speculations on the rites of the second century, and modernists who wish to give the Church the character of our own deplorable epoch. In combination they call themselves 'liturgists'.[29]

There is no doubt that Tolkien was equally as opposed to those who sought to open the windows of the Church to the atmosphere of 'our own deplorable epoch' but, unlike Waugh, he never became embittered and was not tempted to rebellion or stubborn opposition. Instead he exercised the 'virtue of loyalty' to which he had alluded and sought to see the good results of the Council, as well as the bad:

> I find myself in sympathy with those developments that are strictly 'ecumenical', that is concerned with other groups or churches that call themselves (and often truly are) 'Christian'. We have prayed endlessly for Christian re-union ... An increase in 'charity' is an enormous gain. As Christians those faithful to the Vicar of Christ must put aside the resentments that as mere humans they feel ... As a man

whose childhood was darkened by persecution, I find this hard. But charity must cover a multitude of sins! There are dangers (of course), but a Church militant cannot afford to shut up its soldiers in a fortress. It had as bad effects on the Maginot Line.[30]

Tolkien's deep understanding of the ecumenist debate within the Church during the 1960s was exhibited in another letter to his son Michael:

Not that one should forget the wise words of Charles Williams, that it is our duty to tend the accredited and established altar, though the Holy Spirit may send the fire down somewhere else. God cannot be limited (even by his own Foundations) – of which St Paul is the first and prime example – and may use any channel for His grace. Even to love Our Lord, and certainly to call him Lord, and God, is a grace, and may bring more grace. Nonetheless, speaking institutionally and not of individual souls the channel must eventually run back into the ordained course, or run into the sands and perish. Besides the Sun there may be moonlight (even bright enough to read by); but if the Sun were removed there would be no Moon to see. What would Christianity now be if the Roman Church has in fact been destroyed?[31]

This short aside on ecumenism was a footnote added to a long letter to Michael which Tolkien had written in an effort to bolster his son's 'sagging faith'. As well as offering an insight into Tolkien's own faith in the final decade of his life, it expressed an introspectively humble approach to what he perceived as his failings as a father to his children:

I live in anxiety concerning my children: who in this harder crueller and more mocking world into which I have survived must suffer more assaults than I have. But I am one who came up out of Egypt, and pray God none of my seed shall return thither. I witnessed (half-comprehending) the heroic sufferings and early death in extreme poverty of my mother who brought me into the Church; and received the astonishing charity of Francis Morgan. But I fell in love with the Blessed Sacrament from the beginning – and by the mercy of God never have fallen out again: but alas! I indeed did not live up to it. I brought you all up ill and talked to you too little. Out of wickedness and sloth I almost ceased to practise my religion – especially at Leeds, and at 22 Northmoor Road. Not for me the Hound of Heaven, but the never-ceasing silent appeal of Tabernacle, and the sense of starving hunger. I regret those days bitterly (and suffer for them with such patience as I can be given); most of all because I failed as a father. Now I pray for you all, unceasingly, that the Healer (the *Haelend* as the Saviour was usually called in Old English) shall heal my defects, and that none of you shall ever cease to cry *Benedictus qui venit in nomine Domini*.[32]

One cannot help but feel that Tolkien was being unduly harsh in seeing himself as a failure as a father. Whatever shortcomings he exhibited must be countered by the mitigating pleas of those who remembered him as a loving and conscientious parent. One is reminded particularly of the testimony of Simonne d'Ardenne, both an academic colleague and a close family friend. 'All his letters,' d'Ardenne recalled, 'extending over about forty years, tell of his concern about his children's health, their comfort, their future; how best he could help them succeed in life.'[33] 'Tolkien was immensely kind and understanding as a father,' wrote Humphrey Carpenter, 'never shy of kissing his sons in public even when they were grown men, and never reserved in his display of warmth and love.'[34] The fact is that Tolkien did his utmost to ensure that his children enjoyed the security and love which had largely been denied to him through the untimely deaths of his own parents. *The Father Christmas Letters* and *The Hobbit* should serve as adequate evidence to acquit Tolkien of the charges he had levelled against himself.

This domesticated aspect of his personality was, along with his Englishness, at the heart of the 'hobbitness' within him. When he was asked in a radio interview on BBC Radio 4 on 16 December 1970 whether, as his books suggested, he attached importance to 'home, fire, pipe, bed', he replied, with apparently genuine surprise, 'Don't you?'[35] This, in turn, raises the question of his relationship with his wife. His marriage had endured its problems and difficulties, particularly in its infancy, but the teething problems of the first few decades largely resolved themselves in later years. The smouldering resentment which Edith had felt towards her husband's faith, having lapsed herself, and her obdurate opposition to his taking the children to church, had caused tension in their marriage during the '20s and '30s. This occasionally boiled over into furious outbursts, but after one such explosion of anger in 1940 there was a genuine 'clearing of the air' followed by a final reconciliation. Edith explained the complex nature of her feelings and even confessed her desire to resume the practice of her religion. For the rest of her life, though she never attended Mass as frequently or as regularly as her husband, Edith was reconciled to Catholicism and even delighted to take an interest in church affairs.

Another cause of friction within the marriage was the amount of time that Edith believed her husband's work, both in his scholarly and his literary endeavours, was causing him to be apart from her. Yet she shared her children's interest in *The Father Christmas Letters*, *The Hobbit* and *The Lord of the Rings*. Tolkien was conscious of the need to involve her in his creativity and she was the first person to whom he showed two of his stories, *Leaf by Niggle* and *Smith of Wootton Major*, being both warmed and encouraged by her approval.

Edith, at least initially, had resented Tolkien's friendship with C.S. Lewis and the other Inklings, not least because their regular meetings had meant that her husband was away from home for one evening a week, but she was not totally excluded from Tolkien's social life. They shared a number of friends who, for all their academic connections, became as much a part of Edith's life as of her husband's. These included Rosfrith Murray, daughter of the original *Oxford Dictionary* editor Sir James Murray, and her nephew Robert Murray who, partly under Tolkien's influence, went on to become a Jesuit priest. Other mutual friends included Tolkien's former pupils and colleagues such as Simonne d'Ardenne, Elaine Griffiths, Stella Mills and Mary Salu. Some of these had amusing memories of their friendship with the Tolkiens which were recounted in Carpenter's biography. The Tolkiens 'did not always talk about the same things to the same people, and as they grew older each went his or her own way in this respect, Ronald discoursing on an English place-name apparently oblivious that the same visitor was simultaneously being addressed by Edith on the subject of a grandchild's measles. But this was something that regular guests learnt to cope with.'[36]

Perhaps the strongest force in their marriage, bonding them together more than anything else, was the shared love for their children. As both had been orphaned at a young age, they were intent to ensure that their own children enjoyed the strong and conventional family background that they had been denied. They delighted in every detail of the lives of their offspring and, in later life, this delight was evident in their devotion to their grandchildren. They had shared in the pride of parents when Michael had won the George Medal for his action as an anti-aircraft gunner defending aerodromes in the Battle of Britain, and they were overjoyed when John was ordained a priest shortly after the war had ended.

Friends of the Tolkiens remembered the deep affection between them which was visible in the care with which they chose and wrapped each other's birthday presents and the great concern they showed for each other's health. By the 1960s, with the onset of old age, health concerns were becoming an everyday fact of life. 'I have got over my complaints for the present,' Tolkien wrote to his son Michael, 'and feel as well as my old bones allow. I am getting nearly as unbendable as an Ent.'[37] Yet it was his wife's health which was causing most concern.

Edith was becoming increasingly crippled with arthritis and by the beginning of 1968, when she was seventy-nine and he was seventy-six, they decided to move to a more convenient house. A move would also have the added advantage of making Tolkien's whereabouts secret since, by this time, the cult surrounding *The Lord of the Rings* had reached such dimensions that he was being inundated by fan mail, gifts and telephone calls, and was under almost permanent siege from visitors. It was, then, for reasons of both health and privacy that the Tolkiens made their 'escape' to Bournemouth where they bought a modest modern bungalow.

Their new home had a well-equipped kitchen in which Edith could manage to cook in spite of her increasing disability. There was central heating, a 'luxury' they had never had before, and outside there was a verandah where they could sit in the evenings looking out on a large garden that had plenty of room for their roses and even a few vegetables. At the end of the garden was a private gate leading into a small wooded gorge that led down to the sea. Such was the setting for the last three years of their life together.

Edith, in particular, was happy in Bournemouth and Tolkien derived much of his own happiness from hers. He was also free from the incessant harassment of 'fans', allowing him to resume work once more on *The Silmarillion*. There was regular domestic help and Catholic neighbours who often took him to church in their car, yet he confessed to his son Christopher a year after the move to Bournemouth of a lingering loneliness, complaining that 'I see no men of my own kind'.[38] There were also continuing health worries. 'I have horrible arthritis in the *left* hand,' he informed Christopher on 2 January 1969, 'which cannot excuse this scrawl, since, mercifully, my right is not yet affected!'[39] Seven months later, on 31 July, he informed his son that his doctor had 'diagnosed an inflamed/or diseased gall-bladder' which was causing him 'very considerable pain'. 'Usually a cheerful and encouraging doctor, he was alarmingly serious, and the prospect looked dark. We (or at least I) know far too little about the complicated machine we inhabit, and ... underestimate the gall-bladder! It is a vital part of the chemical factory, and apart from all else can cause intense pain, if it goes wrong; and if it is "diseased": well you are "for it".' In spite of initial fears Tolkien made a good recovery and the ominous part of the letter referred to Edith: 'Mummy is ailing, and I fear slowly "declining".'[40]

The decline was indeed slow because Edith lived for another two and a half years, but the end, when it came, was abrupt. She was taken ill on the night of Friday 19 November 1971, aged eighty-two. The cause of her final, fatal illness was an inflamed gall-bladder, putting a prophetic twist on Tolkien's earlier letter. After a few days of severe illness she died in hospital early on Monday 29 November. Later the same day, Tolkien described Edith's final days in a letter to a friend:

> I am grieved to tell you that my wife died this morning. Her courage and determination (of which you speak truly) carried her through to what seemed the brink of recovery, but a sudden relapse occurred which she fought for nearly three days in vain. She died at last in peace.
>
> I am utterly bereaved, and cannot yet lift up heart, but my family is gathering round me and my friends.[41]

It would be many months before Tolkien was able to 'lift up heart' after the loss of Edith. In a letter to Christopher on 11 July 1972, he expressed his love for his wife in the way he had always expressed himself when he had something to say beyond the power of mere facts. He reverted to the language of myth and, more specifically, to the language of the myth she had inspired:

> I have at last got busy about Mummy's grave ... The inscription I should like is:

EDITH MARY TOLKIEN
1889–1971
Lúthien

> : brief and jejune, except for *Lúthien*, which says for me more than a multitude of words: for she was (and knew she was) my Lúthien.

...Say what you feel, without reservation, about this addi-
tion. I began this under the stress of great emotion and regret
– and in any case I am afflicted from time to time (increasingly) with an overwhelming sense of bereavement. I need
advice. Yet I hope none of my children will feel that the use
of this name is a sentimental fancy. It is at any rate not
comparable to the quoting of pet names in obituaries. I never
called Edith *Lúthien* – but she was the source of the story
that in time became the chief part of the *Silmarillion*. It was
first conceived in a small woodland glade filled with
hemlocks at Roos in Yorkshire (where I was for a brief time
in command of an outpost of the Humber Garrison in 1917,
and she was able to live with me for a while). In those days
her hair was raven, her skin clear, her eyes brighter than you
have seen them, and she could sing – and *dance*. But the
story has gone crooked, and I am left, and I cannot plead
before the inexorable Mandos.

I will say no more now. But I should like ere long to have
a long talk with *you*. For if as seems probable I shall never
write any ordered biography – it is against my nature, which
expresses itself about things deepest felt in tales and myths –
someone close in heart to me should know something about
things that records do not record: the dreadful sufferings of
our childhoods, from which we rescued one another, but
could not wholly heal the wounds that later often proved
disabling; the sufferings we endured after our love began – all
of which (over and above our personal weaknesses) might
help to make pardonable, or understandable, the lapses and
darknesses which at times marred our lives – and to explain
how these never touched our depths nor dimmed our memories of our youthful love. For ever (especially when alone) we
still met in the woodland glade, and went in hand many

times to escape the shadow of imminent death before our last parting.[42]

In this heartfelt confession to his son, Tolkien had unwittingly given an evocative exposition of his philosophy of myth which exceeded in poignancy and potency the combined effect of his essay 'On Fairy Stories', his short story *Leaf by Niggle* and his poem 'Mythopoeia'. He was saying, in effect, that the only way to get at the truth of his love for his wife was to enter into the *myth* of Beren and Lúthien which, essentially inspired by that love, was itself the most powerful and poignant expression of it. Truth and myth were intertwined and made 'one body' just as he and Edith had in some mystical and mythical sense become 'one body' in Christian marriage.

Unable to face life in Bournemouth without Edith, Tolkien sought a return to his beloved Oxford. This was facilitated when Merton College invited him to become a resident honorary Fellow, offering him a set of rooms in a college house in Merton Street, where a scout and his wife could look after him. Soon after his return to Oxford he travelled to Buckingham Palace to be presented with a CBE by the Queen. He was deeply moved by the ceremony, as he was by the award in June 1972 of an honorary Doctorate of Letters from his own University of Oxford. Yet the trappings of the world had never satisfied Tolkien even when he was younger. Now that he was old and living his life without Edith, his sense of loneliness and exile must have seemed almost unbearable.

On Tuesday 28 August 1973 he returned to Bournemouth to stay with Denis and Jocelyn Tolhurst, the doctor and his wife who had looked after him and Edith when they had lived there. On the following day he wrote to his daughter, ending with the postscript that 'it is stuffy, sticky, and rainy here at present – but forecasts are more favourable'.[43] The next day he joined in celebrations to mark Mrs Tolhurst's birthday, but he did not feel well and could not eat much, though he drank a little champagne. He was in pain during the night and the next morning he was taken to a private hospital where an acute bleeding gastric ulcer was diagnosed. His family were contacted, but Michael was on holiday in Switzerland and Christopher was in France. Consequently, only John and Priscilla were able to travel to Bournemouth to be with him. By Saturday a chest infection had developed, and he died early on Sunday morning, 2 September 1973. He was eighty-one.

His requiem Mass was held in Oxford four days after his death, in the plain, modern church in Headington which he had attended so often. The prayers and readings were specially chosen by his son John, who was also principal celebrant, assisted by Tolkien's old friend Father Robert Murray and his parish priest Monsignor Doran. He was buried alongside his wife in the Catholic cemetery at Wolvercote, a few miles outside Oxford. The inscription on the granite gravestone reads: *Edith Mary Tolkien, Lúthien, 1889–1971. John Ronald Reuel Tolkien, Beren, 1892–1973.*

Their mortal lives completed and the 'gift of death' accepted, only 'a far off gleam or echo of *evangelium*' remained, most especially in the example of Beren and Lúthien, immortalized in stone on their tomb. It remained in distant echoes of Beren's last words: '"Now is the Quest achieved," he said, "and my doom full-wrought"; and he spoke no more.'[44] Beren's last words, however, were not the end of the story but the beginning: '... thus whatever grief might lie in wait, the fates of Beren and Lúthien might be joined, and their paths lead together beyond the confines of the world.'[45]

The very last words should be left to Tolkien himself, written in a letter to one of his sons:

> Out of the darkness of my life, so much frustrated, I put before you the one great thing to love on earth: the Blessed Sacrament ... There you will find romance, glory, honour, fidelity, and the true way of all your loves on earth, and more than that: Death: by the divine paradox, that which ends life, and demands the surrender of all, and yet by the taste (or foretaste) of which alone can what you seek in your earthly relationships (love, faithfulness, joy) be maintained, or take on that complexion of reality, of eternal endurance, which every man's heart desires.[46]

Epilogue:
Above all Shadows Rides the Sun

Though here at journey's end I lie
in darkness buried deep,
beyond all towers strong and high,
beyond all mountains steep,
above all shadows rides the Sun
and Stars forever dwell:
I will not say the Day is done,
nor bid the Stars farewell.[1]

In 1969, when Tolkien was seventy-seven years old and living in sedate retirement in Bournemouth, he received a letter from Camilla Unwin, his publisher's daughter. Miss Unwin, as part of a school project, had written to ask: 'What is the purpose of life?' Tolkien's reply[2] is here reproduced *in extenso*:

20 May 1969
Dear Miss Unwin,
I am sorry my reply has been delayed. I hope it will reach you in time. What a very large question! I do not think 'opinions', no matter whose, are of much use without some explanation of how they are arrived at; but on this question it is not easy to be brief.

What does the question really mean? *Purpose and Life* both need some definition. Is it a purely human and moral question; or does it refer to the Universe? It might mean: How ought I to try and use the life-span allowed to me? OR: What purpose/design do living things serve by being alive? The first question, however, will find an answer (if any) only after the second has been considered.

I think that questions about 'purpose' are only really useful when they refer to the conscious purposes or objects of human beings, or to the uses of things they design and make. As for 'other things' their value resides in themselves: they ARE, they would exist even if we did not. But since we do exist one of their functions is to be contemplated by us. If we go up the scale of being to 'other living things', such as, say, some small plant, it presents shape and organization: a 'pattern' recognizable (with variation) in its kin and offspring; and that is deeply interesting, because these things are 'other' and we did not make them, and they seem to proceed from a fountain of invention incalculably richer than our own.

Human curiosity soon asks the question HOW: in what way did this come to be? And since recognizable 'pattern' suggests design, may proceed to WHY? But WHY in this sense, implying reasons and motives, can only refer to a MIND. Only a Mind can have purposes in any way or degree akin to human purposes. So at once any question: 'Why did life, the community of living things, appear in the physical Universe?' introduces the Question: Is there a God, a Creator-Designer, a Mind to which our minds are akin (being derived from it) so that It is intelligible to us in part. With that we come to religion and the moral ideas that proceed from it. Of those things I will only say that 'morals' have two sides, derived from the fact that we are individuals (as in some degree are all living things) but do not, cannot, live in isolation, and have a bond with all other things, ever closer up to the absolute bond with our own human kind.

So morals should be a guide to our human purposes, the conduct of our lives: (a) the ways in which our individual talents can be developed without waste or misuse; and (b) without injuring our kindred or interfering with their development. (Beyond this and higher lies self-sacrifice for love.)

But these are only answers to the smaller question. To the larger there is no answer, because that requires a *complete* knowledge of God, which is unattainable. If we ask why God included us in his Design, we can really say no more than because He Did.

If you do not believe in a personal God the question: 'What is the purpose of life?' is unaskable and unanswerable. To whom or what would you address the question? But since in an odd corner (or odd corners) of the Universe things have developed with minds that ask questions and try to answer them, you might address one of these peculiar things. As one of them I should venture to say (speaking with absurd arrogance on behalf of the Universe): 'I am as I am. There is nothing you can do about it. You may go on trying to find out what I am, but you will never succeed. And why you want to know, I do not know. Perhaps the desire to know for the mere sake of knowledge is related to the prayers that some of you address to what you call God. At their highest these seem simply to praise Him for being, as He is, and for making what He has made, as He has made it.'

Those who believe in a personal God, Creator, do not think the Universe is itself worshipful, though devoted study of it may be one of the ways of honouring Him. And while as living creatures we are (in part) within it and part of it, our ideas of God and ways of expressing them will be largely derived from contemplating the world about us. (Though there is also revelation both addressed to all men and to particular persons.)

So it may be said that the chief purpose of life, for any one of us, is to increase according to our capacity our knowledge of God by all the means we have, and to be moved by it to praise and thanks. To do as we say in the *Gloria in Excelsis*: Laudamus te, benedicamus te, adoramus te, glorificamus te, gratias agimus tibi propter magnam gloriam tuam. We praise you, we call you holy, we worship you, we proclaim your glory, we thank you for the greatness of your splendour.

And in moments of exaltation we may call on all created things to join in our chorus, speaking on their behalf, as is done in Psalm 148, and in The Song of the Three Children in Daniel II. PRAISE THE LORD ... all mountains and hills, all orchards and forests, all things that creep and birds on the wing.

This is much too long, and also much too short – on such a question.

With best wishes

J.R.R. Tolkien.

Notes

Preface

1   Humphrey Carpenter (ed.), *The Letters of J.R.R. Tolkien*, London: George Allen & Unwin, 1981, p. 288.

2   Ibid.

3   Ibid.

Chapter 1

1   *Sunday Times*, 26 January 1997.

2   Ibid.

3   *Bookworm*, BBC1, 27 July 1997.

4   *Times Literary Supplement*, 24 January 1997.

5   *Guardian*, 4 March 1997.

6   *Guardian*, 20 January 1997.

7   *Sunday Times*, 26 January 1997.

8   *The Times*, 20 January 1997.

9   *Independent*, 20 January 1997.

10   *Daily Telegraph*, 23 April 1997.

11   *The Times*, 23 April 1997.

12   *Independent*, 20 January 1997.

13   *The Bookseller*, 31 January 1997.

14   *The Times*, 22 January 1997.

15   *Times Educational Supplement*, 24 January 1997.

16   *Independent Education*, 23 January 1997.

17   *Independent*, 22 January 1997.

18 *Independent Education*, 23 January 1997.
19 *Guardian*, 21 January 1997.
20 *Sunday Times*, 26 January 1997.
21 *W Magazine*, Winter/Spring 1997.
22 *Daily Telegraph*, 21 January 1997.
23 *New Statesman*, 31 January 1997.
24 *Daily Telegraph*, 1 February 1997.
25 *Thought for the Day*, BBC Radio 4, 23 January 1997.
26 *Catholic Herald*, 31 January 1997.

CHAPTER 2

1 Humphrey Carpenter, *J.R.R. Tolkien: A Biography*, London: George Allen & Unwin, 1977, p. 9.
2 C.S. Lewis, *Of This and Other Worlds*, London: Fount, 1984, pp. 170–1.
3 J.R.R. Tolkien, *The Lord of the Rings*, London: George Allen & Unwin, one-volume paperback ed., 1978, p. 9.
4 Carpenter, *J.R.R. Tolkien: A Biography*, p. 24.
5 Ibid., p. 30.
6 Ibid., p. 30.
7 Ibid., pp. 30–1.
8 Ibid., p. 32.
9 Brian Rosebury, *Tolkien: A Critical Assessment*, London: St Martin's Press, 1992, p. 122.
10 Carpenter, *J.R.R. Tolkien: A Biography*, p. 36.
11 Carpenter (ed.), *The Letters of J.R.R. Tolkien*, p. 354.
12 Ibid., p. 395.
13 Charles A. Coulombe, *The Lord of the Rings: A Catholic View*, unpublished manuscript, pp. 3–4.
14 Carpenter (ed.), *The Letters of J.R.R. Tolkien*, pp. 353–4.
15 Carpenter, *J.R.R. Tolkien: A Biography*, p. 39.
16 Ibid.

17 Carpenter (ed.), *The Letters of J.R.R. Tolkien*, p. 255.
18 Verlyn Flieger, *Splintered Light: Logos and Language in Tolkien's World*, Grand Rapids, Michigan: William B Eerdmans, 1983, pp. 3–4.
19 Ibid., p. 4.

CHAPTER 3
1   Carpenter (ed.), *The Letters of J.R.R. Tolkien*, p. 53.
2   Carpenter, *J.R.R. Tolkien: A Biography*, p. 48.
3   Ibid., p. 50.
4   Ibid., p. 51.
5   Ibid.
6   Ibid.
7   Ibid.
8   Ibid., pp. 49–51.
9   Carpenter (ed.), *The Letters of J.R.R. Tolkien*, p. 53.
10 Charles Moseley, *J.R.R. Tolkien*, Plymouth: Northcote House Publishers, 1997, pp. 16–17.
11 Ibid., p. 16.
12 Ibid., p. 17.
13 *The Times*, 3 September 1973.
14 Ibid.
15 Ibid.
16 Ibid.
17 Carpenter, *J.R.R. Tolkien: A Biography*, p. 68.
18 Ibid., p. 69.
19 Ibid., p. 70.
20 Ibid., p. 73.
21 Ibid.
22 Ibid., p. 74.
23 Ibid., p. 76.
24 Carpenter (ed.), *The Letters of J.R.R. Tolkien*, p. 53.

25 Ibid.

26 Carpenter, *J.R.R. Tolkien: A Biography*, p. 91.

27 Ibid., p. 89.

28 Moseley, *J.R.R. Tolkien*, p. 10.

29 Mary Salu and Robert T. Farrell (eds), *J.R.R. Tolkien, Scholar and Storyteller: Essays In Memoriam*, Ithaca and London: Cornell University Press, 1979, p. 34.

30 Ibid., p. 33.

31 Ibid., pp. 33–4.

CHAPTER 4

1 G.K. Chesterton in Joseph Pearce, *Wisdom and Innocence: A Life of G.K. Chesterton*, London: Hodder & Stoughton, 1996, p. 83.

2 Carpenter, *J.R.R. Tolkien: A Biography*, p. 161.

3 Ibid., p. 160.

4 *The Listener*, 12 May 1977.

5 Rosebury, *Tolkien: A Critical Assessment*, p. 158.

6 Carpenter (ed.), *The Letters of J.R.R. Tolkien*, p. 60.

7 Ibid., pp. 48–9.

8 Ibid., pp. 51–2.

9 Rosebury, Tolkien: *A Critical Assessment*, pp. 124–5.

10 Carpenter (ed.), *The Letters of J.R.R. Tolkien*, p. 100.

11 Carpenter, *J.R.R. Tolkien: A Biography*, pp. 158–9.

12 Valentine Cunningham, *British Writers of the Thirties*, Oxford: Oxford University Press, 1988, p. 151.

13 Carpenter, *J.R.R. Tolkien: A Biography*, p. 159.

14 C.S. Lewis, *The Four Loves*, London: Fontana, 1963, p. 55.

15 Robert Giddings (ed.), *J.R.R. Tolkien: This Far Land*, London: Vision and Barnes & Noble, 1983, p. 182.

16 Lewis, *The Four Loves*, pp. 57–8.

17 Humphrey Carpenter, *The Inklings: C.S. Lewis, J.R.R. Tolkien, Charles Williams, and their friends*, London: George Allen & Unwin, 1978, pp. 22–3.

18 Ibid., p. 28.

19 Ibid., p. 30.

20 Ibid., p. 32.

21 C.S. Lewis, *Surprised by Joy*, London: Geoffrey Bles, 1955, p. 173.

22 Walter Hooper, interview with the author, Oxford, 20 August 1996.

23 Carpenter, *J.R.R. Tolkien: A Biography*, p. 151.

24 Carpenter, *The Inklings*, p. 44.

25 Lewis, *Surprised by Joy*, pp. 178–9.

26 Carpenter, *The Inklings*, p. 45.

27 Walter Hooper (ed.), *They Stand Together: The Letters of C.S. Lewis to Arthur Greeves (1914–1963)*, London: Collins, 1979, pp. 427–8.

28 Carpenter, *The Inklings*, p. 52.

CHAPTER 5

1 Carpenter (ed.), *The Letters of J.R.R. Tolkien*, p. 64.

2 Stratford Caldecott, 'Tolkien, Lewis and Christian Myth', unpublished manuscript, p. 1.

3 Owen Barfield, interview with the author, Forest Row, 31 December 1996.

4 Lewis, *Surprised by Joy*, p. 180.

5 Ibid., p. 187.

6 Walter Hooper, *C.S. Lewis: A Companion and Guide*, London: HarperCollins*Publishers*, 1996, p. 671.

7 Owen Barfield, interview with the author.

8 Lewis, *The Four Loves*, p. 58.

9 Lewis, *Of This and Other Worlds*, p. 111.

10 C.S. Lewis, 'On Stories', *in Essays presented to Charles Williams*, Oxford: Oxford University Press, 1947, p. 104.

11 Roger Lancelyn Green and Walter Hooper, *C.S. Lewis: A Biography*, London: HarperCollins*Publishers*, 1988, p. 130.

12 Ibid.

13 Christopher Derrick, *C.S. Lewis and the Church of Rome*, San Francisco: Ignatius Press,1981, p. 46.

14 Ibid.

15 Christopher Derrick, interview with the author, Wallington, 26 August 1996.

16 Carpenter, *The Inklings*, p. 50.

17 Walter Hooper, interview with the author.

18 Carpenter, *J.R.R. Tolkien: A Biography*, p. 155.

19 Carpenter (ed.), *The Letters of J.R.R. Tolkien*, p. 96.

20 Carpenter, *J.R.R. Tolkien: A Biography*, p. 154.

21 Ibid.

22 Ibid., p. 173.

23 Ibid., p. 198.

24 Walter Hooper, interview with the author.

25 Carpenter (ed.), *The Letters of J.R.R. Tolkien*, p. 102.

26 Ibid., p. 103.

27 Ibid., p. 95.

28 Ibid., pp. 95–6.

29 Carpenter, *The Inklings*, p. 192.

30 Louis Aragon (ed.), *Authors Take Sides on the Spanish War*, London: Left Review, 1937; quoted in Donat Gallagher (ed.), *The Essays, Articles and Reviews of Evelyn Waugh*, London: Methuen, 1983, p. 187.

31 Peter Alexander, *Roy Campbell: A Critical Biography*, Oxford: Oxford University Press, 1982, p. 151.

32 Roy Campbell, *Light on a Dark Horse: An Autobiography*, London: Hollis & Carter,1951, p. 317.

33 Carpenter, *J.R.R. Tolkien: A Biography*, p. 200.

34 Ibid., p. 201.

35 Carpenter (ed.), *The Letters of J.R.R. Tolkien*, p. 115.

36 Ibid., p. 349.

37 Carpenter, *J.R.R. Tolkien: A Biography*, p. 204.

38 Carpenter (ed.), *The Letters of J.R.R. Tolkien*, p. 352.

39 Carpenter, *J.R.R. Tolkien: A Biography*, pp. 207–8.

40 Carpenter, *The Inklings*, p. 160.

41 *Time and Tide*, August 1954.

42 Chad Walsh in the *New York Times Book Review*, 14 March 1965.

43 Visual Corporation Ltd, *A Film Portrait of J.R.R. Tolkien*, 1992.

44 Ibid.

45 *Daily Telegraph*, 20 January 1996.

46 *New York Times Book Review*, 14 March 1965, pp. 4–5.

47 *University of Portland Review*, 20, No. 1 (1968), p. 43.

48 Philip Yancey (ed.), *Reality and the Vision*, Dallas: Word Publishing, 1990, pp. 29–31.

CHAPTER 6

1 *Time and Tide*, August 1954.

2 T.A. Shippey, *The Road to Middle-Earth*, London: George Allen & Unwin, 1982, p. 176.

3 Ibid.

4 Ibid.

5 Carpenter (ed.), *The Letters of J.R.R. Tolkien*, pp. 109–10.

6 Rosebury, *Tolkien: A Critical Assessment*, p. 97.

7 *The Month*, January 1993.

8 *Crisis*, March 1992.

9 J.R.R. Tolkien, *The Silmarillion*, London: George Allen & Unwin, 1979, paperback ed., p. 15.

10 Richard Jeffery, interview with the author, Oxford, 23 September 1997.

11 Tolkien, *The Silmarillion*, pp. 18–19.

12 Ibid., p. 19.

13 Ibid.

14 Ibid., p. 27.

15 Richard Jeffery, interview with the author

16 Tolkien, *The Silmarillion*, p. 19.

17 Ibid., p. 22.

18 Ibid., p. 34.

19 Ibid., pp. 34–5.

20 Ibid., p. 35.

21 Carpenter (ed.), *The Letters of J.R.R. Tolkien*. p. 283.

22 Ibid., pp. 190–1.

23 Tolkien, *The Silmarillion*, p. 311.

24 Carpenter (ed.), *The Letters of J.R.R. Tolkien*, p. 80.

25 Tolkien, *The Silmarillion*, p. 20.

26 Carpenter (ed.), *The Letters of J.R.R. Tolkien*, p. 99.

27 Visual Corporation Limited, *A Film Portrait of J.R.R. Tolkien*.

CHAPTER 7

1 T.S. Eliot, *Selected Essays, 1917–1932*, New York: Faber & Faber, 1932, p. 218.

2 Carpenter (ed.), *The Letters of J.R.R. Tolkien*, p. 377.

3 George Sayer, interview with the author, 3 September 1997.

4 Carpenter (ed.), *The Letters of J.R.R. Tolkien*, p. 172.

5 Ibid., pp. 171–2.

6 Ibid., p. 172.

7 *The Month*, January 1993.

8 Ibid.

9 Carpenter (ed.), *The Letters of J.R.R. Tolkien*, pp. 99–100.

10 J.R.R. Tolkien (ed. Christopher Tolkien), *The Monsters and the Critics and Other Essays*, London: George Allen & Unwin, 1984, pp. 153–4.

11 Ibid., pp. 156–7.

12 Ibid.

13 *King's Theological Review*, Vol. 12, No. 1, 1989.

14 Stratford Caldecott, 'Tolkien, Lewis, and Christian Myth', p. 15.

15 Carpenter (ed.), *The Letters of J.R.R. Tolkien*, pp. 100–1.

16 Moseley, *J.R.R. Tolkien*, p. 60.

17 Paul Pfotenhauer, *Cresset* (Valparaiso University), 32, No. 3, January 1969, pp. 13–15.

18 *Mythlore*, 3, No. 2, 1975, pp. 3–8.

19 *Mythlore*, 1, No. 1, January 1969, pp. 27–9.

20 Dr Patrick Curry, letter to the author, 30 August 1997.

21 Carpenter (ed.), *The Letters of J.R.R. Tolkien*, p. 172.

22 Ibid., p. 237.

23 Ibid., p. 387.

24 Tolkien, *The Lord of the Rings*, p. 656.

25 Ibid.

26 Carpenter, *J.R.R. Tolkien: A Biography*, p. 89.

27 Tolkien, *The Lord of the Rings*, p. 974.

28 Ibid., p. 976.

29 Ibid., p. 760.

30 *Desert Call*, Colorado, Winter 1992.

31 Caldecott, 'Tolkien, Lewis, and Christian Myth', pp. 4–5.

32 Ibid., p. 6.

33 Ibid.

34 Ibid., p. 8.

35 Tolkien, *The Lord of the Rings*, p. 459.

36 *King's Theological Review*, Vol. 12, No. 1, 1989, p. 6.

37 Ibid., p. 8.

38 Ibid.

39 Tolkien, *The Lord of the Rings*, p. 608 and 618.

40 *King's Theological Review*, Vol. 12, No. 1, 1989, p. 8.

41 Carpenter (ed.), *The Letters of J.R.R. Tolkien*, p. 246.

42 *Mythlore*, 55, Autumn 1988, p. 6.

43 Tolkien, *The Silmarillion*, p. 48.

44 Ibid., pp. 318–19.

45 Ibid., p. 320.

46 Ibid., p. 321.

47 Ibid., p. 47.

48 Carpenter (ed.), *The Letters of J.R.R. Tolkien*, pp. 285–6.

49 *Mythlore*, 55, Autumn 1998, p. 9.

50 Tolkien, *The Lord of the Rings*, pp. 1068–9.

51 Tolkien, *The Silmarillion*, p. 367.

52 Tolkien, *The Lord of the Rings*, p. 1069.

53 Tolkien, *The Silmarillion*, p. 20.

54 Tolkien, *The Lord of the Rings*, p. 1076.

CHAPTER 8

1   G.K. Chesterton, *The Well and the Shallows*, London: Sheed & Ward, 1935, p. 72.

2   Carpenter (ed.), *The Letters of J.R.R. Tolkien*, p. 172.

3   Ibid.

4   Carpenter, *J.R.R. Tolkien: A Biography*, p. 222.

5   Ibid.

6   Carpenter (ed.), *The Letters of J.R.R. Tolkien*, p. 184.

7   Ibid., p. 229.

8   Carpenter, *J.R.R. Tolkien: A Biography*, p. 225.

9   Carpenter (ed.), *The Letters of J.R.R. Tolkien*, p. 230.

10 Lewis, *Of This and Other Worlds*, pp. 73–5.

11 Susan Wood (ed.), *The Languages of the Night*, New York: Berkeley Books, 1979, p. 58.

12 Patrick Curry, 'Tolkien and His Critics: A Critique', unpublished manuscript, p. 2.

13 Ibid.

14 Ibid., p. 3.

15 Ibid.

16 Humphrey Carpenter on the BBC's *Bookshelf*, 22 November 1991.

17 Carpenter (ed.), *The Letters of J.R.R. Tolkien*, p. 63.

18 Ibid., p. 235.

19 Christopher Derrick, interview with the author.

20 Carpenter (ed.), *The Letters of J.R.R. Tolkien*, p. 65.

21 Ibid., pp. 55–6.

22 Ibid., pp. 375–6.

23 Ibid., p. 37.

24 Ibid.

25 Robert Giddings (ed.), *J.R.R. Tolkien: This Far Land*, p. 40.

26 Ibid., p. 73.

27 Ibid., pp. 82–3.

28 Ibid., pp. 189–91.

29 Moseley, *J.R.R. Tolkien*, p. 75.

30 Giddings (ed.), *J.R.R. Tolkien: This Far Land*, p. 119.

31 *The Times*, 20 January 1997.

32 Tolkien, *The Monsters and the Critics and Other Essays*, pp. 147–8.

33 Ibid., p. 159.

34 Gerard Manley Hopkins, *Selected Poems*, Oxford: Oxford University Press 1994, p. 119.

35 Yancey (ed.), *Reality and the Vision*, pp. 35–6.

36 *Crisis*, March 1992.

37 Carpenter (ed.), *The Letters of J.R.R. Tolkien*, p. 255.

38 Tolkien, *The Silmarillion*, p. 31.

39 Maurice Baring, *Have You Anything to Declare?*, London: Heinemann, 1936, p. 147.

40 Emma Letley, *Maurice Baring: A Citizen of Europe*, London: Constable, 1991, p. 217.

41 Laura Lovat, *Maurice Baring: A Postscript*, London: Hollis & Carter, 1947, pp. 4–5.

42 Carpenter (ed.), *The Letters of J.R.R. Tolkien*, pp. 171–2.

43 Father Ricardo Irigaray, 'The Theological Style of J.R.R. Tolkien', unpublished manuscript.

44 Father Charles Dilke, letter to the author, 18 August 1997.

45 Coulombe, *The Lord of the Rings: A Catholic View*, p. 11.

46 J.R.R. Tolkien, *Tree and Leaf*, London: George Allen & Unwin, 1988 ed., p. 64.

CHAPTER 9

1 Carpenter (ed.), *The Letters of J.R.R. Tolkien*, pp. 213–14.

2 Carpenter, *J.R.R. Tolkien: A Biography*, p. 180.

3 Ibid., p. 89.

4 Carpenter (ed.), *The Letters of J.R.R. Tolkien*, p. 88.

5 Ibid., p. 250.

6 Ibid., p. 212.

7 Ibid., p. 218.

8 Ibid., p. 65.

9 Ibid., p. 218.

10 Ibid., p. 213.

11 Ibid., p. 108.

12 Ibid., p. 54.

13 Ibid., p. 288.

14 Visual Corporation Limited, *A Film Portrait of J.R.R. Tolkien*.

15 J.R.R. Tolkien, *The Hobbit*, London: George Allen & Unwin, 1937, p. 32.

16 Ibid., p. 208.

17 Ibid., p. 190.

18 Ibid., p. 235.

19 Ibid., p. 237.

20 Ibid., pp. 284–5.

21 Tolkien, *The Lord of the Rings*, p. 390.

22 Ibid., p. 13.

23 Ibid., p. 657.

24 Ibid., p. 921.

25 Ibid., p. 382.

26 Ibid., p. 494.

27 Ibid., p. 495.

28 Alida Becker (ed.), *The Tolkien Scrapbook*, Philadelphia: Running Press, 1978, p. 26.

29 Paul H. Kocher, *Master of Middle Earth: The Fiction of J.R.R. Tolkien*, Boston, Massachusetts: Houghton Mifflin, 1972, p. 26.

30 Coulombe, *The Lord of the Rings: A Catholic View*, p. 7.

31 Tolkien, *The Lord of the Rings*, p. 935.

32 Ibid., p. 1049.

33 *Observer*, 13 December 1925.

34 G.K. Chesterton, *The Victorian Age in Literature*, London: Williams & Norgate, 1913, pp. 16–17.

35 Ibid.

36 G.K. Chesterton, *William Cobbett*, London: Hodder & Stoughton, 1925, pp. 14–15.

37 Carpenter (ed.), *The Letters of J.R.R. Tolkien*, p. 92.

38 George Sayer, *Jack: C.S. Lewis and His Times*, London: Macmillan, 1988, p. xvi.

39 *South Atlantic Bulletin*, 39, No. ii, May 1974, pp. 10–16.

40 Tolkien, *The Lord of the Rings*, p. 162.

41 Ibid., p. 504.

42   Visual Corporation Limited, *A Film Portrait of J.R.R. Tolkien*.

43   Tolkien, *The Monsters and the Critics and Other Essays*, p. 146.

44   Tolkien, *The Lord of the Rings*, pp. 325–6.

45   *Church Socialist Quarterly*, January 1909.

46   Tolkien, *The Lord of the Rings*, pp. 484–5.

47   G.K. Chesterton, *Tremendous Trifles*, New York: Dodd, Mead & Co., 1909, p. 134.

48   Ibid., pp. 298–303.

49   J.R.R. Tolkien, *The Father Christmas Letters*, London: George Allen & Unwin, 1976.

50   Richard Jeffery, unpublished manuscript of talk to the Oxford C.S. Lewis Society, February 1994, p. 15.

51   J.R.R. Tolkien, *Smith of Wootton Major*, London: George Allen & Unwin, 1967, p. 31.

52   Ibid., p. 56.

53   Carpenter (ed.), *The Letters of J.R.R. Tolkien*, p. 195.

54   Kocher, *Master of Middle Earth*, pp. 164–5.

55   Tolkien, *The Monsters and the Critics and Other Essays*, pp. 156–7.

56   Visual Corporation Limited, *A Film Portrait of J.R.R. Tolkien*.

57   Tolkien, *Tree and Leaf*, p. 88.

58   Ibid., pp. 92–3.

59   Ibid., pp. 100–1.

60   Lin Carter, *Tolkien: A Look Behind The Lord of the Rings*, New York: Ballantine Books, 1969, pp. 93–4.

61   Neil D. Isaacs and Rose A. Zimbardo (eds), *Tolkien and the Critics: Essays on J.R.R. Tolkien's The Lord of the Rings*, Notre Dame and London: University of Notre Dame Press, 1968, pp. 129–30.

62 Ibid., p. 130.

63 Carpenter (ed.), *The Letters of J.R.R. Tolkien*, p. 81.

64 J.R.R. Tolkien, *Farmer Giles of Ham*, London: George Allen & Unwin, 1949, p. 1.

65 Ibid., p. 56.

66 Ibid., p. 13.

67 Tolkien, *The Lord of the Rings*, p. 101.

68 Ibid., p. 170.

69 Ibid., p. 1039.

70 G.K. Chesterton, *The New Jerusalem*, London: Thomas Nelson & Sons, 1920, p. 159.

CHAPTER 10

1 Carpenter, *J.R.R. Tolkien: A Biography*, p. 225.

2 Carpenter (ed.), *The Letters of J.R.R. Tolkien*, p. 223.

3 Ibid.

4 Ibid.

5 Ibid., p. 261.

6 Ibid.

7 Ibid.

8 Salu and Farrell (eds), *J.R.R. Tolkien, Scholar and Storyteller: Essays In Memoriam*, p. 17.

9 *The Times*, 3 September 1973.

10 Salu and Farrell, *J.R.R. Tolkien, Scholar and Storyteller: Essays in Memoriam*, p. 31.

11 *Catholic Herald*, 31 January 1997.

12 Carpenter (ed.), *The Letters of J.R.R. Tolkien*, p. 341.

13 Ibid.

14 Ibid., p. 342.

15 Ibid., p. 349.

16 Ibid., p. 350.

17 Moseley, *J.R.R. Tolkien*, pp. 34–5.

18 Becker (ed.), *The Tolkien Scrapbook*, p. 86.

19 *Independent*, 20 January 1997.

20 Charles W. Moorman, *The Precincts of Felicity: The Augustinian City of the Oxford Christians*, Gainesville: University of Florida Press, 1966, *passim*.

21 Carpenter (ed.), *The Letters of J.R.R. Tolkien*, pp. 401–2.

22 Ibid., pp. 337–9.

23 George Sayer, interview with the author, 3 September 1997.

24 Visual Corporation Limited, *A Film Portrait of J.R.R. Tolkien*.

25 Carpenter (ed.), *The Letters of J.R.R. Tolkien*, p. 419.

26 Ibid., p. 393.

27 Ibid., p. 394.

28 Ibid.

29 *The Spectator*, 23 November 1962.

30 Carpenter (ed.), *The Letters of J.R.R. Tolkien*, pp. 394–5.

31 Ibid., p. 339.

32 Ibid., pp. 339–40.

33 Salu and Farrell (eds), *J.R.R. Tolkien, Scholar and Storyteller: Essays In Memoriam*, pp. 33–4.

34 Carpenter, *J.R.R. Tolkien: A Biography*, p. 161.

35 Interview with Denys Geroult, BBC Radio 4, 16 December 1970.

36 Carpenter, *J.R.R. Tolkien: A Biography*, p. 161.

37 Carpenter (ed.), *The Letters of J.R.R. Tolkien*, p. 340.

38 Carpenter, *J.R.R. Tolkien: A Biography*, p. 251.

39 Carpenter (ed.), *The Letters of J.R.R. Tolkien*, p. 397.

40 Ibid., p. 401.

41 Ibid., p. 415.

42 Ibid., pp. 420–1.

43 Ibid., p. 432.

44 Tolkien, *The Silmarillion*, p. 224.

45 Ibid., p. 225.

46 Carpenter (ed.), *The Letters of J.R.R. Tolkien*, pp. 53–4.

EPILOGUE

1 Tolkien, *The Lord of the Rings*, p. 943.

2 Carpenter (ed.), *The Letters of J.R.R. Tolkien*, pp. 399–400.

Bibliography

The following is intended only as a listing of the principal books by and about Tolkien for those interested in selective further reading. Those requiring a more definitive bibliography of Tolkien's published writings are referred to Appendix C of Humphrey Carpenter's biography. A more exhaustive listing of writings about Tolkien is given in Richard C. West's *Tolkien Criticism: An Annotated Checklist* (Kent State University Press, USA, revised edition 1991).

Works by J.R.R. Tolkien

Sir Gawain and the Green Knight, edited by J.R.R. Tolkien and E.V. Gordon (Oxford: Clarendon Press, 1925)

The Hobbit (London: George Allen & Unwin, 1937)

'On Fairy Stories', an essay by Tolkien in *Essays Presented to Charles Williams*, edited by C.S. Lewis (London: Oxford University Press, 1947)

Farmer Giles of Ham (London: George Allen & Unwin, 1949)

The Fellowship of the Ring, part one of *The Lord of the Rings* (London: George Allen & Unwin, 1954)

The Two Towers, part two of *The Lord of the Rings* (London: George Allen & Unwin, 1954)

The Return of the King, part three of *The Lord of the Rings* (London: George Allen & Unwin, 1955)

The Adventures of Tom Bombadil and other verses from The Red Book (London: George Allen & Unwin, 1962)

Tree and Leaf, containing the essay 'On Fairy Stories' and the short story *Leaf by Niggle* (London: George Allen & Unwin, 1964). Later editions also contain the poem 'Mythopoeia'.

Smith of Wootton Major (London: George Allen & Unwin, 1967)

The Lord of the Rings, first edition in one-volume paperback (London: George Allen & Unwin, 1978)

POSTHUMOUSLY PUBLISHED

The Father Christmas Letters, edited by Baillie Tolkien (London: George Allen & Unwin, 1976)

The Silmarillion, edited by Christopher Tolkien (London: George Allen & Unwin, 1977)

Unfinished Tales of Númenor and Middle-earth, edited by Christopher Tolkien (London: George Allen & Unwin, 1980)

The Letters of J.R.R. Tolkien, edited by Humphrey Carpenter, assisted by Christopher Tolkien (London: George Allen & Unwin, 1981)

Mr Bliss, reproduced from Tolkien's illustrated manuscript (London: George Allen & Unwin, 1982)

Finn and Hengest: The Fragment and the Episode, edited by Alan Bliss (London: George Allen & Unwin, 1982)

The Monsters and the Critics and Other Essays, edited by Christopher Tolkien (London: George Allen & Unwin, 1983)

Between 1983 and 1997 Christopher Tolkien has edited the twelve-volume *History of Middle Earth*, published by George Allen & Unwin.

PRINCIPAL WORKS ON J.R.R. TOLKIEN

Carpenter, Humphrey, *J.R.R. Tolkien: A Biography* (London: George Allen & Unwin, 1977)

Carpenter, Humphrey, *The Inklings: C.S. Lewis, J.R.R. Tolkien, Charles Williams, and their friends* (London: George Allen & Unwin, 1978)

Flieger, Verlyn, *Splintered Light: Logos and Language in Tolkien's World* (Grand Rapids, Michigan: William B. Eerdmans, 1983)

Foster, Robert, *The Complete Guide to Middle Earth: from The Hobbit to The Silmarillion* (New York: Ballantine Books, 1978)

Giddings, Robert (ed.), *J.R.R. Tolkien: This Far Land* (London: Vision and Barnes & Noble, 1983)

Isaacs, Neil D., and Zimbardo, Rose A. (eds), *Tolkien and the Critics* (Notre Dame and London: University of Notre Dame Press, 1968)

Kocher, Paul H., *Master of Middle Earth: The Fiction of J.R.R. Tolkien* (Boston, Massachusetts: Houghton Mifflin, 1972)

Moseley, Charles, *J.R.R. Tolkien* (Plymouth: Northcote House Publishers, 1997)

Rosebury, Brian, *Tolkien: A Critical Assessment* (London: St Martin's Press, 1992)

Salu, Mary, and Farrell, Robert T. (eds), *J.R.R. Tolkien, Scholar and Storyteller: Essays In Memoriam* (Ithaca and London: Cornell University Press, 1979)

Shippey, T.A., *The Road to Middle-Earth* (London: George Allen & Unwin, 1982)

INDEX

Ackerman, Forrest J., 183
aggiornamento, 196–7
agnosticism, 57
Albrow, Desmond, 10, 185–6
Aldrich, Kevin, 118, 123
Alice in Wonderland (Carroll),
  15, 66
Americo-cosmopolitanism, 135
Andersen, Hans, 15
Animal Farm (Orwell), 5, 140
anti-industrialism, 155 *et*
  passim
Aquinas, St Thomas, 47, 178
Ariosto, 127–8
Aristotle, 47, 54
Atkins, Anne, 9
Auden, W.H., 80, 129–30, 154–5
Augustine, St, 84, 190
Augustinian theology, 88, 93,
  109, 190
Austen, Jane, 3

Bailey, George, 188
Ball and the Cross, The
  (Chesterton), 171
Ballad of the White Horse, The
  (Chesterton), 163–4
Barfield, Owen, 62–5, 71, 77, 187
Baring, Maurice, 149–50, 181

Barnes, Ann, 5
Beethoven, Ludwig van, xii
Belloc, Hilaire, 160, 181
Bent, Horace, 4
Birmingham Oratory, 19–20,
  27–8, 38
Blake, William, 160, 162
Bookseller, The, 4
Bookworm (BBC), 2
Bradbury, Sue, 3
Bratt, Edith, *see* Tolkien, Edith
Bretherton, Christopher, 188
Brewerton, George, 31
Brodax, Al, 183
Byron, Lord, 78

C.S. Lewis and the Church of
  Rome (Derrick), 67
C.S. Lewis Society, 89, 170
Caldecott, Stratford, 61,106,
  115–6
Campbell, Roy, 72–6, 190
Canterbury Tales, The
  (Chaucer), 152
Carey, John, 3, 46–8
Carpenter, Humphrey, 3, 21–4,
  29, 39, 45–7, 58, 61, 81, 133,
  200–1
Carter, Father Douglas, 102, 195

Carter, Lin, 177

Catcher in the Rye, The (Salinger), 5

Catholic Herald, 10, 185

Catholicism, xiii, 10, 16–25, 34–6, 67–9, 83 *et passim*, 100 *et passim*, 148 *et passim*, 190 *et passim, see also* Christianity

Centre for Faith and Culture, Oxford, 61

Chamberlain, Joseph, 18

Chaucer, Geoffrey, 31

Cherryman, A.E., 128

Chesterton, G.K., 8, 15, 26, 58, 62, 150, 160 *et passim*, 191, 195

Choruses from 'The Rock' (Eliot), 189

Christian marriage, Tolkien's view of, 47–51

Christianity, xiii, 9–10, 15, 31, 57–60, 83 *et passim*, 100 *et passim*, 150–1, 209–12, *see also* Catholicism

Church of England, 34–5, 66

Cicero, 32, 54

Clausen, Christopher, 164

Cleese, John, 141

Clute, John, 190

Coat Without Seam, The (Baring), 150

Cobbett, William, 160, 162

Coghill, Nevill, 70

Coulombe, Charles A., 20, 152, 160

Country Life, 128

Craigie, Sir William, 52

Cunningham, Valentine, 52

Curry, Patrick, 8, 109, 132–3

Daily News, 169

Daily Telegraph, 3, 7, 8, 80, 126

Dante Alighieri, 100, 117, 172, 177

Darby and Joan (Baring), 149

D'Arcy SJ, Martin, 72

d'Ardenne, Simonne, 43, 199, 201

David Copperfield (Dickens), 3

Davidman, Joy, 186–7

Dawson, Christopher, 75

Debray, Regis, 141

Defending Middle Earth (Curry), 8, 109

Demosthenes, 33

Derrick, Christopher, 67, 134

Dickens, Charles, 3, 166

Dilke, Father Charles, 151

Disney, Walt, 183

Distributist League, 160–1

Divine Comedy, The (Dante), 62, *see also Paradiso* and *Purgatorio*

Dollfuss, Engelbert, 160

Drabble, Margaret, 132

Dundas-Grant, James, 187

Duns Scotus, Johannes, 146

Dylan, Bob, 140

Dyson, Hugo, 57–8, 65

ecumenism, 197–8

Eliot, T.S., 100, 188–90

Elizabeth II, Queen, 206

Encyclopedia of Fantasy, The (Clute), 190

Engels, Friedrich, 141
'Englishness', 153 *et passim*
Essays Presented to Charles Williams (Tolkien, Lewis *et al*), 77, 103
Ethics (Aristotle), 47
Ethics of Revolution, The (Marcuse), 141
eucatastrophe, concept of, 103–4
Everlasting Man, The (Chesterton), 58–9, 62, 178–9
Exeter College, Oxford, 32, 57

Farrer, Katherine, 79
fascism, 73–6, 137–40
Father Brown stories (Chesterton), 171
feminism, 5–6, 142–4
First World War, 37–40, 112
Flieger, Verlyn, xiii, 24
Flying Inn, The (Chesterton), 179–81
Folio Society, 3–4
Four Loves, The (Lewis), 53–5, 64
Four Quartets (Eliot), 189
Franco, General Francisco, 73–5
Freudianism, 11–12, 21–2, 141–3

Glover, Willis B., 109
Golden String, The (Griffiths), 63
Golding, William, 12
Goldthwaite, John, 133
Goodman, Paul, 6–8
Grahame, Kenneth, 126
Great Divorce, The (Lewis), 79
Green, Peter, 126
Green, Roger Lancelyn, 78

Greer, Germaine, 6–8
Greeves, Arthur, 55, 60
Griffiths, Dom Bede (Alan), 62–4
Griffiths, Elaine, 201
Guardian, 2, 5–6
Guevara, Che, 140
Gunton, Colin, 106, 116–8

HarperCollins*Publishers*, 4
Hastings, Peter, 94
Havard, R.E., 65, 71, 187
Have You Anything to Declare? (Baring), 149
Heath-Stubbs, John, 133
Helbeck of Bannisdale (Ward), 150
Hemingway, Ernest, 80
Hitler, Adolf, 74, 76, 135, 138
Hollis, Christopher, 75
homosexuality, 54–5
Hooper, Walter, 57, 68, 70
Hopkins SJ, Gerard Manley, 146
Howard, Leslie, 185

Iliad, The (Homer), 62
Illustrated London News, 129
Incledon, May (aunt), 16, 20
Incledon, Walter (uncle), 16
Inglis, Bob, 1
Inglis, Fred, 137–8
Inklings, the, 64–5, 69 *et passim*, 164, 181, 187, 201
inscape, concept of, 146
Irigaray, Father Ricardo, 151
Isherwood, Christopher, 80

Jacobson, Howard, 1
Jeffery, Richard, 89, 91, 170
Jeffreys, Susan, 1, 3

Jones, Griff Rhys, 2
Joyce, James, 2

Kerr, Graham, 2
Kilby, C.S., 109
King's College, London, 106
Knox, Monsignor Ronald, 75, 190
Kocher, Paul, 159, 172, 177
Krog, Helge, 75

Lambert, J.W., 127
Lang, Andrew, 15, 32
Lawhead, Stephen R., 81, 146–7
Lawlor, John, 187
Lawrence, D.H., 19
Lawson, Mark, 2–3
Le Guin, Ursula, 132
Lee, Martin, 2
Leeds University, 41
Lenin, V.I., 138
Leo XIII, Pope, 160
Levin, Bernard, 129–30
Lewis, C.S., 11–12, 21–2, 47, 52
    et passim, 61 et passim, 83–7,
    91, 120, 123, 127–32, 164,
    177–8, 181, 186–90, 192, 201
Lewis, Major Warren 'Warnie',
    65, 68, 71, 77
Library Association, 4
Life and Passion of St Julienne,
    The, 43
Lion, the Witch and the
    Wardrobe, The (Lewis), 78,
    80, 82
Listener, The, 46–7
Literary Review, 3
London Oratory, 151

Lord of the Flies, The (Golding),
    12
Lunn, Arnold, 75

Macdonald, George, 15, 32, 177
McGrath, Sean, 114, 116
Magdalen College, Oxford, 52,
    57, 65, 71
Major, John, 2
Manalive (Chesterton), 171,
    178–9
Manchester Guardian, 128
Mao Tse-Tung, 138
Marcuse, Herbert, 141
Marx, Karl, 138, 141
Master of Middle Earth
    (Kocher), 172
Mathew, Father Gervase, 77
Mauriac, François, 150
Merton College, Oxford, 55, 206
Middle Earth (see separate
    index, pp. 241–2)
Millar, Victoria, 5
Mills, Stella, 201
Milton, John, 84
Moorman, Charles W., 190
Morgan, Father Francis Xavier,
    19–21, 26–31, 34, 38, 45–6, 51,
    199
Morte d'Arthur, Le, 152
Moseley, Charles, 30–2, 40, 108,
    189
Muir, Edwin, 127, 130–1
Murray, Sir James, 101, 201
Murray SJ, Robert, 88, 100–2,
    126, 150, 201, 207
Murray, Rosfrith, 201
Mussolini, Benito, 138

myth, philosophy of, xiii–xiv,
57–62, 86–7, 103–7, 206

Napoleon of Notting Hill, The
(Chesterton), 179
'Narnia' (Lewis), 78–9, 127
Nation, The, 130
National Association for the
Teaching of English, 5
Nazism, 74–5
Nesbit, E.M., 52
New Statesman, 8, 138–9
New York Times, 129
New York Times Book Review,
80, 131
Newman, John Henry, Cardinal,
19
Nickolds, Andrew, 6
Nineteen Eighty-Four (Orwell),
2, 5, 140
Noyes, Alfred, 75, 191

Observer, The, 127, 130
Odyssey, The (Homer), 62, 79
Orange Order, 68
Orwell, George, 2–3, 5, 74, 140
*Oxford Companion to English
Literature, The*, 132
*Oxford Concise Companion to
English Literature, The*, 132
Oxford Magazine, 72
Oxford Times, 128

Paradiso (Dante), 177
Partridge, Brenda, 54, 142–3
Perelandra (Lewis), 82
Pfotenhauer, Paul, 108–9
philology, Tolkien and, xii, 15,
33, 37, 56, 70, 93, 184–5

Pied Piper, The, 15
Pilgrim's Regress, The (Lewis),
66–7
Pius X, St, 194
Pius XI, Pope, 160
Planer, Nigel, 2
Plato, 62
political views, Tolkien's, 133 *et
passim*
possessiveness, 156–7
Preface to Paradise Lost, A
(Lewis), 84–5
Pride and Prejudice (Austen), 3
Princess and Curdie, The
(Macdonald), 32
Princess and the Goblin, The
(Macdonald), 15, 32
Prohibition, 181
Purgatorio (Dante), 172, 177

Quadragesimo anno (Pius XI),
160

racism, 135–7
Rackham, Arthur, 183
Reading University, 57, 65
recovery, Tolkien's concept of,
166
Reilly, Robert J., 177–8
Reporter, The, 188
Rerum Novarum (Leo XIII), 160
Reynolds, Nigel, 80
Richards, Jeffrey, 8
Rigoletto (Verdi), 182
Road to Middle Earth, The
(Shippey), 84, 165
Robinson, Derek, 144
Roddenberry, Gene, 144
Ronald, Amy, 191

Rosebury, Brian, 18, 46, 51, 87–8
Ruskin, John, 8

Salazar, Antonio de Oliviera, 160
Sale, Roger, 159
Salinger, J.D., 5
Salu, Mary, 201
Sassoon, Siegfried, 191
Saunders, Andrew, 132
Sayer, George, 100, 164, 187, 194
Sayers, Dorothy L., 77, 190
'scale of significance', Tolkien's, xii
Schall SJ, James V., 88, 147
Schumacher, E.F., 159
Second Vatican Council, 194–8
Shadowlands, BBC and Hollywood productions of, 187
Shelley, Percy Bysshe, 162
Shimmon, Ross, 4
Shippey, T.A., xiii, 84–5, 165
Short Oxford History of English Literature, The, 132
Sitwell, Edith, 191
Small is Beautiful (Schumacher), 159
Somme, Battle of the, 37–9
Spanish Civil War, 74
Speaight, Robert, 150
Spectator, The, 197
Splintered Light: Logos and Language in Tolkien's World (Flieger), 24
Spring, Howard, 128
Stalin, Josef, 74

Star Trek, 144, 147
Sunday Times, 1, 127
Surprised by Joy (Lewis), 56, 63

Temperance movement, 181
That Hideous Strength (Lewis), 70
theism, 57
Thompson, E.P., 138
Thought for the Day (BBC), 9
Time and Tide, 129
Times, The, 33, 140, 144, 184, 186
Times Educational Supplement, 5
Times Literary Supplement, 2
Today (BBC), 2
Tolhurst, Denis, 206
Tolhurst, Jocelyn, 206–7
Tolkien: A Critical Assessment (Rosebury), 18, 87
Tolkien, Arthur (father), 12–14
Tolkien, Christopher (son), 40, 70–1, 80, 86, 96, 99, 102, 155, 203–4, 207
Tolkien, Edith (wife), 26 *et passim*, 45–7, 51, 101, 200 *et passim*
Tolkien, Hilary (brother), 12–13, 21, 26
Tolkien, J.R.R.,
    LIFE: birth, 12; christening, 12; death of father, 13; education, 14–17; early influences, 15; moves to village of Sarehole, 14, 18–19; mother's conversion to Roman Catholicism, 15–16;

family returns to Birmingham, 17–19; First Communion, 19; death of mother, 19–25; Father Francis Morgan becomes legal guardian, 19–21; holidays in Dorset, 26, 45; courtship, 26–32; at Exeter College, Oxford, 32, 37; invents Elvish language, 33; engagement to Edith Bratt, 34; marriage, 37–8; active service in First World War, 37–40; appointment to Leeds University, 41; married life, 45–7, 51–3; return to Oxford, 52; friendship with C.S. Lewis, 52 et passim; membership of the Inklings, 64–5, 69; visits Italy, 182; international success of The Lord of the Rings, 183 et passim; retirement and valedictory address at Oxford, 184–5; reaction to Lewis's marriage, 186–7; and Lewis's death, 187–8; old age, 190 et passim; and Second Vatican Council, 194–8; married life in old age, 200 et passim; moves to Bournemouth, 202–3; Edith's death, 204–6; return to Oxford, 206; awarded CBE, 206, death, 206–8

WORKS: 'Albarion and Erendis', 51; Farmer Giles of Ham, 168, 178–81; Father Christmas Letters, The, 41–3,
168–70, 200–1; Fellowship of the Ring, The (see The Lord of the Rings); Hobbit, The, 4, 40, 43, 65–6, 80, 136, 155–7, 200–1; Leaf by Niggle, 79, 106, 123, 168, 171–8, 201, 206; Lord of the Rings, The, passim; anti-modernism of, 8; Christianity and, 9–10, 100 et passim; conflict of good and evil in, 111, 116–18, 122; critical reaction to, xi–xii, 1–10, 126 et passim; 'escapism' and, 78, 144 et passim; 'flight from reality' and, 6–8; influence of his marriage on, 51; life and death in, 111, 118–25; politics and, 7; sacrifice and free will in, 111–16, 122; sexuality in, 47–8, 142–4; spiritual values in, 8; time and eternity in, 111, 118–25; 'Mythopoeia', 61, 106, 176–7, 206; 'On Fairy Stories', 103–6, 131, 144, 163, 173, 176, 206; Return of the King (see The Lord of the Rings); Silmarillion, The, 40–1, 56, 58, 70, 83 et passim, 119–20, 124–5, 148, 174, 203, 205; Smith of Wootton Major, 51, 168, 170–1, 175, 201; Tree and Leaf, 106, 176; Two Towers, The (see The Lord of the Rings)

Tolkien, Father John (son), 40–1, 194, 202, 207

Tolkien, Mabel (mother), 12–20, 199

Tolkien, Michael (son), 39, 40, 135, 155, 188, 191, 195, 198, 202, 207

Tolkien, Priscilla (daughter), 40, 80 102, 163, 170, 174, 182, 187, 206–7

Tolkien Society, 2

traditionalism, 167–8, 195–6

Treasure Island (Stevenson), 15

Truth, 128, 130

Ulysses (Joyce), 2

University of Portland Review, 81

Unwin, Camilla, 209

Unwin, Rayner, 154

Verdi, Giuseppe, 182

Victoria, Queen, 195

Volsungasaga, 32

W Magazine, 6

Wagner, Richard, 133, 137

Walmsley, Nigel, 140–1

Walsh, Chad, 80

Ward, Mrs Humphry, 150

Waste Land, The (Eliot), 189–90

Waterstone's poll, xi, 1–10, 80, 144, 190

Waugh, Auberon, 3

Waugh, Evelyn, 3, 74, 138–9, 191, 194, 197

Weinig, Sister Mary Anthony, 81

Westminster College, Oxford, 61

Williams, Charles, 69–72, 76–7, 80–2, 177, 188, 190, 198

Wilson, Angus, 9

Wilson, Colin, 190

Wilson, Edmund, 130

Winsness, Erling, 75

Woodhead, Chris, 4, 8

Woolf, Virginia, 149

Wordsworth, William, 72

Zimmerman, Morton Grady, 183

Index of Characters and Places
in Tolkien's Middle Earth

Ainur, the, 84, 88 *et passim*,
    120, 122, 125
Aman, 121
Aragorn, 32, 51, 115, 125, *see
    also* Strider
Arwen, 32, 51

Baggins, Bilbo, *see* Bilbo Baggins
Baggins, Frodo, *see* Frodo
    Baggins
balrog, 114
barrow wights, 78
Beleriand, 85
Beren, 32, 51, 56, 97, 206–8
Bilbo Baggins, 140
Bombadil, Tom, 78, 124, 165
Boromir, 114, 183

Cirith Ungol, 129
Cotton, Rosie, *see* Rosie Cotton
Cracks of Doom, 113, 183

Dark Lord, *see* Sauron
Durin, 167
dwarves, 116, 120, 156, 164

Eldar, the, 85, 96–7, 124–5
Elrond, 51
elves, 78, 85–6, 89 *et passim*,
    116 *et passim*, 143, 157, 164

ents, 51, 78, 117, 202, *see also*
    Treebeard and Quickbeam
entwives, 51
Eru, 89, 95, 110, 122 *see also*
    Ilúvatar
Estë, 148

Frodo Baggins, 95, 111 *et
    passim*, 123, 129, 138, 142–3,
    148, 151, 158, 161, 180–1

Galadriel, 101, 138, 142, 151,
    159, 164
Gamgee, Sam, *see* Sam Gamgee
Gandalf, 114, 117–18, 123, 138,
    164, 167, 171, 191
Golden Perch at Stock, 180
Gollum, 10, 111, 151, *see also*
    Smeagol
Gondor, 182

hobbits, 8, 130, 153, 157, *see
    also* Bilbo Baggins, Frodo
    Baggins, Merry, Pippin, Rosie
    Cotton and Sam Gamgee

Ilúvatar, 85, 88 *et passim*,
    119–22, 125, *see also* Eru
Isengard, 159

Khazad-Dûm, 114

Lórien, 151, 157, 183
Lúthien, 32, 51, 56, 97, 204–8

Mandos, 119, 205
Manwë, 92
Master of Lake Town, 156–7
Melkor, 84, 91 *et passim*,
 119–20, 122, 148–9, *see also*
 Morgoth
Meneltarma, 122
Merry, 124, 168
Mithlond, 124
Mordor, 7, 8, 111–12, 133, 158,
 161, 180–9
Morgoth, 85, 91 *et passim*,
 120–1, *see also* Melkor
Moria, 167
Mount Doom, 113, 117

Nazgûl, 114
Nienna, 148
Noldor, the, 92
Númenor, 120–2

orcs, 94–5, 120, 143
Orthanc, 159

Pippin, 124, 168, 180

Prancing Pony at Bree, 72, 180
Quickbeam, 165, 175, *see also*
 ents

ring-wraiths, 117
Rosie Cotton, 51

Sam Gamgee, 40, 51, 95, 111 *et*
 passim, 124, 142–3, 148, 153,
 158, 161, 180–1
Saruman, 138, 159
Sauron, 108, 112, 117, 122, 133,
 138
Shelob, 113, 142–3
Shire, the, xiii, 7, 14, 115, 153 *et*
 passim
Smaug, 156
Smeagol, 114, *see also* Gollum
Strider, 72, *see also* Aragorn

Tar-Ancalimon, 122
Thorin, 156
Treebeard, 70, 94–5, 159, 165,
 167–8, 195, *see also* ents

Valar, the, 89 *et passim*, 110,
 119–21, 148
Valinor, 119–20

Wormtongue, 157, 180